Currency Crises

NEW HORIZONS IN MONEY AND FINANCE

Series Editor: Mervyn K. Lewis, *University of South Australia*

This important series is designed to make a significant contribution to the shaping and development of thinking in finance. The series will provide an invaluable forum for the publication of high quality works of scholarship on a breadth of topics ranging from financial markets and financial systems to monetary policy and banking reform, and will show the diversity of theory, issues and practices.

The focus of the series is on the development and application of new original ideas in finance. Rigorous and often path-breaking in its approach, it will pay particular attention to the international and comparative dimension of finance and will include innovative theoretical and empirical work from both well-established authors and the new generation of scholars.

Titles in the series include:

Banking Reforms in South-East Europe
Edited by Zeljko Sevic

Russian Banking
Evolution, Problems and Prospects
Edited by David Lane

Currency Crises
A Theoretical and Empirical Perspective
André Fourçans and Raphaël Franck

Currency Crises

A Theoretical and Empirical Perspective

André Fourçans

Professor of Economics
ESSEC Business School
Paris, France

and

Raphaël Franck

Research Fellow, Aharon Meir Centre for Banking
Bar Ilan University
Ramat Gan, Israel

New Horizons in Money and Finance

Edward Elgar
Cheltenham, UK • Northampton, MA, USA

Published by
Edward Elgar Publishing Limited
Glensanda House
Montpellier Parade
Cheltenham
Glos GL50 1UA
UK

Edward Elgar Publishing, Inc.
136 West Street
Suite 202
Northampton
Massachusetts 01060
USA

MK

A catalogue record for this book
is available from the British Library

Library of Congress Cataloguing in Publication Data

Fourçans, André .
Currency crises : a theoretical and empirical perspective / André Fourçans and Raphaël Franck.
p. cm. —Mathematical models. I. Franck, Raphaël, 1976- II. Title. III. New horizons in money and finance.

HG3851.3.F68 2004
332.4'56—dc22

2003061593

ISBN 1 84376 433 4

Printed and bound in Great Britain by MPG Books Ltd, Bodmin, Cornwall

To Claire and Paul

To my parents and my sisters

Contents

Figures

Tables

Introduction

There are three broad categories of financial crises: debt crises, banking crises and currency crises.[1] Debt crises occur when countries cannot service their sovereign or private foreign debt. Banking crises take place when actual or potential bank runs or bankruptcies force banking institutions to suspend the convertibility of their liabilities, or make the government and monetary institutions intervene so as to prevent such situations from happening. Currency crises are characterised by speculative attacks where speculators sell the currency of a country and deplete the monetary authorities' foreign exchange reserves. These attacks lead to a devaluation or revaluation in a fixed exchange system or to a shift from a fixed exchange rate to a floating exchange rate. They may compel the government or the monetary authorities to defend the national currency so as to avoid falls or hikes in the exchange rate.

Ever since the pioneering study by Krugman (1979), many theoretical and empirical analyses have been put forward to explain currency crises. There have also been several attempts at classifying them, either in the form of articles or of chapters in books. However these surveys cannot always provide a comprehensive view of the field in a limited number of pages: they emphasise some aspects while overlooking others.[2] This book takes a more general approach and provides an extensive perspective on currency crises. It should appeal to graduate students and researchers interested in the evolution of currency crisis research.

The collapse of the Bretton Woods agreements in 1971 led to an increase in the number of currency crises. Several theories which claim to reflect their main features have been suggested to explain their outbreak and spread. In the end of the 1970s and during the following decade, most, though not all currency crises, occurred in Latin America. According to the first models of speculative attacks, they stemmed from lenient monetary policies that are incompatible with a fixed exchange rate regime.

Currency crises in the 1990s called into question those analyses which consider that policymakers cause speculative attacks and that market participants are not to blame. The crises of the European Monetary System

(EMS) in 1992 and 1993 cannot be ascribed to expansionary monetary policies since European countries conducted restrictive and converging policies in line with the Bundesbank in order to promote the single European currency. The first models of speculative attacks were then declared null and void: they should be replaced by formalisations where market participants' self-fulfilling expectations trigger currency crises and cause them to spread across countries.

In December 1994, Mexico was hit by a speculative attack that compelled the government to abandon the parity between the peso and the US dollar. The Mexican government's economic policies were far from being optimal. The domestic macroeconomic situation had been worsening for the past two years. Still market participants' self-fulfilling expectations are held responsible for the outbreak of the crisis. By attacking the peso, they compelled the Mexican authorities to let the exchange rate go. Had speculators not launched an attack, the crisis would have been avoided.

This is an explanation of the Mexican crisis, and of currency crises more generally. It is at odds with the 1997 East Asian crisis and the subsequent attacks in Russia, Brazil, Turkey and Argentina in 1998, 1999, 2000 and 2001. Current research tries to provide an explanation of these crises by assessing the responsibilities of the policymaker in the worsening of the macroeconomic situation and the responsibilities of market participants in the increase of speculative pressures.

There is actually a double controversy on the causes of currency crises. The first aspect of this controversy tries to determine whether attacks are triggered or spread across countries by deteriorated economic fundamentals, by market participants' self-fulfilling expectations or by economic policies. The second aspect of this controversy is related to the links between crises and the nature of the macroeconomic equilibrium. Is there a single or several equilibria for the same market conditions? This question is all the more important as currency crises result from deteriorated fundamentals in models with a unique equilibrium while they stem from speculators' expectations or the policymaker's economic policy choices in models with multiple equilibria. Given these two features, this book asserts that models on the outbreak and the spread of currency crises share similarities and may be studied together.

By building on the typology developed by Eichengreen, Rose and Wyplosz (1996a, 1996b), theoretical developments in the currency crisis literature lead to three types of models being distinguished. First-generation models assume that deteriorated fundamentals in a unique-equilibrium economy are the single cause of attacks. Second-generation models state that multiple equilibria exist. In this framework, speculators' self-fulfilling expectations trigger crises, even though fundamentals are not deteriorated.

Third-generation models analyse interactions between fundamentals, speculators' expectations and the policymaker's economic choices, but remain divided on the nature of the macroeconomic equilibrium.

Part 1 focuses on first-generation models. Chapter 1 describes the canonical framework of first-generation models. Chapter 2 discusses aspects of the policymaker's behaviour while Chapter 3 presents extensions to this framework.

Part 2 deals with second-generation models. Chapter 4 discusses models of self-fulfilling currency crisis outbreak and Chapter 5 those of self-fulfilling currency crisis contagion. Chapter 6 questions the relevance of second-generation models by confronting them with empirical studies on currency crises and investigating the rationale for the existence of multiple equilibria.

Part 3 tackles third-generation models. Chapter 7 focuses on the policymaker's role in third-generation currency crisis models. Chapter 8 discusses contagion that is warranted by fundamental links between countries. Chapter 9 deals with the interactions between deteriorated fundamentals and speculators' expectations.

Part 4 discusses the manner in which the currency crisis literature casts light on recent crises in emerging crises and its normative implications, that is, how the international financial system is to be reformed in order to prevent currency crises. Chapter 10 provides a case study on the spread of the East Asian currency crisis to Russia and Brazil. Chapter 11 focuses on exchange rate regimes in relation to speculative attacks. Chapter 12 deals with international financial institutions.

Let it be noted that throughout this study, the 'policymaker' is the agent who decides to keep or abandon the fixed exchange rate, who judges the appreciation or depreciation of the flexible exchange rate. Agents who cause speculative attacks and currency crises are indifferently referred to as 'speculators', 'market participants' or 'private agents'.

There are not enough letters in the Latin and Greek alphabets for us to be entirely consistent, although we believe our notation is largely standard. Some letters are bound to have more than one meaning throughout the book. We have tried to make it as clear as possible when the signification of a letter changes.

Numerous discussions with friends and colleagues helped us in improving this book. We would like to thank, without implication, Agnès Benassy-Quéré, Damien Besancenot, Henri Bourguinat, Elise Brezis, Michele Fratianni, Paul de Grauwe, Bertrand Lemmenicier, Abraham Lioui, Alessandro Prati, Dominick Salvatore, Aimé Scannavino, Radu Vranceanu and Warren Young. An anonymous referee was also helpful in improving this book.

We would also like to thank Alexandra Minton and Nep Athwal at Edward Elgar Publishing. Ms Minton has been supportive of our project since its beginning. Her advice was crucial in turning the manuscript into a complete book. Ms Athwal's help was crucial in the final stages of the writing.

NOTES

1. For discussions on these definitions, see Bordo (1986), Bordo, Eichengreen, Klingbiel and Martinez-Peria (2001), Eichengreen and Rose (1998).
2. Surveys dealing with the outbreak of currency crises include Agénor, Bhandari and Flood (1992), Blackburn and Sola (1993), Garber and Svensson (1994), Sutherland (1995), Obstfeld and Rogoff (1996), Flood and Marion (1998a), Agénor and Montiel (2000), Jeanne (2000) and Sarno and Taylor (2002). Claessens, Dornbusch and Park (2000) and de Bandt and Hartmann (2000) analyse models of contagion. Rangvid (2001) only deals with very specific models, the so-called second-generation models. Pesenti and Tille (2000) discuss recent studies that focus on the role of the banking and financial sector, as well as on the channels of currency crisis spread across countries. Kaminsky, Lizondo and Reinhart (1997) and Berg, Borensztein, Milesi-Feretti and Patillo (1999) survey empirical studies on currency crises. Heinemann (2002) reviews studies using the game-theoretical 'global game' approach in currency crisis studies.

PART ONE

First-generation Models of Currency Crises

Research on currency crisis starts with first-generation models. Most of them were designed in the late 1970s and during the 1980s to account for speculative attacks in developing countries. Those crises almost always resulted from macroeconomic imbalances.

The pioneering studies by Krugman (1979) and Flood and Garber (1984b) constitute the canonical framework of these models. It is assumed that the policymaker conducts an expansionary monetary policy that is a priori incompatible with a fixed exchange regime. Speculative attacks do not stem from the irrational behaviour of speculators. On the contrary currency crises result from their rational assessment of a forthcoming collapse in the exchange rate. Speculators anticipate that the fixed exchange rate regime cannot be indefinitely maintained. They launch an attack before the foreign exchange reserves the Central Bank owns are exhausted.

First-generation models view currency crises as 'runs' on the policymaker's foreign exchange reserves where speculators sell the domestic money they own against foreign-denominated currencies before the fall of the fixed exchange rate regime. Jeanne (2000) shows the analogy between the canonical Krugman–Flood–Garber currency crisis framework and the seminal study of Diamond and Dybvig (1983) on banking crisis.

The relevance of this comparison between these two frameworks is undeniable. Some of their features are however clearly opposed. The models of Krugman (1979) and Flood and Garber (1984b) are in a continuous time framework and with a unique equilibrium. The study by Diamond and Dybvig (1983) has a discrete-time framework with multiple equilibria.

Unlike Diamond and Dybvig (1983), first-generation models assert that crises do not result from speculators' self-fulfilling expectations. They stem from monetary or fiscal policies that are a priori incompatible with a fixed exchange rate regime. As can be seen, first-generation models rest on strong assumptions. Their features often resemble the characteristics of currency crises that occurred in the 1970s and 1980s. This is shown by the empirical studies of Blanco and Garber (1986), Goldberg (1994) and Melick (1996) that analyse the repeated devaluations that took place in Mexico in the 1970s and the work of Cumby and van Wijnbergen (1989) that deals with the speculative attacks against the Argentinean currency between 1979 and 1982. It is more difficult to explain the 1990s currency crises, notably those in East Asian countries, in the light of first-generation models.

Chapter 1 describes the main assumptions of first-generation models. The incompatibility between the growth in domestic credit and a fixed exchange regime is shown. The moment the speculative attack takes place is determined, under the assumption that agents have perfect foresight expectations.

Chapter 2 focuses on the behaviour of the policymaker, in spite of the assumption common to first-generation models that monetary policy is incompatible with a fixed exchange rate regime. The defences that the policymaker may use to delay and prevent speculative attacks are analysed. The impact of different exchange rate regimes, after a first devaluation, on possible future exchange rate crises are then examined. Finally the policymaker's behaviour is investigated in a stochastic framework.

Chapter 3 deals with studies that extend the framework of Krugman (1979) and Flood and Garber (1984b). They tackle market imperfections, i.e., price stickiness and imperfect substitution between goods and assets, the real effects of speculative attacks and the banking sector. These analyses cannot prevent first-generation models from being called into question.

1. Main Assumptions of First-generation Models

In order to determine the factors that compel a country to abandon a fixed peg and let the exchange rate go, studies by Krugman (1979) and Flood and Garber (1984b) start from the model of exhaustible resources developed by Salant and Henderson (1978). In the latter model, the authorities try to prevent a fall in the gold price by using their reserves. They show that this strategy is bound to fail since private agents end up buying the whole stock of gold.[1]

Krugman (1979) suggests that similarities exist between the model of exhaustible resources of Salant and Henderson (1978) and currency crises viewed as balance-of-payment crises.[2] Both are related to attacks on foreign exchange reserves held by the government. Prior to the crisis, speculators modify their portfolio allocations: they trade their domestic currency for foreign currency. This leads to a progressive depletion of the government's foreign exchange reserves. Speculators anticipate that, at some point in time, the policymaker will have no more reserves to keep the exchange rate fixed. They thus launch a speculative attack that compels the policymaker to let the exchange rate go.

Krugman (1979) shows that currency crises do not stem from speculators' irrationality. They originate from monetary policies that are incompatible with a fixed exchange rate regime. However some non-linearities in his model prevent him from computing the date the speculative attack occurs. Flood and Garber (1984b) determine it, thus providing the canonical form of first-generation models.

1.THE GROWTH IN DOMESTIC CREDIT

In a continuous-time framework where agents have perfect foresight expectations, a small country, known as the domestic country, fixes the price of its currency against the currency of another country, which is assumed to be bigger. There are no private banks. Hence the money supply equals the sum of:

- the domestic credit provided by the Central Bank;
- the value in domestic currency of foreign exchange reserves which do not produce any interest.

The model is based upon the following equations:

$$m_t - p_t = -\alpha i_t \quad (1.1)$$

$$m_t = d_t + r_t \quad (1.2)$$

$$\dot{d} = \mu \quad (1.3)$$

$$p_t = p_t^* + s_t \quad (1.4)$$

$$i_t = i_t^* + E_{t-1}\Delta s_t \quad (1.5)$$

where m_t represents the domestic money supply, i_t the domestic interest rate, p_t the price level in the domestic country, d_t the domestic credit, μ the growth rate in domestic credit that is assumed to be constant and strictly positive, r_t the foreign exchange reserves, s_t the spot exchange rate. The index t indicates that the variable is measured at time t. Variables with an asterisk are from the foreign country. A dot above a variable indicates a derivative in relation to time: $\dot{d}$ is thus the rate of domestic credit growth. E_t is the conditional expectation operator of the information available at time t; Δs_t represents the change in the exchange rate between dates t and t-1. All variables are expressed in logarithm except for the interest rate and $-\alpha i$ that represents the agents' demand for money.

Equation (1.1) describes the equilibrium condition in the money market. The left-hand side of the equation represents the real money supply while the right-hand side defines the real demand for money as a negative function of the domestic interest rate. Equation (1.2) asserts that the supply of nominal money equals the sum of foreign exchange reserves and domestic credit. The latter increases at a constant and strictly positive rate μ, as equation (1.3) indicates. Lastly the price level and domestic interest rate follow the conditions of international arbitrage. Equations (1.4) and (1.5) respectively indicate that the price level follows the purchasing power parity rule and that the interest rate obeys the uncovered interest parity rule.

Under the assumption of perfect foresight, and assuming the exchange rate is fixed and equal to $\underline{s}$, then:

$$E_{t-1}\,\Delta s_t=0$$
$$i_t = i_t^*$$

Replacing (1.2), (1.4) and (1.5) into equation (1.1) leads to:

$$r_t + d_t - p_t^* - \underline{s} = -\alpha(i_t^* + E_{t-1}\Delta s_t) \tag{1.6}$$

By assumption, the exchange rate $\underline{s}$ before the attack, the foreign price level p_t^* and the foreign interest rate i_t^* are constant. Deriving the previous equation and following equation (1.3), the depletion rate of foreign exchange reserves $\dot{r}$ equals:

$$\dot{r} = -\mu \tag{1.7}$$

with $\dot{r}$ the rate of variation in foreign exchange reserves. Rewriting equation (1.7) in relation to time, it follows that:

$$r_t = r_0 - \mu t \tag{1.8}$$

where r_0 represents the level of reserves that the authorities initially own at time t=0.

Equation (1.8) shows that reserves decrease proportionally to the growth in domestic credit. It asserts that the government finds it impossible to keep the exchange rate fixed when credit growth exceeds money demand. Thus any stock of foreign exchange reserves is bound to be exhausted in a finite period of time.

This framework suggests an explanation for the progressive depletion of exchange reserves and the outbreak of speculative attacks. It rests upon two implicit assumptions. First domestic credit d_t is the only monetary policy instrument that is available to the authorities. They cannot either raise the interest rate or manipulate the quantity of money through a policy of sterilisation.[3]

The second implicit assumption is related to the level of reserves the policymaker is willing to commit in defence of the peg. It is assumed that the policymaker finds it optimal to let the exchange rate go once a predetermined level of reserves is reached. Let $\underline{r}$ be a level of reserves such that:

$$0 \le \underline{r} < r_0 \tag{1.9}$$

The fixed exchange rate system is maintained at time *t* if $r_t > \underline{r}$; if not, the policymaker lets the exchange rate go.

The model explains why crises occur before the total depletion of foreign exchange reserves. It shows that currency crises stem from the rational behaviour of market participants. The latter know the level $\underline{r}$ with perfect-foresight expectations. These participants anticipate that the policymaker will let the exchange rate go, when the level $\underline{r}$ is reached, even if no speculative attack takes place. Thus they launch an attack in order not to incur losses when the shift to a floating exchange rate system occurs. Under perfect foresight, the moment this attack happens may be determined.

2. THE OUTBREAK OF SPECULATIVE ATTACKS

In order to determine the moment when the speculative attack takes place, the 'backward induction' process is used. It enables the assessment the exchange rate that would prevail in a flexible exchange regime when foreign exchange reserves hit the level $\underline{r}$. It is called the shadow exchange rate and is denoted $\tilde{s}$.

In equilibrium and under perfect foresight, the exchange rate does not 'jump' when an attack occurs. If it did, speculators would benefit from infinite arbitrage opportunities. Indeed if:

$$\tilde{s} < \underline{s} \tag{1.10}$$

speculators incur immediate capital losses when buying reserves and triggering a speculative attack. Conversely if:

$$\tilde{s} > \underline{s} \tag{1.11}$$

market participants instantaneously realise capital gains. These two situations are incompatible with the assumption of perfect foresight and are consequently eliminated through arbitrage. The floating exchange rate that prevails immediately after the attack is therefore equal to the fixed exchange rate that existed when the crisis happened. This implies that the shift to a flexible exchange rate system occurs when the fixed exchange rate equals the shadow exchange rate, that is when:

$$\tilde{s} = \underline{s} \tag{1.12}$$

From the shadow exchange rate $\tilde{s}$, it is possible to assess the benefits market participants may obtain when a currency crisis happens. It is the price that speculators pay when buying foreign exchange reserves. It must also be noted that the shadow exchange rate $\tilde{s}$ justifies the uniqueness of the equilibrium: it stabilises the foreign exchange market following a speculative attack that provokes a shift to a flexible exchange rate system.

The shadow exchange rate $\tilde{s}$ is now computed in order to determine the time T when the currency crisis occurs.

Let it be noted that under perfect foresight:

$$E_{t-1}\, \Delta s_t = \dot{s} \tag{1.13}$$

where $\dot{s}$ represents the expected exchange rate on the foreign exchange market.

At the moment when the speculative attack compels the policymaker to let the exchange rate go, domestic credit keeps on growing at rate μ. This implies that:

$$\dot{s} = \mu \tag{1.14}$$

From the uncovered interest parity in equation (1.5), it follows that:

$$i_t = i_t^* + \mu \tag{1.15}$$

To simplify computations, it is assumed without loss of generality that:

$$i_t^* = 0$$
$$p_t^* = 0$$
$$\underline{r} = 0$$

Equality $\underline{r} = 0$ suggests that foreign exchange reserves are completely exhausted at the end of the speculative attack. This assumption is made by Flood and Garber (1984b) in order to determine the equilibrium of the model more easily. It does not however call into question the main assumptions in Krugman (1979). Equation (1.6) becomes:

$$d_t - \tilde{s} = -\alpha(E_{t-1}\Delta s_t) \tag{1.16}$$

The shadow exchange rate $\tilde{s}$ equals:

$$\tilde{s} = \alpha\mu + d_t \tag{1.17}$$

In Figure 1.1, equation (1.17) and the fixed exchange rate that prevails before the crisis are represented. It appears that a speculative attack only happens if equality (1.12) holds. The abscissa of the intersection point between the two lines indicates the time *T* when the currency crisis occurs.

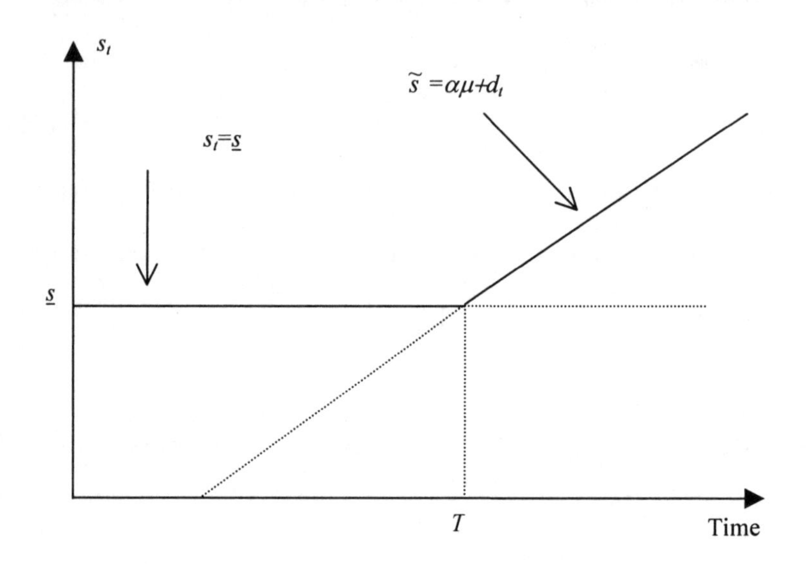

Figure 1.1 The evolution of the exchange rate s_t *before and after a speculative attack*

At time *T*, the speculative attack triggers a fall in the money supply. Both the attack and the fall are of size $-\Delta r$. This collapse in the money supply entails a drop in money demand. These two phenomena, which equilibrate the foreign exchange market, are summed up in the following equation:

$$\Delta r=-\alpha\mu \qquad (1.18)$$

If equality (1.18) holds, reserves are exhausted at time *T*. Moreover rewriting equation (1.8) as a function of *T* leads to:

$$-\Delta r=r_0-\mu T \qquad (1.19)$$

Equations (1.18) and (1.19) are the necessary conditions for an attack to happen. The time *T* of the attack is given by:

$$T=(r_0-\alpha\mu)/\mu \qquad (1.20)$$

Equation (1.20) shows that the fall of the fixed exchange rate system is delayed when initial reserves are high and the expansion rate of domestic credit is low. Figure (1.2) illustrates the evolution of reserves r_t, domestic credit d_t, and money stock m_t before and after the crisis, with d_0 and r_0 being the initial levels in domestic credit and reserves.

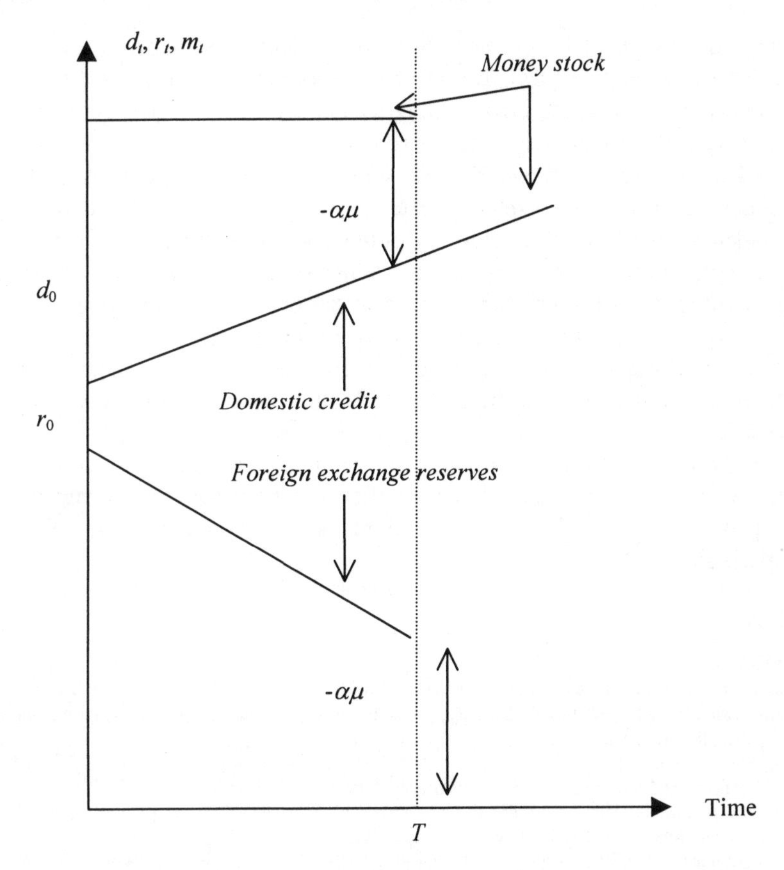

Figure 1.2 Evolution of domestic credit, foreign exchange reserves and money stock before and after a speculative attack

Prior to the crisis, the quantity of money remains constant but its composition varies: domestic credit grows at rate μ while reserves decrease at rate $-\mu$. The speculative attack occurs at time *T* just before the shift to the floating exchange rate system. After the crisis, the money stock equals domestic credit since reserves have been assumed to be null.

This model provides a convincing explanation of currency crisis outbreaks. But it relies on several strong assumptions, the most crucial being that the policymaker conducts a monetary policy that eventually leads to the fall of the fixed exchange rate system.

3. CHAPTER SUMMARY

The framework of first-generation models stems from papers by Krugman (1979) and Flood and Garber (1984b). Speculative attacks result from an expansionary domestic credit policy leading to a progressive exhaustion of the government's foreign exchange reserves.

Under perfect foresight, market participants anticipate that the policymaker lets the exchange rate go when reserves hit a known and predetermined level. But before the policymaker opts for a flexible exchange rate system, each agent forecasts that other speculators are going to sell the amount of national currency they own in order to avoid losses. In this context, all speculators launch an attack on the currency at the same time. Using backward induction, it is possible to determine the moment when the fixed exchange rate system collapses in this unique-equilibrium currency crisis.

These models rely on strong assumptions. Fundamentals are confined to monetary policy variables while the policymaker's behaviour is exogenous to the model. These limits will be amended by subsequent research on speculative attacks.

NOTES

1. Salant (1983) and Flood and Garber (1984a) suggest several extensions to Salant and Henderson (1978).
2. The balance-of-payments measures exchanges in goods and services, as well as capital inflows and outflows, between a country and the rest of the world.
3. In Krugman (1979) and Flood and Garber (1984b), sterilisation policies fail because speculators immediately adjust their behaviours in order to lessen the effects of these policies. Modelling sterilisation in first-generation models requires additional assumptions. See Chapter 2, Section 1.3, Sterilisation and rise in interest rates.

2. Aspects of the Policymaker's Behaviour

The policymaker conducting an expansionary monetary policy which is a priori incompatible with a fixed exchange rate regime is the central assumption of the standard first-generation model presented in Chapter 1. Despite this strong hypothesis, various studies analyse the policymaker's behaviour prior to the outbreak of speculative attacks.

A first strand of research focuses on the defences that the policymaker may use to prevent currency crises, though his policies lead to the collapse of the peg. Various strategies for the defence of the peg are dealt with: establishing capital controls, borrowing to finance foreign exchange reserves, sterilisation and hikes in interest rates.

Other studies deal with the choice of the exchange rate regime in the wake of a speculative attack. They show that some exchange rate systems may lead to the outbreak of a subsequent currency crisis just after the first collapse of a peg.

Another type of extension tackles the policymaker's behaviour in a stochastic framework. In spite of his expansionary monetary policy, uncertainty allows the policymaker to postpone the outbreak of the currency crisis. The collapse of the peg is not certain any more.

1. DEFENCES AGAINST SPECULATIVE ATTACKS

Some first-generation models consider different defences of a fixed exchange rate system. They analyse whether capital controls, foreign exchange reserves financing through borrowing on capital markets, sterilisation and rise in interest rates may postpone and even prevent speculative attacks.

1.1. Capital Controls

In order to limit reserve losses, the policymaker may institute temporary or permanent capital controls. Temporary capital controls have minor economic costs on domestic activity but may be less efficient than permanent capital controls in preventing the collapse of a fixed peg.

To introduce permanent capital controls in the standard first-generation model presented in Chapter 1, Agénor, Bhandari and Flood (1992) suggest replacing equation (1.5) – the uncovered interest rate parity condition – by:

$$i_t = (1-\theta)(i_t^* + E_{t-1}\Delta s_t) \tag{2.1}$$

where θ is the tax rate on profits.

Equation (2.1) shows the influence of capital controls in the deviations from uncovered interest rate parity. Introducing equation (2.1) in the model of Chapter 1 so as to determine the time T when the speculative attack takes place leads to:

$$T = \frac{r_0 - (1-\vartheta)\alpha\mu}{\mu} \tag{2.2}$$

In equation (2.2), a high capital control tax, represented by a high value of θ, delays the outbreak of the currency crisis.

Such permanent capital controls entail costs.[1] They limit a country's capital inflows, and consequently its investment capacities. A solution lies in establishing temporary capital controls in times of speculative pressures and to remove them when the currency is not subjected to attacks. Another possibility consists in instituting partial capital controls that only apply to a certain category of private agents. For instance Wyplosz (1986) analyses the case in which residents cannot hold foreign currencies but where non-residents may hold domestic currency. The latter trigger a speculative attack when the amount of domestic currency they hold equals the level of foreign exchange reserves owned by the Central Bank. In such a framework, Wyplosz (1986) suggests that the policymaker does not need capital controls to keep the exchange rate fixed. He must however create some uncertainty about the level of foreign exchange reserves so that risk-averse speculators are only willing to commit limited amounts to a speculative attack. Hence capital controls may prevent the fall of a peg by putting a lid on the volume of speculative transactions.

However, the analysis of Wyplosz (1986) is called into question by Bacchetta (1990). He considers that private agents' expectations change when the policymaker announces the establishment of temporary capital controls. A current account deficit follows since capital outflows and an increase in imports occur jointly. A speculative attack may even occur just before capital controls are set up. Establishing capital controls may then bring about the very outcome that these regulations are meant to avoid. Such a debate is given another perspective in the framework of second-generation models of currency crises (see Chapter 6, section 1, Regulatory implications of second-generation models).

1.2. Borrowing to Finance Foreign Exchange Reserves

In the standard first-generation model of Chapter 1, it is assumed that foreign exchange reserves decrease until a given level where the policymaker lets the exchange rate go. Yet if he has access to perfect capital markets, he may borrow to finance his reserves. His intertemporal budget constraint may still hold even though reserves become infinitely negative. Such a framework allows the exchange rate regime to be maintained. Its relevance is however limited.

All countries do not have access to perfect capital markets. As in Obstfeld (1986a) and van Wijnbergen (1991), they face budgetary constraints that limit their ability to create reserves. The growth rate in domestic credit cannot always be maintained above the international interest rate since the government would violate its intertemporal budget constraint: an expansionary monetary policy thus leads to the fall of the fixed exchange rate system.

Even if capital markets are perfect, Buiter (1987) shows that borrowing may not prevent attacks. His study suggests that the moment when the policymaker borrows influences the time when the currency crisis occurs. Let the policymaker's simplified intertemporal budget constraint be:

$$\dot{d} + \dot{h} = g_t + i_t^* + h_t \tag{2.3}$$

with g_t the primary deficit which is assumed to be constant,[2] h_t the domestic debt, $\dot{h}$ the derivative of h_t in relation to time, $\dot{d}$ the rate of domestic credit growth.

From equations (1.3) and (1.7), it is found that:

$$\dot{r} = -\dot{d} \tag{2.4}$$

Introducing equation (2.4) into equation (2.3) leads to:

$$\dot{r} = \dot{h} - g_t + i_t^* + h_t \tag{2.5}$$

Equation (2.5) shows that borrowing on financial markets increases foreign exchange reserves by the amount of the contracted debt.

It is assumed that the policymaker decides to finance foreign exchange reserves by only borrowing once and for all at time z. In that case, $\dot{h}=0$. This leads to:

$$\dot{d} = g_t + i_t^* + h_z \tag{2.6}$$

and

$$r_t = -(g + i_t^* + h_z) \tag{2.7}$$

Given (2.6) and (2.7), the amount of domestic credit at time t after the policymaker has borrowed at time z is:

$$d_t = d_z + (g_t + i_t^* + h_z)(t\text{-}z)\,,\ t \geq z \tag{2.8}$$

At time T when the speculative attack occurs, $d_T = 0$ by assumption. Since equation (1.9) states that the fixed exchange rate and the shadow exchange rate are equal when the speculative attack happens, it follows that:

$$\underline{s} = -\alpha(g_t + i_t^* + h_z) + d_Z \tag{2.9}$$

From equations (2.8) and (2.9), it is possible to determine the time interval between time z (the moment the policymaker borrows) and time T (the moment the fixed exchange rate regime collapses):

$$T - z = \frac{\underline{s} + \alpha(g_t + i_t^* + h_z)}{g_t + i_t^* + h_z} \tag{2.10}$$

Equation (2.10) shows that borrowing on foreign exchange markets cannot be said to either delay or precipitate currency crises for certain. Foreign exchange reserves are increased, but so are the debt service and the growth rate in domestic credit. If borrowing is done shortly before the expected date of the speculative attack, the first effect exceeds the second: the crisis is delayed. But if borrowing is done long before the crisis, the second effect outdoes the first, and the fall of the fixed exchange rate regime is hastened.

To sum up, borrowing to finance exchange rate reserves does not always postpone speculative attacks. The policymaker may have to rely on other means to defend the fixed exchange rate regime.

1.3. Sterilisation and Rise in Interest Rates

At first glance, it seems inappropriate to jointly deal with sterilisation and rises in interest rates. These procedures try to prevent falls in the exchange rate: sterilisation by preventing capital outflows, interest rate rises by increasing capital inflows. However these two defence methods against speculative attacks have often been similarly formalised in the framework of first-generation models and rely on similar assumptions.

When the policymaker undertakes a sterilisation policy, he hopes he may defer, and even prevent, a currency crisis by compensating reserve losses using another counterpart of the domestic money supply. This conflicts with the standard first-generation model of Chapter 1 developed by Krugman (1979) and Flood and Garber (1984b). They assume that no fixed peg may hold if the policymaker sterilises an attack: under perfect foresight, speculators immediately guess his intentions and thwart his sterilisation policies. Likewise a rise in interest rates is inefficient because agents know that the policymaker cannot compensate for all his reserve losses by increasing capital inflows.

Several studies deal with the effects of interest rate increases in the framework of first-generation models.[3] Flood and Jeanne (2000) build on Flood, Garber and Kramer (1996) where an illiquid bond is traded on the asset markets. They show that a rise in interest rates before the outbreak of the currency crisis systematically hastens the speculative attack following the deterioration of the fiscal situation.The relevance of the analysis in Flood and Jeanne (2000) is called into question by Lahiri and Végh (2003). They consider that bonds whose interest rate has risen are still liquid. An interest rate increase would lead to a rise in the real demand for money.

This section draws on Lahiri and Végh (2003) to analyse the effects of an interest rate defence on the outbreak of currency crises. The model rests on the following equations:

$$m_t - p_t = h(i_t) + g(i_t - i_t^g) \tag{2.11}$$

$$\dot{r} = -\mu d_0 \exp(\mu t) \tag{2.12}$$

$$p_t = p_t^* + s_t \tag{1.4}$$

$$i_t = i_t^* + E_{t-1} \Delta s_t \tag{1.5}$$

with $h(.)$ and $g(.)$ the demand for cash and liquid bonds, i_t the 'pure' interest rate, i_t^g the interest rate on liquid bonds. Partial derivatives of functions h and g are such that:

$$\partial g/\partial i_t < 0$$
$$\partial g/\partial i_t^g > 0$$
$$\partial h/\partial i_t < 0$$

It is also assumed for simplicity that:

$$i_t^* = 0$$
$$p_t^* = 0$$
$$\underline{r} = 0$$

with $\underline{r}$ the threshold level of reserves where the policymaker lets the exchange rate go.

Equation (2.11) defines the money market equilibrium. Equation (2.12) describes the evolution of international reserves: it states that along paths with a fixed exchange rate and expanding domestic credit, foreign exchange reserves will fall at an increasing rate. Equations (1.4) and (1.5) are those of the model in Chapter 1. Also in line with Chapter 1, the exchange rate is assumed to be fixed at level $\underline{s}$.

The model departs from the standard first-generation model of Chapter 1 by assuming that the policymaker may lead an active interest rate policy. He sets the interest rate on liquid bonds i_t^g but lets the market determine the composition of cash and liquid bonds – his liabilities. This leads to the following money market equilibrium:

$$m_t - s_t = h(i_t) + g(i_t - i_t^g) \tag{2.13}$$

In this framework, the policymaker sets the exchange rate and the interest on liquid bonds. The private sector then chooses real money demand, which determines through equation (2.13) the nominal money supply (H+G) with H=$h(.)$ and G=$g(.)$. The nominal money supply determines in turn the respective levels of H and G.

In this model, an interest rate defence of the peg consists in increasing the policy-controlled interest rate so as to make domestic assets more attractive. It is assumed that the policymaker announces at time $t = 0$ that he will adjust the interest rate on liquid bonds i_t^g if the nominal interest rate i_t changes so that:

$$\Delta i_t^g = \gamma \Delta i_t \tag{2.14}$$

where γ is a policy parameter that is optimally chosen by the policymaker in the interval $[0;\gamma^{+}]$ such that:

- if $\gamma = 0$, the policymaker's interest rate policy is completely passive. This is the model of Chapter 1;
- if $\gamma = \gamma^{+}$, money demand does not vary even if i_t-i_t^g falls.

Equation (2.14) describes the rule that governs interest rate policy. It enables the discussion of the effects of an interest rate hike on the outbreak of speculative attacks.

In this framework where it is assumed the currency crisis occurs at time T, the timing of events is defined as follows:

- Before time T when the currency crisis occurs, the policymaker loses reserves at an increasing rate following equation (2.12).
- After time T, the policymaker maintains a floating exchange rate system and the domestic currency depreciates at the constant rate of monetary expansion μ.

Hence the rate of currency depreciation δ_t follows:

$$\delta_t = \begin{cases} 0, & 0 \leq t < T \\ \mu, & t \geq T \end{cases} \tag{2.15}$$

Given the uncovered interest parity in equation (1.5), the private sector expects the nominal interest rate after time T to be worth:

$$i_T = i_t^{*} + \mu \tag{2.16}$$

With the policy rule in equation (2.14), equation (2.16) implies that the interest rate on liquidity bonds is:

$$i_T^g = i_0^g + \gamma\mu \tag{2.17}$$

Combining equations (2.16) and (2.17) leads to:

$$i_T - i_T^g = i_t^{*} \text{-} i_0^g + (1\text{-}\gamma)\mu \tag{2.18}$$

From equation (2.18), γ^{+}, that is the value of γ such that real money demand at time T does not vary, may be said to satisfy the following condition:

$$h(i_t^*) - h(i_t^* + \mu) = g[i_t^* - i_0^g + (1-\gamma^+)\mu] - g(i_t^* - i_0^g) \qquad (2.19)$$

For any given μ that is strictly positive, the left-hand side of equation (2.19) is a positive constant while its right-hand side is a strictly increasing function of γ (and negative for $\gamma = 0$). Thus γ^+ exists and is unique.

Equation (2.19) also allows the money market equilibrium at the time of the collapse to be determined. Assuming that equation (1.9) holds, i.e., the exchange rate does not jump at the time of the crisis, it follows that:

$$h(i_t^* + \mu) + g[i_t^* - i_0^g + (1-\gamma)\mu] = d_0 \exp(\mu T) - \underline{s} \qquad (2.20)$$

where the left-hand side of equation (2.20) denotes real money demand at time T and the right-hand side, real money supply at time T.

Equation (2.20) also defines T as a strictly increasing function of γ, i.e., $T = \overline{T}(\gamma)$. It may thus be analysed whether an increase in interest rates delays, and even prevents, a currency crisis, i.e., whether there is a monotonic and positive relationship between the moment T of the crisis and the degree γ of policy activism. Computing the slope of $\overline{T}(\gamma)$ leads to:

$$\overline{T}(\gamma) = \frac{-g'[i_t^* - i_0^g + (1-\gamma)\mu]}{d_0 \exp(\mu T)} \qquad (2.21)$$

Several cases, which are represented on Figure 2.1, may be distinguished:

- if $\gamma = 0$, the policymaker does not implement an interest rate defence of the exchange rate. Then $\overline{T}(0) = T^k$: the crisis occurs at time T^k.
- if $\gamma = \gamma^+$, the interest rate policy is such that real money demand does not change. The policymaker delays the crisis as long as he finds it possible, i.e., from T^k to T^+. When the fixed exchange rate system is abandoned at time T^+, no run on foreign exchange reserves occurs. Such a situation results from the influence of γ on the desired change in real money demand. The higher γ is, the smaller the variation in real money demand is, since the change in opportunity cost of holding liquid bonds becomes smaller. Because the desired change in real money demand determines the size of the attack, a higher γ implies a smaller speculative attack that is therefore more easily postponed.

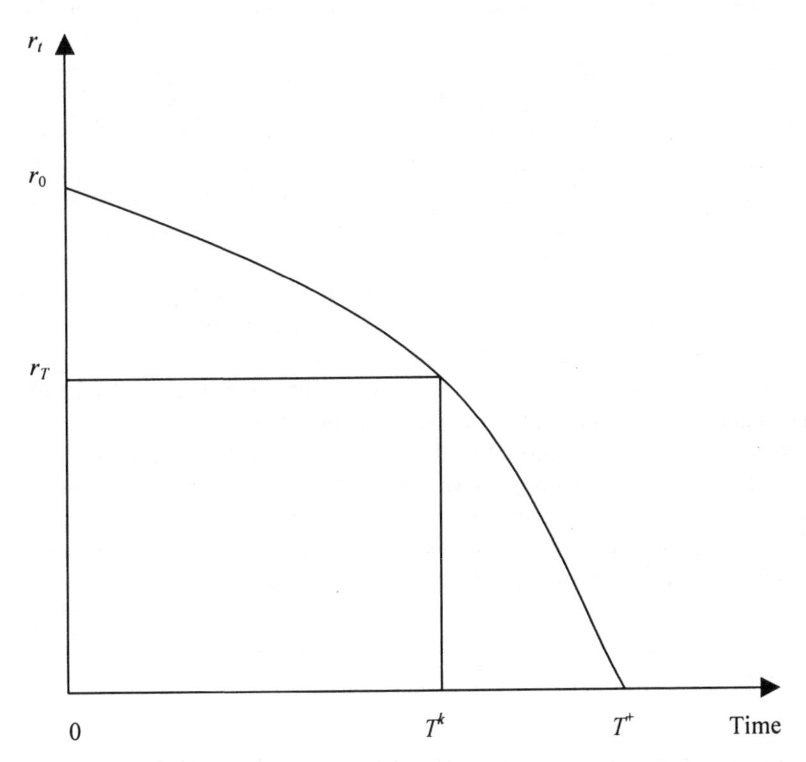

Figure 2.1 Sterilisation and the timing of the speculative attack

The analysis by Lahiri and Végh (2003) on the optimal rise in interest rates is disputed by Drazen (2000a) insofar as it does not take into account the costs born by the government through its intertemporal budget constraint following a fixed exchange rate defence. This increase in costs is even absent from their main model. Hence the maximum rise in interest rates is always optimal. Lahiri and Végh (2003) however admit that the intertemporal budget constraint imposes interest rate payments that must be financed by a future inflation tax.[4] The maximum rise in interest rates is therefore no longer optimal, but a partial defence may be. Still the relevance of such an analysis is limited since the model of Lahiri and Végh (2003) only takes into account parts of the costs that follow a rise in interest rates, especially the negative effects on consumption and the domestic product.[5]

The relevance of a sterilisation policy in a first-generation-model framework is also questionable. Flood, Garber and Kramer (1996) show that a sterilisation policy is efficient in a perfect foresight expectation model if national and foreign assets are not perfectly substitutable. Their idea is developed by Flood and Marion (1998a, 1998b) who replace equation (1.5) by a formula that incorporates a risk premium. But they acknowledge that introducing a risk premium in a perfect foresight model is an anomaly.

Flood and Marion (1998a, 1998b) consider that a complete sterilisation policy is only efficient if the initial amount of foreign exchange reserves is sufficiently high. Flood, Garber and Kramer (1996) however consider that losses may be sterilised for different levels of foreign exchange reserves left to the policymaker's appreciation. But this strategy is not necessarily efficient: Mexican authorities used it unsuccessfully during the peso crisis in December 1994.[6] If sterilising the money supply cannot prevent foreign exchange reserve losses and capital outflows, increasing the interest rate may foster capital inflows and raise the amount of reserves.

To sum up, research dealing with sterilisation policies and rise in interest rates considers that these strategies of fixed peg defences are inefficient in first-generation models, since monetary policy is a priori incompatible with a fixed exchange rate regime. These studies also relax an over-simplifying assumption of the model presented in Chapter 1, i.e., the policymaker never tries to prevent the fall in the exchange rate. But in most instances, policymakers try to avoid collapses of the peg. Likewise it is assumed in Chapter 1 that a flexible exchange rate system is always established after a speculative attack. However, the policymaker may opt for other exchange rate systems.

2. THE CHOICE OF AN EXCHANGE RATE REGIME AFTER SPECULATIVE ATTACKS

In the first-generation model of Chapter 1, it is assumed that an attack always triggers a shift to a float. Yet the policymaker may choose to establish other exchange rate regimes after a crisis. Blanco and Garber (1986) consider that a devaluation allows him to establish a new fixed exchange rate regime. He may also opt for a crawling peg as Dornbusch (1987) and Savastano (1992) suggest. The choice of an exchange rate regime may also influence the moment the crisis occurs. Under perfect foresight, Obstfeld (1984) and Djajic (1989) analyse the situation where a speculative attack leads to a period of floating before a new fixed exchange rate is established. It is assumed that the policymaker lets the currency float during a temporary period τ, then re-establishes a fixed exchange rate regime at rate $\underline{s}'$, such that:

$$\underline{s}' > \underline{s} \qquad (2.22)$$

with $\underline{s}$ is the exchange rate at time T. Variables T and $\underline{s}$ are known by speculators who have perfect foresight expectations, with

$$s_T = \underline{s} \tag{2.23}$$

and

$$s_{T+\tau} = \underline{s}' \tag{2.24}$$

By assumption the shadow exchange rate during the transitory period of floating follows:

$$\widetilde{s}_t = \alpha\mu + d_t + \chi\exp(t / \gamma) \tag{2.25}$$

where χ is an arbitrary constant.

Consequently the exchange rates at time T and $T+\tau$ are:

$$s_T = \alpha\mu + d_0 + \mu T + \chi\exp(T/\gamma) \tag{2.26}$$

and

$$s_{T+\tau} = \alpha\mu + d_0 + \mu(T+\tau) + \chi\exp[(T+\tau)/\gamma] \tag{2.27}$$

To satisfy equations (2.23) and (2.24) in equilibrium, the constant χ must equal

$$\chi = s_{T+\tau}.\exp[-(T+\tau)/\gamma] \tag{2.28}$$

Therefore the moment T when the speculative attack occurs is:

$$T = \frac{r_0 - \alpha\mu}{\mu} - \frac{\tau.\exp(\tau / \gamma)}{1 - \exp(-\tau / \gamma)} \tag{2.29}$$

Under perfect foresight, equation (2.29) shows that the moment the crisis takes place is related both to monetary policy and to the length of the floating period:

- The bigger the expected devaluation, the earlier the speculative attack takes place.
- The influence of the floating period τ on T is uncertain. If τ is high, $\partial T/\partial\tau > 0$; if τ is low, $\partial T/\partial\tau < 0$.

To sum up, if the period of floating is very short, or the expected devaluation is large, the speculative attack happens as soon as private agents understand that the fixed exchange rate regime cannot be maintained for ever.

Studies that deal with the choice of the exchange rate regime after a crisis point out the importance of the perfect foresight assumption in first-generation models. It must then be investigated whether the main results of these models still hold when this assumption is relaxed and a stochastic framework is introduced.

3. SPECULATIVE ATTACKS IN A STOCHASTIC FRAMEWORK

Most first-generation models rest on the assumption that agents have perfect foresight expectations. They rightly anticipate the policymaker's behaviour. For instance they know the threshold level of reserves where the policymaker lets the exchange rate go. They are also knowledgeable about the monetary policies he implements before and after the crisis. But in an imperfect world, it is unlikely that speculators know for certain what the policymaker plans to do, let alone when he is going to let the exchange rate go.

For example it is likely that market participants ignore the amount of reserves the policymaker is willing to commit in defence of the peg. Krugman (1979) believes this situation may entail a series of crises and renewals of confidence on foreign exchange markets. Willman (1989) considers that the process the policymaker uses to determine the threshold level $\underline{r}$ influences the speculators' behaviour. If $\underline{r}$ stems from a stochastic computation, the currency crisis consists of several distinct speculative attacks throughout time. When $\underline{r}$ is set in advance, but remains unknown to market participants, the speculative attack only takes place once.

Introducing a stochastic framework also modifies the analysis of monetary policy. Flood and Garber (1984b) develop a random process of domestic credit growth in a discrete time model of currency crises. Their analysis departs from the model in Chapter 1 by assuming that speculators launch an attack when they believe at time t that the growth in domestic credit at time t+1 will trigger a depreciation of the exchange rate if a speculative attack occurs. Therefore a currency crisis only happens if the shadow exchange rate $\tilde{s}$ undergoes a depreciation relative to the fixed exchange rate. The speculative attack occurs if:

$$s_t > \underline{s} \quad (2.30)$$

As a result the specific domestic growth creation process influences the probability ${}_t\pi_{t+1}$ at time t of an attack at time $t+1$:

$$ {}_t\pi_{t+1} = \text{Prob}\,(s_{t+1} > \underline{s}) \tag{2.31} $$

Next the expected depreciation in the exchange rate is determined:

$$ E_t s_{t+1} - s_t = {}_t\pi_{t+1}\left[E_t(s_{t+1}|s_{t+1} > \underline{s}) - \underline{s}\right] \tag{2.32} $$

with $E_t(s_{t+1}|s_{t+1}>\underline{s})$ the speculators' conditional expectations of the exchange rate at time $t+1$.

The expected depreciation rate hinges on variables that have an impact on s_t. It expands before the outbreak of the crisis since ${}_t\pi_{t+1}$ and $E_t(s_{t+1}|s_{t+1}>\underline{s})-\underline{s}$ increase before a speculative attack.

Let $g_t(s_{t+1})$ be the density probability function at time t of s_{t+1}. Equations (2.31) and (2.32) become:

$$ {}_t\pi_{t+1} = \int_{\underline{s}}^{+\infty} g_t(s_{t+1})ds_{t+1} \tag{2.33} $$

and

$$ E_t(s_{t+1}|s_{t+1} > \underline{s}) = \int_{\underline{s}}^{+\infty} g_t(s_{t+1})s_{t+1}ds_{t+1} \tag{2.34} $$

The probability ${}_t\pi_{t+1}$ at time t of an attack at time $t+1$ rises before the outbreak of a speculative attack. It depends on $E_t(s_{t+1}|s_{t+1}>\underline{s})$, which is the speculators' expected value at time t of the exchange rate at time $t+1$, that itself hinges on the expected value at time t of the domestic credit at time $t+1$. Thus the growth of the domestic credit at each time period entails a rise in the nominal interest rate which becomes more significant as the outbreak of the currency crisis is closer. This is an empirical feature of currency crises which is absent from currency crisis models with perfect foresight expectations, as Blanco and Garber (1986) note.

Their study, which deals with the periodic devaluations in Mexico between 1973 and 1982, shows that the stochastic nature of domestic growth creation influences agents' expectations and the moment of the attack. Their estimations do not however provide a definite assessment of the credit growth process. They assume that the monetary base follows an auto-regressive process that is independent of the exchange rate. Flood and Garber (1984b) assume that the domestic credit follows an exponential distribution:

its high increase immediately entails important reserve losses. This implies that a speculative attack may suddenly compel the policymaker to give up on the fixed exchange regime, even though the initial amount of exchange reserves is high. But according to Dornbusch (1987), high reserves may help avoid a currency crisis if the domestic credit growth process follows a uniform distribution and has an upper bound.

As can be seen, the stochastic framework influences the fall of the fixed exchange rate regime which is not even certain. Consequently Flood and Garber (1984b) and Dornbusch (1987) agree that it is impossible to determine the moment the policymaker lets the exchange rate go, since the speculative attack does not necessarily happen. Pastine (2002) even asserts that a currency collapse may be avoided in a first-generation framework if the policymaker is of a forward-looking type: he introduces uncertainty in the speculators' decisions and the attack is not sudden any more. Instead there is a prolonged period of speculation and uncertainty such that the policymaker may eventually keep the exchange rate fixed.

All in all, a stochastic approach to the framework of first-generation models shows how these models are questionable. Grilli (1986) states that uncertainty influences speculators' expectations such that changes in exchange rate regimes occur independently of the evolution of monetary aggregates. Obstfeld (1986b) also establishes that, because of uncertainty, a speculative attack may happen and trigger a float, even though macroeconomic fundamentals are compatible with a fixed exchange rate system. Grilli (1986) and Obstfeld (1986b) deduce from their models that the fall of a fixed exchange rate regime does not result from unsound monetary and fiscal policies, but from the speculators' self-fulfilling expectations. Their analyses are a turning point in currency crisis studies and call into question the whole relevance of first-generation models, in spite of their various extensions.

4. CHAPTER SUMMARY

In first-generation models, the policymaker's behaviour is exogenous. His fiscal and monetary policies are by assumption at the root of speculative attacks. Yet some studies investigate what the policymaker may do in times of currency crises. They deal with potential defences against speculative attacks, the choice of an exchange rate system after a crisis, and the effects of uncertainty on economic policies.

Several types of fixed-exchange-rate defences against speculative attacks are dealt with in this framework. Wyplosz (1986), Bacchetta (1990) and Gros (1992) study the effectiveness of capital controls. Buiter (1987), Grilli

(1990), and Mizen (1999) examine the effects of financing foreign exchange reserves by borrowing on foreign exchange markets. Flood, Garber and Kramer (1996) discuss the pros and cons of sterilisation. Flood and Jeanne (2000) and Lahiri and Végh (2003) examine the effectiveness of an interest rate defence of fixed exchange rate systems. But given that an expansionary monetary policy is a priori incompatible with a fixed exchange rate system in these models, such defences cannot eventually prevent a fall in the exchange rate.

Authorities may choose the exchange rate regime that is to prevail when a devaluation has just occurred. Studies by Obstfeld (1984), Dornbusch (1987), Djajic (1989) and Savastano (1992) examine which exchange rate system the policymaker should opt for just after a speculative attack. Obstfeld (1984) and Djajic (1989) show that the policymaker's willingness to restore a fixed exchange system after a short period of float influences the launching of the speculative attack leading to a flexible exchange rate system.

All these models assume that private agents know exactly which economic policies are implemented. Several other papers, e.g., Flood and Garber (1984b), Cumby and Wijnbergen (1989), depart from the perfect foresight assumption and use a stochastic framework to study the policymaker's behaviour. They find it impossible to determine the moment when the speculative attack occurs. Actually it is not even certain that the currency crisis will happen.

In addition Grilli (1986) and Obstfeld (1986b) state that the introduction of a stochastic framework in the first-generation models calls into question the very assumptions of these studies. Currency crises should not result from expansionary fiscal and monetary policies, but from the speculators' self-fulfilling expectations.

NOTES

1. See Isard (1995) for a general discussion on the effects of capital controls. See also Drazen (2000b) on the political incentives governments may have to establish capital controls.
2. The primary deficit is the deficit free from the interest paid on the public debt.
3. There are studies on interest rate rises in the framework of third-generation models. See Chapter 7, Section 1, The policymaker's optimal commitment to exchange rate stability.
4. See Sargent and Wallace (1981) for an analysis of the future inflation tax.
5. Lahiri and Végh (2003) criticise Flood and Jeanne (2000) for not discussing the optimality of an interest rate defence policy. It must be remembered that in first-generation models, the optimality of a policy decision is never discussed since the policymaker's behaviour is exogenous. Even though Lahiri and Végh (2003) do not provide the government with a loss function, discussing welfare maximisation leads their study to depart from the canonical framework of first-generation models while Flood and Jeanne (2000) remain closer to it.
6. On this matter, see Kumhof (2000). For an account of the 1994 Mexican crisis, see Dornbusch, Goldfajn and Valdés (1995) and Sachs (1995).

3. Extensions of First-generation Models

Although the model of Chapter 1 provides some insights into the causes of speculative attacks, some of its assumptions seem over-simplifying. It overlooks various side issues of currency crises. This is why several studies attempt to refine the analysis of speculative attacks by providing extensions to the standard first-generation model.

A first type of extension concerns the causes of speculative attacks. Instead of focusing on the effects of an expansionary monetary policy, some analyses emphasise fiscal deficits as a source of speculative attacks.

A second strand of research deals with the real effects of speculative attacks. It is often assumed that a devaluation positively influences real output, provided the Marshall–Lerner conditions are satisfied. However it seems that currency crises may also bring about recessions.

Other studies relax an over-simplifying assumption of first-generation models: they introduce banks in the framework presented in Chapter 1. They consider that an increase in banking loans precipitates crises, following excessive governmental domestic credit creation, or that the banking debts which are warranted by public guarantees are a source of speculative attacks.

A fourth type of extension deals with the coordination of speculative attacks and the possibility of contagion. By introducing imperfect communication among market participants, it is shown that the moment when the speculative attacks occur is postponed. Currency crises may thus hit more than one country.

1. FISCAL SOURCES OF SPECULATIVE ATTACKS

The standard first-generation model of Krugman (1979) and Flood and Garber (1984b) presented in Chapter 1 considers that an expansionary monetary policy is the single cause of speculative attacks. Indeed fundamentals are confined to monetary policy variables. A logical extension of the model in Chapter 1 then involves analysing the effects of expansionary fiscal policies on the outbreak of currency crises.

Drawing on Burnside, Eichenbaum and Rebelo (2001a), a model of fiscal-related speculative attacks in presented here:

$$m_t - p_t = -\alpha i_t \tag{3.1}$$

$$p_t = p_t^* + s_t \tag{3.2}$$

$$i_t = i_t^* + E_{t-1} \Delta s_t \tag{3.3}$$

$$m_t = s_t . \exp(-\alpha i_t) \tag{3.4}$$

where m_t represents the domestic money supply, i_t the domestic interest rate, i_t^* the foreign interest rate, p_t the price level in the domestic country, p_t^* the price level in the foreign country, μ the growth rate in domestic credit that is assumed to be constant and strictly positive, s_t the exchange rate, and Δs_t the change in the exchange rate between dates t and t-1. All variables are expressed in logarithm except for the interest rate and $-\alpha i$ that represents the agents' demand for money.

The first three equations in the model stem from Chapter 1 and are renamed here to avoid cross-references. Equation (3.1) describes the equilibrium condition in the money market. Equations (3.2) and (3.3) respectively indicate that the price level follows the purchasing power parity rule and that the interest rate obeys the uncovered interest parity rule. Equation (3.4) states the equality between money supply and money demand.

It is assumed that the foreign price level, domestic real income and the money supply are constant. Hence the government is unable to use seigniorage as a means to increase its revenues.[1] In line with the model of Chapter 1, a shift to a flexible exchange rate system is unavoidable. The source of currency crises does not however stem from monetary policy. Speculative attacks result from present and, most importantly, future fiscal imbalances: these are the so-called 'prospective fiscal deficits'. In this framework, the time T when the speculative attack takes place hinges on two aspects of the government's policy:

1. The government's rule on abandoning the fixed exchange rate. It is assumed that the shift to a flexible exchange rate regime takes place when public debt reaches a finite upper bound. As such, this threshold rule can be interpreted as a short-run borrowing constraint on the government: it limits the amount of reserves. Such a rule amounts to letting the exchange rate go when the amount of domestic money sold

by private agents in exchange of foreign currency exceeds χ percent of the initial money supply.

2. The government's monetary policy after the collapse. At some point in time $t = t^*$ after the crisis, the policymaker increases the money supply by an amount equal to γ percent of m_t as defined in equation (3.4). This discrete rise makes the money supply grow at rate μ. The evolution of the money supply hence follows a two-equation rule.

a. If $T \leq t < t^*$:

$$m_t = \exp(-\chi).m_{t-1} \tag{3.5}$$

b. If $t \geq t^*$:

$$m_t = \exp[\gamma + \mu(t - t^*)].m_{t-1} \tag{3.6}$$

Equations (3.5) and (3.6) define the timing of events: the endogenous time when the speculative attack occurs depends on the moment the policymaker implements its new monetary policy.[2]

Next the time of the speculative attack is determined.[3] Following the derivation in Sargent and Wallace (1973), equation (3.1), which describes the money demand function, becomes:

$$p_t = \alpha i_t + \frac{1}{\alpha}\int_t^{+\infty} \exp[-(s_t - t)/\alpha]m_s ds \tag{3.7}$$

By assumption the government lets the exchange rate go at time T. Equation (2.7) hence implies that the price level after T is:

$$p_T = \alpha i_t + \frac{1}{\alpha}\int_T^{+\infty} m_s \exp[-(s_t - T)/\alpha] ds \tag{3.8}$$

Before the devaluation, money demand implies that (2.1) holds. Assuming continuity of the price level at T, that is:

$$p_t = p_T \tag{3.9}$$

it is found from equations (2.7) and (2.8) that:

$$m_t = \frac{1}{\alpha}\int_T^{+\infty} m_s \exp[-(s_t - T)/\alpha]\,ds \qquad (3.10)$$

It is assumed that the government abandons the peg when χ percent of the foreign exchange reserves are sold. Whence it follows from equations (3.5) and (3.6) that:

$$\frac{1}{\alpha}\int_T^{+\infty} m_s \exp[-(s_t - T)/\alpha]\,ds =$$

$$m_t - \chi[1 - \exp(-(t^* - T)/\alpha)] + (\gamma + \mu\alpha)\exp[-(t^* - T)/\alpha] \quad (3.11)$$

The time T of the speculative attack may be determined by substituting equation (3.11) into equation (3.10):

$$T = t^* - \alpha(\chi + \gamma + \mu\alpha)/\chi \qquad (3.12)$$

In this framework, there are two jumps in real money balances. The first one occurs at time T and triggers a devaluation. The second one happens at time t^* when the government increases the money supply by γ. Assuming fixed values of t^* and γ, the government's simplified intertemporal budget constraint is satisfied if:

$$\varphi = \int_{t^*}^{+\infty} (\dot{m}_t + \pi_t m_t)\exp(-i.t)dt + \exp(-i.T)\dot{m}_T dt + \exp(-i.t^*)\dot{m}_{t^*} \qquad (3.13)$$

Equation (3.13) is a simplified version of the government intertemporal budget constraint. The interest rate i is assumed to be constant. There are no nonindexed governmental liabilities and no seigniorage is collected between T and t^*.

After time t^*, the inflation rate is constant and equals μ, the growth rate in domestic credit. Real balances are also constant and equal to $\exp[-\alpha(i+\mu)]$. The government's intertemporal budget constraint in equation (3.13) may then be rewritten as:

$$\varphi = \exp(-i.t^*).(\mu/i).\exp[-\alpha(i+\mu)] + \exp(-iT).\,\dot{m}_T + \exp(-i.t^*).\,\dot{m}_t \quad (3.14)$$

The model is solved by determining the two unknowns T and μ in equations (3.12) and (3.14).

Equations (3.12) and (3.14) suggest that the currency crisis occurs before the government implements a rise in domestic money supply: $T<t^*$. If all other things are equal, t^* is larger:

- the longer the government delays implementing its new monetary policy, that is the larger is T;
- the more willing to accumulate debt the government is, that is the higher χ is; moreover other things being equal, T is smaller;
- the higher the interest elasticity of money demand, that is the larger α is;
- the more money the government prints in the future, that is the higher γ and μ are.

'Prospective fiscal deficits', which are also associated with banking crises (see in this chapter, section 3, Influence of the banking sector) in the study of Burnside, Eichenbaum and Rebelo (2001a), are not the single source of speculative attacks from fiscal imbalances. Prior studies emphasise that market imperfections, i.e., price stickiness and imperfect substitution between assets, may also cause fiscal-related currency crises.

Flood and Hodrick (1986), Blackburn (1988), Willman (1988) and Goldberg (1991) study the effects of price stickiness and imperfect substitution between assets. Unlike Chapter 1's model, prices are no longer assumed to be flexible while domestic and foreign assets are not perfect substitutes anymore. Goldberg (1991) abandons the purchasing power parity condition. She suggests that it should be replaced by another equation where purchasing power parity is not satisfied in the short–run. Thus Blackburn (1988), Flood and Hodrick (1986) and Willman (1988) use a price-adjustment equation that is inspired by the exchange rate dynamic model of Dornbusch (1976). Blackburn (1988) develops a currency crisis model where quick price adjustments and high capital mobility hasten the outbreak of speculative attacks. Willman (1988) refines the analyses of Blackburn (1988) by taking into account public spending that may be a possible source of the balance-of-payments deficit. Speculative attacks are shown not only to result from the policymaker's unsound monetary policies, but also from his inconsequent fiscal policies. Willman (1988) thus casts light on some additional causes of currency crises, especially their real effects.

2. REAL EFFECTS OF CURRENCY CRISES

While the framework of first-generation models ignores the real effects of speculative attacks, empirical studies by Blanco and Garber (1986), Cumby and van Wijnbergen (1989) and Goldberg (1994) show that large trade balance and current account movements occur before and after speculative attacks. These studies consider that a deficit in the current account[4] signals approaching speculative attacks since market participants modify their consumption behaviour and their portfolio allocations – they choose safer currencies – when they expect a crisis. These portfolio adjustments explain why attacks are often preceded by periods where the decreasing rate of foreign exchange reserves is, in absolute value, superior to the growth rate in domestic credit. These empirical studies corroborate theoretical analyses dealing with the real effects of currency crises.

The presentation in this section draws on Osakwe and Schembri (2002), using elements of the stochastic model of speculative attacks that is presented in Chapter 2, section 3, Speculative attacks in a stochastic framework:

$$m_t - p_t = -\alpha i_t + \gamma y_t \tag{3.15}$$

$$y_t = \beta\left(p^* + s_t - p_t\right) - \lambda \rho_t + u_t \tag{3.16}$$

$$\bar{y} = \beta\left(p^* + s_t - p_t\right) - \lambda E_{t\text{-}1}\rho_t + E_{t\text{-}1}u_t \tag{3.17}$$

$$i_t^* = x_t + \zeta \tag{3.18}$$

$$m_t = d_t + r_t \tag{3.19}$$

$$\dot{d} = \mu \tag{3.20}$$

$$p_t = p_t^* + s_t \tag{3.2}$$

$$i_t = i_t^* + E_{t-1}\Delta s_t \tag{3.3}$$

where m_t represents the domestic money supply, i_t the domestic interest rate, p_t the price level in the domestic country, μ the growth rate in domestic credit, s_t the exchange rate, y_t real output, $\bar{y}$ full employment output, ρ_t the real interest rate, ζ a constant. The shocks u_t and x_t are mutually and serially uncorrelated shocks that have null means and constant variances σ_u^2 and σ_x^2. The index t indicates that the variable is measured at time t, E_t is the conditional expectation operator of the information available at time t, Δs_t represents the change in the exchange rate between dates t and t-1.

Equation (3.15) is a modified version of equation (3.1): it states that real money balances depends on the nominal interest rate i_t and on real output y_t.

In equation (3.16), real output depends positively on the relative price of foreign to home goods and negatively on the real interest rate ρ_t. Equation (3.17) shows how domestic prices are determined. At time t-1 the domestic price for period t is such that expected demand equals full employment output $\bar{y}$. Equation (3.18) describes the evolution of the foreign nominal interest rate.

Equations (3.2), (3.3), (3.19) and (3.20) are those of the model of Chapter 1 and are renamed here to avoid any cross-references. Equations (3.2) and (3.3) respectively indicate that the price level follows the purchasing power parity rule and that the interest rate is governed by the uncovered interest parity rule. In equation (3.19), the supply of money equals the sum of foreign exchange reserves and domestic credit. In equation (3.20), domestic credit increases at a constant and strictly positive rate μ.

In line with the model of Chapter 1, the threshold level of reserves $\underline{r}$ when the government lets the exchange rate go equals zero. From equations (3.2), (3.3) and equations (3.15) to (3.20), a first-order stochastic equation is obtained:

$$s_t = k_0 + k_1 d_{t-1} + k_2 x_t + k_3 u_t \tag{3.21}$$

This equation is solved for the flexible exchange rate with the method of undetermined coefficients (see the appendix to this chapter).

$$k_0 = \left(1+\alpha+\frac{\lambda}{\beta}\right)\mu - \frac{\lambda}{\beta}\mu + \left(\alpha+\frac{\lambda}{\beta}\right)i^* - p^* \tag{3.22}$$

$$k_1 = 1 \tag{3.23}$$

$$k_2 = \frac{\alpha+\gamma\lambda}{\alpha+\gamma\lambda+\gamma\beta} \tag{3.24}$$

$$k_3 = \frac{-\gamma}{\alpha+\gamma\beta+\gamma\lambda} \tag{3.25}$$

From equations (3.22) to (3.25), it appears that:

- a positive demand shock induces a nominal real exchange appreciation;
- a rise in (lagged) domestic credit and a foreign interest rate shock (consistent with capital outflows) lead to a nominal real exchange depreciation.[5]

Following Flood and Hodrick (1986), the conditional variance of real output is used as a measure of the variability of output across exchange rate regimes:

$$\text{Var}_{t-1}(y_t) = E_{t-1}(y_t - E_{t-1}y_t)^2 \tag{3.26}$$

To simplify the analysis, let $\bar{y}=E_{t-1}y_t$ and $E_{t-1}y_t=0$. Using equation (3.16) that defines real output, the conditional variance of real output under a permanently fixed exchange rate regime is:

$$\begin{aligned}\text{Var}_{t-1}(y_t)|_{\text{Flex}} = {} & (\beta+\lambda)^2\text{Var}_{t-1}(s_t)+\lambda^2\text{Var}_{t-1}(x_t)+\text{Var}_{t-1}(u_t) \\ & -2(\beta+\lambda)\lambda\text{Cov}_{t-1}(s_t,x_t)+2(\beta+\lambda)\text{Cov}_{t-1}(s_t,u_t)\end{aligned} \tag{3.27}$$

with $\text{Cov}_{t-1}(s_t,x_t)$ being the conditional covariance between the exchange rate and the foreign interest rate shock, and $\text{Cov}_{t-1}(s_t,u_t)$ being the conditional covariance between the exchange rate and the demand shock.

In a fixed exchange rate regime, the variance of the exchange rate and the related covariances are null. The variance of real output under a permanently fixed exchange rate regime therefore equals:

$$\text{Var}_{t-1}(y_t)|_{Fix} = \lambda^2\text{Var}_{t-1}(x_t)+\text{Var}_{t-1}(u_t) \tag{3.28}$$

Equations (3.27) and (3.28) do not provide a definitive answer on the exchange rate regime with the lower conditional variance from real output. This results from covariances between the flexible exchange rate and the two shocks being negative.

Such uncertainty about the relationship between the conditional variance for output and the type of exchange rate regimes is all the more straightforward, when equations (3.27) and (3.28) are rewritten using the solution for the flexible exchange rate in equations (3.22) to (3.25) and the definitions of the shocks:

$$\text{Var}_{t-1}(y_t)|_{\text{Flex}} = \left(\frac{\alpha}{\alpha+\gamma\lambda+\gamma\beta}\right)^2\left(\beta^2\sigma_x^2+\sigma_u^2\right) \tag{3.29}$$

and

$$\text{Var}_{t-1}(y_t)|_{\text{Fix}} = \lambda^2\sigma_x^2+\sigma_u^2 \tag{3.30}$$

From equations (3.29) and (3.30), $\beta<\lambda$ is a sufficient but not necessary condition for the flexible exchange rate regime to have a lower real output variance than the fixed peg. Moreover it implies that under a permanently flexible exchange rate regime, the domestic and foreign interest rates are equal. Shocks to the foreign interest rate fully affect the domestic interest rate, and through λ, the variability of aggregate demand and output. Under a permanently fixed exchange rate, foreign interest rate shocks affect aggregate demand indirectly, through the exchange rate, via β.

This analysis however lays an implicit assumption when analysing the variance of real output: the flexible or the fixed exchange rate regime is chosen, and then lasts indefinitely. But what happens if the fixed exchange rate is assumed to collapse at some point in time? If the assumption of perfect foresight is relieved, speculators form expectations about future exchange rates, anticipating that the peg may collapse in the near or distant future. In order to determine the probability of the fixed exchange rate regime according to speculators, the shadow flexible exchange rate has to be computed.

Maintaining the assumption that $\underline{r} = 0$, the shadow exchange rate $\tilde{s}$ equals:

$$\tilde{s}_t = \tilde{k}_0 + k_1 d_{t-1} + k_2 x_t + k_3 u_t \tag{3.31}$$

with:

$$\tilde{k}_0 = \left(1 + \alpha + \frac{\lambda}{\beta}\right)\mu - \frac{\lambda}{\beta}\mu + \left(\alpha + \frac{\lambda}{\beta}\right)i^* - p^* \tag{3.32}$$

and k_1, k_2 and k_3 as defined in equations (3.23), (3.24) and (3.25).

Following the stochastic framework defined in Chapter 2, section 3, Speculative attacks in a stochastic framework, speculators benefit from a speculative attack if the shadow flexible exchange rate is greater than the fixed peg. Therefore the probability of a speculative attack is the likelihood that the shadow flexible exchange rate is greater than the fixed peg:

$$\pi_{t-1} = \text{Prob}_{t-1}\left(\tilde{s} > \underline{s}\right) \tag{3.33}$$

Given the definition of the shadow flexible exchange rate in equation (3.31), it follows that:

$$\pi_{t-1} = \text{Prob}_{t-1}\left(Z_t > v_{t-1}\right) \tag{3.34}$$

with:

$$Z_t = k_2 x_t + k_3 u_t \tag{3.35}$$

and:

$$v_{t-1} = \underline{s} - \widetilde{k}_0 - k_1 d_{t-1} \tag{3.36}$$

Given π_{t-1}, the expectation at time t-1 of the exchange rate at time t, denoted $E_{t-1}\Delta s_t$, is a weighted average of:

- the exchange rate when the peg is abandoned, that is the value of the shadow flexible exchange rate and of
- the exchange rate when the peg is not abandoned, that is the current fixed exchange rate.

As such $E_{t-1}\Delta s_t$ equals:

$$E_{t-1}s_t = (1-\pi_{t-1})\underline{s} + \pi_{t-1}E_{t-1}(\widetilde{s}_t|C_t) \tag{3.37}$$

with $E_{t-1}(\widetilde{s}\,|C_t)$ being the expectation at time t-1 of the exchange rate at time t conditional on a collapse at time t. This leads to the following expression of the conditional variance of output under a fixed exchange rate regime:

$$\begin{aligned}\mathrm{Var}_{t-1}(y_t)|_{\mathrm{CFix1}} = {} & (\beta+\lambda)^2.\, E_{t-1}(\Delta s_t^2) + \lambda^2.E_{t-1}(x_t^2) + E_{t-1}(u_t^2) \\ & -2(\beta+\lambda)[\lambda.E_{t-1}(s_t x_t) - E_{t-1}(s_t, u_t)]\end{aligned} \tag{3.38}$$

A second definition of the conditional variance of output under a collapsing fixed exchange rate regime may be used: the conditional variance of output in a regime that is expected to collapse but has not yet. This variance would be estimated using a sample of observations for an exchange rate regime that eventually collapses, but the sample does not actually include the point of the collapse. This conditional variance is denoted $\mathrm{Var}_{t-1}(y_t)|_{\mathrm{CFix2}}$ and is worth:

$$\mathrm{Var}_{t-1}(y_t)|_{\mathrm{CFix2}} = (\beta+\lambda)^2.\, E_{t-1}(\Delta s_t^2) + \lambda^2.E_{t-1}(x_t^2) + E_{t-1}(u_t^2) \tag{3.39}$$

Following Osakwe and Schembri (2002), an estimate of equation (3.38) may be interpreted as an estimate of the asymptotic conditional variance of output under the collapsing regime; an estimate of equation (3.39) may be viewed as an estimation of equation (3.38) on a small sample.

Osakwe and Schembri (2002) show, by estimating equation (3.38), that the variance of output in a fixed exchange rate regime that is expected to collapse (*C*Fix1) lies between the variance of output in a permanent flexible exchange rate regime and the variance of output in a permanent fixed exchange rate regime. The lower (respectively higher) the probabilities of collapse, the closer the variance of output under a collapsing fixed exchange rate regime is to the variance of output under a permanently fixed (respectively flexible) exchange rate regime. Under a fixed exchange rate regime that is expected to collapse, the variance of output is a weighted average of the variances under the two permanent regimes, where the weights are a nonlinear function of the probability of collapse.

Osakwe and Schembri (2002) also estimate equation (3.39) and show that the variance of output under a fixed exchange rate regime that is expected to collapse but has not yet (*C*Fix2) is higher than the variance of output in the permanently fixed and flexible exchange rate systems. Such a result stems from prediction errors that increase as the probability of a crisis rises and generate a price level that is relatively far from the one that would equate aggregate demand to the full employment level of output in equation (3.17). For instance in the expectation of a collapse and of a depreciation in the exchange rate, the domestic price level is set higher to equate aggregate demand to the full employment level of output. But if no crisis occurs, then the output gap will be positive and the trade balance will be reduced. In such a case, the conditional variance of output rises as the prediction errors for the exchange rate grow larger.

Such a result illustrates a phenomenon that appears in the empirical studies of Blanco and Garber (1986), Cumby and van Wijnbergen (1989) and Goldberg (1994). Before the collapse, i.e., when the likelihood of a speculative attack is high, economic variables are far from their long-run equilibrium values. Domestic output may be slumping, imports may increase and the trade balance deficit may widen.

There are other studies dealing with the real effects of speculative attacks. Connoly and Taylor (1984) and Goldberg (1991) analyse the situation where there are traded and non-traded goods. Calvo (1987) and Claessens (1988) examine how the agents' intertemporal consumption variations influence their crisis expectations. Flood and Hodrick (1986), Blackburn (1988) and Willman (1988) deal with the real effects of speculative attacks in a small country where there is some price stickiness.

Willman (1988) analyses the situation where domestic production, via demand, is a positive function of the real exchange rate and a negative function of the interest rate. The trade balance positively hinges on the real exchange rate and negatively on the domestic product. In addition, prices are influenced by wages, which are previously set following either 'backward looking' or 'forward looking' schemes.[6] In such a framework, and under perfect foresight, Willman (1988) shows that a currency crisis brings about changes in the real and financial sectors. In particular, when contracts are of the 'forward-looking' type, private agents who expect a currency crisis provoke a rise in prices and a decrease in domestic product before the fall of the fixed peg. Domestic competitiveness deteriorates and increases the trade deficit. It will progressively diminish once the crisis is over. Thus Willman (1988) provides many an insight on some empirical features of speculative attacks, notably on current account deficits and empirical outflows.

Penati and Pennachi (1989) give another explanation of capital movements before and after the outbreak of a crisis. They apply the Capital Asset Pricing Model (CAPM) to an intertemporal monetary framework so as to determine private agents' optimal consumption and investment decisions. They assume that the policymaker is systematically subjected to reserve losses before a currency crisis, as a result of an expansionary monetary policy. This excessive creation of domestic credit provides incentives to market participants to hedge against the risk of a devaluation by buying foreign-currency denominated bonds. The expected fall of the exchange rate leads to a depreciation and a 'jump' in the domestic price level. The expected inflation rate then becomes positive, while the nominal interest rate rises and the demand for domestic money decreases. This analysis explains some features of the 1976 Italian and the 1983 French currency crises.

Studies by Conolly and Taylor (1984) and Calvo (1987) also try to explain another empirical characteristic of currency crises, one that relates to the evolution of the prices of traded and non-traded goods.[7] They suggest that the price of traded goods remains constant because the exchange rate is assumed to be continuous and the international price of traded goods is supposedly constant. Hence only the price of non-traded goods varies before and after the attack. The fall in the real exchange rate entails a decrease in the price of non-traded goods relatively to the price of traded goods. No country gains a trade advantage, even a temporary one, from a devaluation. Calvo (1987) considers that this result is not paradoxical, though it may appear to be so, since the framework of first-generation models does not take into account the labour market. Currency crises may stem from a rise in unemployment if prices and wages are downwardly rigid.

It must be said that studies dealing with non-traded and traded goods in currency crises remain peripheral. There are on the other hand several papers that analyse the influence of banking institutions on the outbreak of speculative attacks.

3. INFLUENCE OF THE BANKING SECTOR

Several empirical studies by Demirgüç-Kunt and Detragiache (1998), Glick and Hutchinson (1999), Kaminsky (1999) and Kaminsky and Reinhart (1999) state that currency crises often entail banking crises, and conversely. Some first-generation models introduce banks in the standard first-generation model of Chapter 1. They analyse whether the banking sector has any influence on the outbreak and the magnitude of speculative attacks.[8]

Drawing on Miller (1999), it is possible to analyse how banks may finance speculative attacks in the framework of first-generation models. It is assumed that banks are not indebted. They may increase their loans following a rise in interest rates caused by the continuous increase in domestic credit. Under perfect foresight speculators anticipate the devaluation of the domestic currency.

The model relies on the following equations:

$$\eta\text{-}\beta n_t + m_t - p_t = -\alpha i_t \quad (3.40)$$

$$m_t = \delta d_t + (1-\delta) r_t \quad (3.41)$$

$$p_t = p_t^* + s_t \quad (3.2)$$

$$i_t = i_t^* + E_{t-1} \Delta s_t \quad (3.3)$$

$$\dot{d} = \mu \quad (3.20)$$

where $\eta - \beta n_t$ is a linear approximation of the monetary multiplier. It is linearised around the reserve/deposit ratio, denoted n_t. All these variables are in logarithm, with the exception of interest rates and of n_t. To simplify computations, it is assumed without loss of generality that:

$i_t^* = 0$
$p_t^* = 0$

Equation (3.40) describes the money market equilibrium. Equation (3.41) is a log-linear approximation of the monetary base. Equations (3.2), (3.3) and (3.20) were dealt with in the previous section. Equation (3.2) indicates that the price level follows the purchasing power parity rule. In equation (3.3), the interest rate is governed by the uncovered interest parity rule. In equation (3.20), domestic credit increases at a constant and strictly positive rate μ.

The banking sector is assumed to be competitive: banks may always grant additional loans at the market interest rate. But there is an unavoidable gap between granted loans and loans that fall due. Banks may therefore not always be able to increase their reserves. When the actual ratio n_t^d (reserves / deposits) is higher than n_t, banks adjust their reserves following :

$$\dot{n}_t = \phi(n_t^d - n_t) \tag{3.42}$$

where ϕ is the finite speed of reserves' adjustment, with $\phi \in]0;1[$. The ratio n_t^d (reserves/deposits) thus describes the evolution of banks' profits:

$$n_t^d = \lambda - v i_t \tag{3.43}$$

where λ and v are positive constants. The interest rate i_t measures the opportunity cost of keeping bank reserves.

The fixed exchange rate under equilibrium $\underline{s}$ and the decreasing rate of reserves $\dot{r}$ can now be computed. Using equation (3.43) with equations (3.40), (3.41), (3.2), (3.3) and (3.20), it is found that:

$$\eta - \beta\lambda + m_t = s_t - (\gamma + \beta v)\dot{s}_t \tag{3.44}$$

If the exchange rate is fixed, then:

$$\dot{s}_t = 0 \tag{3.45}$$

From equations (3.40), (3.41), (3.44), the fixed exchange rate under equilibrium $\underline{s}$ becomes:

$$\underline{s} = \eta - \beta\lambda + \delta d_0 + (1-\delta) r_0 \tag{3.46}$$

The decreasing rate of reserves under a fixed exchange regime therefore equals:

$$\dot{r} = -\frac{\delta\mu}{(1-\delta)} \tag{3.47}$$

The shadow exchange rate $\tilde{s}$ is then determined by using the method of indeterminate coefficients (see the appendix to this chapter):

$$\tilde{s} = (\alpha + \beta v + t)\delta + \eta - \beta\lambda + \delta d_0 \tag{3.48}$$

Following equation (1.12) (see Chapter 1, section 2, The outbreak of speculative attacks), the speculative attack occurs when $s_t = \underline{s}$. From equations (3.46) and (3.48), the currency crisis happens at time T:

$$T = \frac{(1-\delta)r_0}{\delta\mu} - (\alpha + \beta v) \tag{3.49}$$

Equation (3.49) shows that a balance-of-payments crisis is hastened when initial reserves are low while the growth rate in domestic credit and the interest rate elasticity of money demand are high. It is also shown that the fall of the fixed exchange rate system is hastened when banks finance a large share of the attack. This share depends upon v that denotes the sensitivity of reserves to variations in the interest rate. The higher v is, the lower the level in domestic credit that is required for the outbreak of a currency crisis. It is not however necessary for banks to directly finance the attack for a currency crisis to occur: they only have to increase their loans following a rise in the interest rate.

The consistency of this model rests on the assumption that banks increase their credit supply when a rise in interest rate occurs. Such a situation is possible when banking risks are mismanaged. Miller (1999) suggests regulating banking loan activities so as to avoid currency crises. In first-generation models, such regulations may be relevant since the policymaker is assumed to let domestic credit grow.

But speculative attacks may not always result from excessive domestic creation. As demonstrated by Velasco (1987), budgetary deficits caused by guarantees on the private banking sector's debts may trigger speculative attacks. He shows how indebted banks hasten the outbreak of such attacks. When the policymaker seeks to bail out banks, banking panics may entail currency crises. The rise in liquidity that stems from governmental action is usually incompatible with keeping the exchange rate fixed. Such an analysis is meant to explain the repeated failures of stabilisation programmes in Latin American countries during the 1970s, which almost always ended in speculative attacks. Other studies have tried to analyse the role of banks in the light of the 1990s East Asian and Russian crises.

Buch and Heinrich (1999) analyse the effects of unhealthy banks on speculative attacks. They remain close to the framework of Flood and Garber (1984b), although the assumption of domestic growth being incompatible with a fixed peg is not as central to their model as it is in Miller (1999).

Burnside, Eichenbaum and Rebelo (2001a) introduce the banking sector in the stochastic framework dealt in Chapter 3, Section 1, Fiscal sources of speculative attacks. The shift in speculators' expectations triggers a joint banking and currency crises. A major limitation of their study, which also exists in Buch and Heinrich (1999), lies in the assumption that financial institutions' bankruptcies and speculative attacks always occur simultaneously.

Such a hypothesis is rejected by Flood and Marion (2001) in a framework where bank and currency collapses are connected. However as one of them does not necessarily happen as a consequence of the other, their study tries to take into account some features of the East Asian crisis. It emphasises the role of commercial banks in the financial system, the fiscal costs of restructuring financial institutions and private foreign-currency denominated debts.

In these studies, just like in most first-generation models of currency crises, the coordination of attacks is not really dealt with: it rests upon the assumption of perfect foresight. Statements on the outbreak of speculative attacks may not be straightforward when this hypothesis is rejected.

4. COORDINATION OF SPECULATIVE ATTACKS AND CONTAGION

In the model of Chapter 1, all speculators launch an attack against the peg at the same time because they are assumed to have perfect foresight expectations. Yet it is less straightforward to determine the moment the attack occurs when there is imperfect communication between speculators. It may take a long time before successful coordination among speculators is achieved. Building on Botman and Jager (2002), this section analyses coordination of speculative attacks in a two-country extension of the model of Chapter 1 where the assumption of perfect foresight is rejected.

It is assumed that there are two identical countries A and B whose situation is described by the standard first-generation model of Chapter 1. They peg their exchange rate to a third country, known as the anchor country. As of $t = 0$, both countries are likely to be hit by a currency crisis since their monetary policy is a priori incompatible with a fixed exchange rate regime. In this framework, it is assumed that no speculator is large enough to trigger a currency crisis on his own. As such, a certain number of speculators must attack the same currency, as it is the only way to gather sufficient resources to buy the government's foreign exchange reserves.

Let ϕ be the total amount of speculative funds held by speculators. There is a continuum of speculators normalised on [0;1]. Their initial beliefs at $t = 0$ are such that a fraction of speculators ρ_0^A (respectively $\rho_0^A = 1-\rho_0^B$) takes a costless short position in the currency of country A (B). Without loss of generality, it is assumed that $\rho_0^A > \rho_0^B$.

The total value of all the short positions taken against a currency at the beginning of a period implies a corresponding drop in the country's reserves. If the total value of the short positions is not large enough to trigger a currency crisis, these positions are cancelled at the end of the period, and the stock of reserves returns to the level it would have had in the absence of speculation. In this situation, reserves change:

- from one period to the next because of the growth of domestic credit that entails a decrease in reserves at rate $-\mu$ and,
- during each period as a result of speculation by $-\rho_t^i\psi$, with $i = A, B$.

The equation of country i's reserves is:

$$r_0^i = r_0 - \mu t - \rho_t^i \psi \tag{3.50}$$

with r_0 the level of reserves at the beginning of time $t = 0$. Rewriting equation (3.50) leads to:

$$\Delta r_t^i = -\mu - \Delta\rho_t^i \psi \tag{3.51}$$

If no currency crisis occurs, the short positions are cancelled. At the beginning of period t+1, the stock of reserves equals the level from the previous period:

$$r_{t+1} = r_0 - \mu t \tag{3.52}$$

At the beginning of each period, speculators choose in which of the two currencies they want to take a position. They know that a currency crisis only occurs if a sufficiently high number of market participants launch an attack against the peg. Hence they take a short position in the currency in which the bulk of speculators took a short position in the previous period, as reflected in that country's temporary drop in reserves. In this framework, coordination between speculators is made possible by trading.

The analysis of coordination hinges on the dynamic process that governs selection among alternatives. But whatever the process, coordination is a lengthy procedure. It begins as soon as a currency becomes misaligned and ends when a sufficient number of speculators have selected the same currency. To solve the model, the required value of short positions that make an attack successful is first determined, then the actual value of short positions per currency over time is calculated.

It is assumed that the total value of financial funds for all speculators, ϕ, is such that the required fraction of these funds, $\rho_0^i(r)$, needed for a successful attack against the peg in country i, $i = A,B$, at $t = 0$, equals 1. In other words, an attack at $t = 0$ is only successful if all speculators coordinate their activities on the same currency. Thus, $\phi = r_0 = \underline{r}$ denotes the threshold level of reserves where the policymaker lets the exchange rate go. A successful attack happens in country i, i=A,B when:

$$\rho_t^i \geq \rho_t^i(r) \tag{3.53}$$

Countries A and B both lead monetary policies that are a priori incompatible with a fixed exchange rate regime. Their foreign exchange reserves fall and the required fraction of speculators for an attack to be successful decreases such that:

$$\rho_t^i(r) = \rho_t^i(r) - \frac{\mu t}{r_0} = 1 - \frac{\mu t}{r_0} \tag{3.54}$$

At time t, when inequality (3.53) holds, a high number of market participants take short positions in the currency of country i so that a crisis occurs. But in order to determine ρ_t^i in inequality (3.53), communication among speculators by means of trading has to be formalised. The signal received by speculator $k \in [0;1]$ at time t may be defined as:

$$z_{k,t} = \rho_{t-1}^A - \rho_{t-1}^B + \varepsilon_{k,t} \tag{3.55}$$

where $\varepsilon_{k,t}$ is an idiosyncratic noise term with cumulative distribution function F and corresponding probability density function f.

For simplicity it is assumed that the speculators who receive a signal opt for a short position against currency A. The fraction of speculators receiving a positive signal equals $1\text{-}F(\rho_{t-1}^B\text{-}\rho_{t-1}^A)$, assuming F is a monotonically non-decreasing function. The equation for the dynamics of coordination for currency A at time t is therefore:

$$\rho_t^A = 1 - F\left(\rho_{t-1}^B - \rho_{t-1}^A\right) \tag{3.56}$$

The moment of successful coordination is determined by substituting equations (3.56) and (3.54) in inequality (3.53):

$$F\left(2\rho_{t-1}^A - 1\right) \geq 1 - \frac{\mu t}{r_0} \tag{3.57}$$

Botman and Jager (2002) show that the left-hand side of equation (3.57) increases with time while its right-hand side decreases with time. This indicates that it takes longer for a speculative attack to succeed:

- if the initial gap between the volume of short positions between the two currencies is small, i.e., when ρ_0^i is close to 0.5, with i=*A*,*B*; each speculator then finds it hard to determine which country was attacked by the bulk of speculators at the previous time period;
- if the domestic growth rate is smaller relative to the initial amount of reserves; in that case, the required fraction of speculators for an attack to be successful diminishes less quickly;
- if communication between speculators becomes noisier; each market participant then finds it difficult to determine the currency that most investors attacked in the previous period.

These results rest on the assumption that initial beliefs determine which currency is to come under attack first. It is also supposed that multiple equilibria may appear, in sharp contrast to the standard first-generation model of Chapter 1. There is another caveat in this analysis. In practice reserve fluctuations do not only result from other market participants' speculative positions. They may also stem from current account imbalances.

Nevertheless this study of speculators' behaviour in a first-generation model provides an interesting perspective on the outbreak of currency crises, but also on their propagation. When country *A* lets its exchange rate go, it is likely that country *B* will be hit faster by a successful speculative attack. Compared to country *A*, it loses less reserves in the final attack, experiences a larger period of overvaluation of the currency prior to the attack, and undergoes a larger devaluation at the moment of the attack.

5. CHAPTER SUMMARY

In order to gain a more realistic view on speculative attacks, studies refine the canonical first-generation models presented in Chapter 1.

Some studies view fiscal imbalances as a possible cause of speculative attacks. Burnside, Eichenbaum and Rebelo (2001a) identify 'prospective fiscal deficits' as sources of these attacks. Willman (1988) shows that, under the assumption of imperfect substitution between domestic and foreign exchange assets, a high-level of capital mobility hastens the fall in the exchange rate. Blackburn (1988) completes this analysis by showing that quickly adjusting prices precipitates speculative attacks.

These studies also investigate the effects of market imperfections: the price level rises, the country competitiveness worsens, output drops while the trade deficit rises. The exchange rate appreciates until the speculative attack occurs, and depreciates once the policymaker opts for a flexible exchange rate system. They also provide insights on the real effects of speculative attacks that are analysed by Osakwe and Schembri (2002), amongst others.

Other research focus on the role of banks before currency crises. Velasco (1987) examines how debts of financial institutions create public deficits when the government guarantees banks' borrowings. Conversely Miller (1999) argues that speculative attacks may indirectly result from relatively healthy banks. The banking sector is indeed provided with incentives to lend when an anticipated devaluation provokes a rise in interest rates. This requires that the policymaker keeps on increasing domestic credit, in line with the standard first-generation model.

Another assumption of this standard model is that speculators have perfect foresight expectations. But if there is imperfect communication between speculators, as Botman and Jager (2002) suggest, then the outbreak of speculative attacks is postponed.

6. APPENDIX

This appendix provides an outline of the 'method of undetermined coefficients' developed by Agénor, Bhandari and Flood (1992) to determine the shadow exchange rate in a first-generation model of currency crises. Their demonstration has been used in several other studies since. It relies on equations from the standard first-generation model of Chapter 1 but may be easily adapted to its extensions.

Assuming that there are no bubbles, the shadow flexible exchange rate is said to follow the forward expansion:

$$s_t = d_t + E_{t-1}\Delta s_t - \left(\frac{1}{\alpha}\right)\int_t^{+\infty} \exp\left(\frac{t-k}{\alpha}\right).(E_{t-1}d_k)dk \qquad (3.58)$$

Under perfect foresight, equation (3.58) becomes:

$$s_t = \left(\frac{1}{\alpha}\right)\int_t^{+\infty} \exp\left(\frac{t-k}{\alpha}\right).[d_t + (k-t)\mu]dk \qquad (3.59)$$

If equation (1.3), which states that domestic credit d_t grows at a constant rate μ, is assumed to hold, then computations yield equation (1.17):

$$s_t = \alpha\mu + d_t \qquad (1.17)$$

There is an alternative method of computing the shadow exchange rate that builds upon the 'method of undetermined coefficients'. It is assumed that the shadow exchange rate follows:

$$s_t = \kappa_0 + \kappa_1 m_t \tag{3.60}$$

where κ_0 and κ_1 are constant parameters.
Under perfect foresight, the expected change in the exchange rate is:

$$E_{t-1} s_t = \kappa_1 \mu \tag{3.61}$$

In the wake of the collapse of the peg, the exchange rate follows:

$$s_t = m_t + \alpha \kappa_1 \mu \tag{3.62}$$

Between equations (3.60) and (3.62), it is found that:

$\kappa_0 = \alpha\mu$
$\kappa_1 = 1$

With equation (1.2), which holds that $m_t = d_t + r_t$, and equation (1.3), equation (1.17) is obtained.

NOTES

1. Even if it is assumed that the foreign price level or the domestic real income can grow, the argument essentially remains the same. The present values of seigniorage revenues stemming from these sources are included into the government's pre-crisis intertemporal budget constraint.
2. In equilibrium, the parameters γ and μ must be such that the government's intertemporal budget constraint holds.
3. To determine the time T of the attack, it is assumed that the exchange rate is a continuous function of time, that the purchasing power parity rule holds and that the price level is also continuous.
4. It should be remembered that: Current Account + Net Foreign Direct Investment + Other Capital Entries = Foreign Exchange Reserves Variation.
5. Following either the increase in domestic credit or the foreign interest rate shock, exchange rate movements are likely to mitigate the effects of the shocks on output.
6. On backward and forward looking schemes, see Calvo (1983a).
7. See Calvo (1983b) for an empirical study.
8. It must be noted that some third-generation models also deal with the joint outbreak of currency crises and banking crises. Studies on these so-called 'twin crises' are tackled in Chapter 9, section 1, Currency crises and financial crises, and provide a different perspective on speculative attacks.

PART TWO

Second-generation Models of Currency Crises

A self-fulfilling expectation is a temporal phenomenon where a forecast has an immediate influence on current events and determines the conditions of its own realisation in the future.[1] Second-generation models apply this concept to currency crises which may occur independently of the evolution of macroeconomic fundamentals. They therefore call into question the relevance of first-generation models and the uniqueness of the economic equilibrium. They consider that the equilibrium on foreign exchange markets is undetermined. There are at least two equilibria for the same market conditions; only the speculators' self-fulfilling expectations determine the realisation of one of them. The occurrence of multiple equilibria on foreign exchange markets is thus the cause of self-fulfilling attacks. They compel the policymaker to let the exchange rate go, despite the state of macroeconomic fundamentals.

This part of the book deals with second-generation models. They became popular following the 1992 and 1993 European Monetary System (EMS) crises. Eichengreen and Wyplosz (1993) had at the time a decisive influence on the general orientation of these researches. They stated that attacks against the EMS could not stem from the strict monetary policies led by European governments. The causes of the crises were to be found in market participants' self-fulfilling expectations.[2]

Chapter 4 examines the links between the outbreak of currency crises and speculators' self-fulfilling expectations. Abandoning the perfect foresight assumption and adopting a stochastic framework in first-generation models allows Grilli (1986) and Obstfeld (1986b) to show that speculative attacks result from mismanaged monetary and fiscal policies, which still remain exogenous to the model. The policymaker's behaviour becomes endogenous in the escape clause models of Obstfeld (1991,1994). In this setting, speculators provoke a crisis when they observe a perturbation such that, in their view, the policymaker finds it optimal to give up the fixed exchange rate regime. Yet this analysis ignores macroeconomic fundamentals. It is amended by Irwin and Vines (1995), Cole and Kehoe (1996) and Obstfeld (1996) following the 1994 devaluation of the Mexican peso. These authors consider that crises always result from speculators' self-fulfilling expectations and multiple equilibria, but only occur when the macroeconomic situation is paradoxically both compatible with upholding and leaving the fixed exchange regime.

This framework is used by pure contagion models presented in Chapter 5. They attempt to account for the East Asian currency crisis contagion and the subsequent devaluations in Russia and Brazil in 1998 and 1999. They rely on research on investors' behaviour. These studies assert that crises are spread across countries by speculators who are facing financial constraints and informational asymmetry on foreign exchange markets. Macroeconomic links between countries do not play any role in this type of currency crisis contagion.

The contribution of second-generation models to currency crisis studies is far from negligible. They show the importance of self-fulfilling expectations in currency outbreak and contagion. Escape clause models are especially crucial as far as they endogenise the policymaker's behaviour. Yet some assumptions of second-generation models seem strong. They consider that the policymaker has no incentives to abandon a fixed exchange rate. In such a framework, crises result from speculators' self-fulfilling expectations and multiple equilibria while fundamentals do not have any influence.

For these reasons the relevance of second-generation models is dubious. Chapter 6 shows that their regulatory implications are questionable. It also tackles empirical studies on currency crises whose results imply that speculative attacks are likely to occur when fundamentals are deteriorated and not when their macroeconomic situation is sound. Chapter 6 finally deals with multiple equilibria, as some studies cast doubt on their relevance: it seems that they do not occur as often as second-generation models suggest.

NOTES

1. Azariadis (1981) first developed self-fulfilling expectations in a macroeconomic framework, and Cass and Shell (1983) in a microeconomic setting. See Farmer (2001) for a survey.
2. This interpretation is simplistic because European states also conducted lenient fiscal policies. In that line of research, Eichengreen (2000) provides an analysis of the 'EMS crisis in retrospect' that has more moderate conclusions.

4. Self-fulfilling Expectations and the Outbreak of Currency Crises

In second-generation models, the outbreak of a currency crisis in a country is not related to its macroeconomic situation. It results from speculators whose self-fulfilling expectations make them launch an attack. The policymaker is compelled to let the exchange rate go. He thus warrants speculators' expectations about a forthcoming fall in the exchange rate.

Grilli (1986) and Obstfeld (1986b) formalise self-fulfilling attacks in a stochastic framework related to first-generation models. Their perspective differs, since they consider that the policymaker is not responsible for speculative attacks though he conducts an expansionary monetary policy. Only the speculators' self-fulfilling expectations trigger crisis.

A limit in the studies by Grilli (1986) and Obstfeld (1986b) is in the assumption that the policymaker's economic policies are exogenous to their models. Yet governmental policies are endogenous in the escape clause models that originate in the studies by Obstfeld (1991, 1994). The policymaker is given an objective function so that his choices in times of speculative pressures become more straightforward. In this line of research, two types of models may be distinguished. 'Early' escape clause models consider that speculators may trigger self-fulfilling currency crises, whether or not the macroeconomic situation is deteriorated. 'Late' escape clause models state that self-fulfilling speculative attacks may only occur when a paradoxical situation prevails in the country: fundamentals are deteriorated but the policymaker may keep the exchange rate fixed as long as speculators do not launch self-fulfilling attacks against the currency.

1. SELF-FULFILLING SPECULATIVE ATTACKS

Grilli (1986) and Obstfeld (1986b) first developed stochastic models of currency crises with self-fulfilling expectations that are closely related to first-generation studies. The fall of the fixed exchange rate regime occurs when the amount of reserves reaches a given predetermined threshold; the fundamental variables that are taken into account only relate to monetary policies.

The two authors' approach differs from first-generation studies. They assert that crises do not result from unsound economic policies but from the speculators' self-fulfilling expectations and from the existence of multiple equilibria. There exist for the same market conditions at least two equilibria: one allowing the upholding of the fixed exchange rate regime, the other leading to a devaluation. Speculators' self-fulfilling expectations provoke the 'jump' moving the economy from the fixed exchange rate equilibrium to the crisis equilibrium. Such a framework relies on strong assumptions, i.e., the occurrence of multiple equilibria and the existence of a 'jump' between equilibria, which call into question the pertinence of these studies (see below, Chapter 6, section 3, Theoretical and empirical problems with multiple equilibria, for a discussion on multiple equilibria and on the relevance of the 'jump').

Savastano (1992) extends the analyses of Grilli (1986) and Obstfeld (1986b) to a framework where self-fulfilling attacks are related to the policymaker's fiscal policies, with tax receipts that follow the Laffer curve. Artus (1994) formalises attacks on a 'strong' currency. His study shows that a currency crisis is necessarily self-fulfilling in this situation. The speculative attack entails the exchange rate depreciation: the value of the exchange rate is precisely the cause of the attack because market participants consider that its too high value prevents the upholding of the exchange rate.

The stochastic model of Grilli (1986) rests on the following equations:

$$m_t - p_t = \beta + \gamma y_t - \alpha i_t + w_t \tag{4.1}$$

$$m_t = d_t + r_t \tag{4.2}$$

$$i_t - i_t^* = E_t s_{t+1} - s_t \tag{4.3}$$

$$p_t - p_t^* = s_t + u_t \tag{4.4}$$

where m_t, s_t, p_t and p_t^* are respectively the logarithms of the money stock, the nominal exchange rate, the domestic and foreign price levels; i_t and i_t^* are the domestic and foreign interest rates; E_t is a conditional operator of expectations on information available at time t; u_t and w_t are random shocks.

Equation (4.1) represents the money market equilibrium. Equation (4.2) describes the evolution of the money stock m_t whose sources are domestic credit d_t and exchange rate reserves r_t. Equation (4.3) asserts that the uncovered interest rate parity is upheld in this model. Equation (4.4) describes the evolution of the exchange rate driven by the deviation from purchasing power parity. By combining these four equations, the first-order differential equation of the exchange rate may be determined:

$$(1+\alpha)s_t - \alpha E_t s_{t+1} = h_t \tag{4.5}$$

with $h_t = \log[d_t + r_t] - \beta - \gamma y_t + \alpha i_t^* - w_t - p_t^* - u_t$.

In a flexible exchange rate regime, the equilibrium value of the exchange rate is obtained by solving the following equation:

$$s_t = \frac{1}{1+\alpha} \sum_{j=0}^{+\infty} \left(\frac{\alpha}{1+\alpha} \right)^j E_t h_{t+j} \tag{4.6}$$

The current exchange rate hinges on the agents' expectations of the present and future values of the fundamentals.

Grilli (1986) considers that the policymaker fixes the exchange rate at a given level $\underline{s}$ and that two types of speculative attacks are possible: 'buying attacks' and 'selling attacks'. During the former, speculators purchase the policymaker's foreign exchange reserves until they reach a threshold $r_{\min}$ where the currency is devalued. When the latter occurs, speculators sell foreign currencies to the Central Bank until foreign exchange reserves reach a level $r_{\max}$ where the domestic currency is re–evaluated. Obviously $0 \le r_{\min} < r_{\max}$.

'Buying attacks' happen when speculators anticipate the depreciation of the exchange rate, while 'selling attacks' result from appreciation expectations. Devaluations and re–evaluations occur independently of the evolution of monetary aggregates and macroeconomic fundamentals.

This study by Grilli (1986) criticises first-generation models by establishing that currency crises result exclusively from the speculators' self-fulfilling expectations. It does not however include multiple equilibria. It is assumed that speculators are large enough so that the coordination of their actions is not necessary for an attack to be successful. This seems to be a strong assumption which suggests that multiple equilibria are necessary in order for crises with self-fulfilling expectations to happen.

Obstfeld (1986b) rejects the argumentation of Grilli (1986). He assumes that each speculator is not sufficiently large to provoke a speculative attack on his own. In that case, there are multiple equilibria.

By building on Flood and Garber (1984a) who deal with exhaustible resources, Obstfeld (1986b) suggests that the speculators' expectations, who cause multiple equilibria and ultimately crises, are influenced by the variations in the money creation process. In his analysis, money creation follows the rule:

$$d_t = d_0 + v_t \tag{4.7}$$

where the perturbation v_t follows the stationary covariance auto-regressive process AR(1):

$$v_t = \rho v_{t-1} + \varepsilon_t \tag{4.8}$$

with $0 \leq \rho \leq 1$, and where innovations ε_t are independently and identically distributed (i.i.d.) with $E_{t-1}(\varepsilon_t) = 0$.

Other formalisations are possible. Willman (1988) considers that there exists a probability q that the policymaker maintains a monetary policy rule that is incompatible with a fixed exchange rate system, e.g., $\dot{d} = \mu$ as in equation (1.3) of the model of Chapter 1, and a probability $(1-q)$ that he upholds a rule that is compatible with a fixed exchange rate regime, e.g., $\dot{d} = 0$.

Jeanne (1996a, 2000) analyses the changes in the monetary creation process that result from the policymaker's reactions to potential speculative attacks. It is assumed that the values in domestic credit are respectively d_0 and d_1 at two distinct dates $t = 0,1$. Monetary policy conducted in $t=1$ stems from the policymaker's decision to devalue or keep the exchange rate fixed at time $t = 0$. He chooses d^f at time $t = 1$ if he maintained the exchange rate fixed at time $t = 0$ and d^d otherwise. The policymaker's reaction function takes the following form:

- If there is a devaluation at time $t = 0$, then:

$$d_1 = d^d \tag{4.9}$$

- If there is no devaluation at time $t = 0$, then:

$$d_1 = d^f \tag{4.10}$$

Jeanne (2000) assumes that monetary policy is more expansionary at time $t = 1$ than in $t = 0$. The policymaker thus provides speculators with an ex post validation of their expectations. To justify this assumption, the author follows Obstfeld (1986a) and van Wijnbergen (1991), and states that an expansionary monetary policy may be optimal in a flexible exchange rate regime. By so doing, the policymaker monetises the public debt when borrowing on capital markets is no longer possible. Such a policy also warrants the existence of two equilibria in the model. In the first equilibrium, the currency is not under attack at time $t = 0$ and the policymaker conducts a moderate domestic credit policy at the following time period. In the second equilibrium, a speculative attack occurs at time $t = 0$ and the policymaker implements a more expansionary policy in the following period.

The analysis of Jeanne (2000) rests upon the existence of multiple equilibria. In line with other studies on self-fulfilling attacks, it does not explain the element(s) that lead(s) the speculators' expectations towards a currency crisis equilibrium rather than towards a fixed exchange rate equilibrium. This theoretical weakness is also found in escape clause models.

2. ESCAPE CLAUSE MODELS

Escape clause models originate in the studies by Obstfeld (1991, 1994) and were developed subsequently by Davies and Vines (1995) and Ozkan and Sutherland (1994, 1995, 1998). They constitute a landmark in currency crisis research since the policymaker is given an explicit objective function.

Their approach stems from works by Kydland and Prescott (1977) and Barro and Gordon (1983) on the dynamic inconsistency of monetary policy.[1] These studies assume that the policymaker intends to conduct an inflationary policy so as to increase national income. But if agents expect a rise in inflation, they adjust their wage demands and cancel the effects of inflation on the national product. The policymaker is led to implement a non-inflationary policy allowing continuous growth in the economy. If he does not, his inflationary policy brings about a recession.

Escape clause models consider that the policymaker faces tradeoffs between several economic policy objectives, while providing guarantees to private agents that the exchange rate will remain fixed. Yet this commitment is revocable. The policymaker may change his exchange rate policy if he wants to. But speculators are aware of the policymaker's tradeoff. They may expect and trigger a devaluation even though the policymaker's economic policies are compatible with a fixed exchange rate regime.

Escape clause models do not all tackle self-fulfilling currency crises in the same way. The 'early' escape clause models of Obstfeld (1991, 1994) and Ozkan and Sutherland (1994, 1995, 1998) consider that self-fulfilling expectations are solely responsible for the outbreak of currency crises. The 'late' escape clause models of Davies and Vines (1995) and Obstfeld (1996) state that self-fulfilling speculative attacks occur when the macroeconomic situation deteriorates, but paradoxically enough, at the same time compatible with keeping and abandoning the fixed exchange rate regime.

2.1. 'Early' Escape Clause Models

This section develops a simplified version of the study of Obstfeld (1994), following the reinterpretation of Flood and Marion (1998b) so as to synthesise the main aspects of escape–clause models. The policymaker follows an exchange rate policy with the social loss function L:

$$\text{Min } L = \frac{\omega}{2}\delta_t^2 + \frac{(\delta_t - E_{t-1}(\delta_t) - u_t - k)^2}{2} \tag{4.11}$$

where δ_t is the currency depreciation rate, $E_{t-1}(\delta_t)$ the expected depreciation rate based on available information in the previous period, u_t the shock hitting the domestic economy at time t that follows a normal law with null mean and variance σ^2, k a measure of distortion and ω the relative weight attached to price changes.

Equation (4.11) exhibits the policymaker's tradeoff between currency defence costs and exit costs from the fixed exchange rate regime. In the first case, the policymaker aims at maintaining the fixed exchange regime such that $\delta_t=0$. Private agents formulate their expectations while taking this into account so that:

$$E_t(\delta_t^{\text{Fix}})=0 \tag{4.12}$$

The expected value $E_t(L^{\text{Fix}})$ of the loss function when this fixed exchange rule is followed is:

$$E_t(L^{\text{Fix}}) = \frac{\sigma^2 + k^2}{2} \tag{4.13}$$

In the second case, the policymaker intervenes in a discretionary manner. Private agents anticipate his actions and adjust their expectations so that:

$$E_t(\delta_t^{\text{Flex}})=k/\omega \tag{4.14}$$

Assuming $\omega=1$ to simplify computations, the expected value of the policymaker's loss function becomes:

$$E_t(L^{\text{Flex}}) = \frac{\sigma^2}{4} + k^2 \tag{4.15}$$

Equations (4.13) and (4.15) show that the social loss is lower under a monetary policy rule than under a discretionary intervention, when no shock occurs in the economy ($\sigma^2 = 0$). However if there are shocks, discretion may be superior to regulation. This is especially true for high values of σ^2.

In this framework, the policymaker finds it optimal to keep the exchange rate fixed, unless speculators launch a self-fulfilling attack against the currency. When this happens, the policymaker lets the exchange rate float: it is said that he invokes his escape–clause. The following condition is then satisfied:

$$E_t[L^{\text{Fix}}(u_t)] > E_t[L^{\text{Flex}}(u_t)] + \frac{C^2}{2} \tag{4.16}$$

where C is the lump sum that the policymaker bears when he abandons the fixed exchange rate regime. The variable C represents various factors, such as the policymaker's financial losses from debts denominated in foreign currency, or the loss in political credibility entailed when the fixed exchange rate system is abandoned. It may easily be assumed that C is known by the policymaker, but it remains uncertain whether speculators know its exact value. Studies by Flood and Marion (1997) and Obstfeld (1994, 1996) do not provide an explicit solution to this issue. Ozkan and Sutherland (1994, 1995, 1998) state that agents may determine C while Bensaïd and Jeanne (1997) assume the opposite.

Equation (4.16) is partially non-linear. It comprises the problems of agents formulating their expectations over the value of the currency depreciation rate. Speculators choose the currency depreciation rate before knowing what policies the policymaker adopts. They compute a probability weighted by the expected rate chosen under the economic policy rule, $E_t(\delta_t^{\text{Fix}})=0$, and by the expected rate chosen under discretionary intervention $E_t(\delta_t^{\text{Fix}})>0$. They trigger a self-fulfilling attack when perturbations u_t equal $\underline{u}$ or $\overline{u}$, with $\underline{u}<\overline{u}$, assuming that perturbations u_t are uniformly distributed.[2]

In this framework, a rise in the exit costs C from a fixed exchange rate regime is likely to increase speculators' trust in the policymaker's willingness to keep the exchange rate fixed. He is provided with incentives not to invoke his escape–clause since he then unavoidably bears the political and economic consequences of a currency crisis. Ozkan and Sutherland (1995) consider that a rise in C promotes the stability of the system since the agents perceive that it will be harder for the policymaker to change the exchange rate regime. He gets incentives and is compelled to guarantee the fixed peg insofar as the interest differential between domestic and foreign currencies has decreased. For Flood and Marion (1997), an increase in exit costs increases the probability of a currency crisis. In an economy where multiple equilibria are likely to occur, a rise in C entails an increase in $\overline{u}$, but a decrease in $\underline{u}$, and thus increases the probability of a currency crisis occurrence.

'Early' escape–clause models assume that crises result from speculators' self-fulfilling expectations. Yet some studies reject the idea that attacks are not related to the macroeconomic situation and develop escape–clause models that include macroeconomic fundamentals.

2.2. 'Late' Escape Clause Models

Unlike 'early' escape–clause models, the analyses of Davies and Vines (1995), Cole and Kehoe (1996) and Obstfeld (1996) assume that self-fulfilling currency crises happen in a macroeconomic situation characterised by, at least, two equilibria: one allowing the fixed peg to be maintained, the other when it is abandoned. These 'late' escape–clause models try to reconcile the main assumptions of escape–clause models with the 1994 Mexican currency crisis. According to Cole and Kehoe (1996), the speculative attack against the Mexican peso stemmed from speculators' self-fulfilling expectations who considered that the domestic debt compelled the government to let the exchange rate go.[3] But from the country's macroeconomic situation, the fixed exchange rate could have been maintained, had the speculative attack not been launched.[4]

The studies by Davies and Vines (1995), Cole and Kehoe (1996) and Obstfeld (1996) rest on a formalisation that departs from the framework of 'early' escape–clause models. They suggest that there are three intervals of values of fundamentals. Multiple equilibria may appear in only one of these three intervals. In the interval with multiple equilibria, fundamentals are at the same time compatible with keeping and abandoning the fixed exchange rate.

This paradoxical situation may be explained by following Jeanne (2000). The relative influence of the shock u_t and of the variable θ_t, which synthesises the various macroeconomic fundamentals, is modified. The policymaker minimises the loss function:

$$L=(y_t)^2+\delta C \qquad (4.17)$$

under the constraint:

$$y_t=u_t-\alpha(s_t-E_{t-1}\Delta s_t) \qquad (4.18)$$

The policymaker uses his escape–clause when the following condition holds:

$$L^{\text{Fix}} > L^{\text{Flex}} \qquad (4.19)$$

If speculators do not expect a collapse of the fixed exchange rate regime, then $E_{t-1}\Delta s_t=0$. The policymaker's losses under a fixed and a flexible exchange rate system respectively equal:

$$L^{\text{Fix}} = (u_t)^2 \qquad (4.20)$$

and:

$$L^{\text{Flex}} = (u_t - \alpha\delta)^2 \qquad (4.21)$$

The escape clause is satisfied if:

$$\frac{C}{\alpha\delta} - 2u_t > \alpha\delta \qquad (4.22)$$

If speculators expect a devaluation, then $E_{t-1}\Delta s_t=\delta$. The policymaker's losses under a fixed and a flexible exchange rate system respectively equal:

$$L^{\text{Fix}} = (u_t + \alpha\delta)^2 \qquad (4.23)$$

and:

$$L^{\text{Flex}} = (u_t)^2 + C \qquad (4.24)$$

The escape clause is satisfied if:

$$\frac{C}{\alpha\delta} - 2u_t < \alpha\delta \qquad (4.25)$$

Let θ_t be the variable that synthesises the domestic macroeconomic situation at time t, with $\theta_t=(C/\alpha\delta)-2u_t$. Let θ_A and θ_B be threshold values of the fundamental θ_t such that $\theta_A=-\alpha\delta$ and $\theta_B=\alpha\delta$. There are three situations and four macroeconomic equilibria whose occurrence depends on the shock u_t via the fundamental θ_t:

- if $\theta_t \in]-\infty;\theta_A[$, macroeconomic fundamentals are such that the policymaker is compelled to let the exchange rate go. There is a unique equilibrium perfectly anticipated by agents with rational expectations;
- if $\theta_t \in [\theta_A;\theta_B]$, there are two equilibria stemming from speculators' self-fulfilling expectations. The first one implies that the fixed exchange rate can be maintained, the second one that the currency must be devalued. The first equilibrium is often considered as a 'good equilibrium' while the second one is dubbed as a 'bad equilibrium';[5]
- if $\theta_t \in]\theta_B;+\infty[$, there exists a unique equilibrium perfectly anticipated by agents. This equilibrium allows the exchange rate to remain fixed until the next time period.

Some characteristics of these models need to be refined because neither the jump from the fixed exchange rate equilibrium to the crisis equilibrium, nor the coordination of speculators' self-fulfilling expectations are explained.[6]

Escape–clause models provide a major contribution to currency crisis research. By giving the policymaker an objective-function, they show that the arbitrages he faces makes the fixed exchange rate regime inherently unstable.

Other features of escape clause models are also questionable. It is said that the policymaker undergoes attacks but does not provoke them, even though he may have incentives to let the exchange rate go. And if his objective is to prevent crises, he is likely to try to influence speculators' expectations. He may try to convince them that his macroeconomic policies are compatible with a fixed exchange regime. However, the policymaker is considered to remain passive in escape clause models.

3. CHAPTER SUMMARY

Second-generation models originate in the studies of Grilli (1986) and Obstfeld (1986b). They mirror in many ways first-generation models. For instance the only variables that are taken into account are related to monetary and fiscal policies. Yet this research is quite distinct from first-generation models insofar as it assumes that currency crises do not stem from economic policies that are incompatible with a fixed peg. They result from speculators' self-fulfilling expectations.

Escape–clause models provide a major contribution to currency crisis research. By giving the policymaker an objective-function, they show that the arbitrages he faces make the fixed exchange rate regime inherently unstable. Currency crises hence occur when speculators launch a self-fulfilling attack on the peg, though the policymaker's policies may be compatible with a fixed peg. In the 'early' escape clause models of Obstfeld (1991, 1994) and Ozkan and Sutherland (1994, 1995, 1998), such self-fulfilling speculative attacks may occur at any time period whatever the state of fundamentals. In the 'late' escape clause models of Davies and Vines (1995) and Obstfeld (1996), crises may only happen in a peculiar macroeconomic situation with multiple equilibria, where the policymaker can keep the exchange rate fixed if speculators do not launch an attack. But if they do, the policymaker lets the exchange rate go, thus warranting the speculators' expectations about a future currency crisis.

NOTES

1. For surveys on the policymaker's dynamic inconsistency in monetary policy, see Cukierman (1992) and Drazen (2000b).
2. In this framework, if perturbations u_t are assumed to be normally distributed, then there are three values of u_t such that the policymaker finds it optimal to invoke his escape–clause.
3. Cole and Kehoe (1996) use a public debt model that can easily be reinterpreted as a currency crisis model. For a differing analysis of this model, see Jeanne (1999).
4. The analysis of the Mexican crisis by Cole and Kehoe (1996) is criticised by Dornbusch, Goldfajn and Valdès (1995) and Sachs, Tornell and Velasco (1996a, 1996b).
5. In this formalisation, there are only two equilibria in the interval of fundamentals where multiple equilibria occur, just like in most escape–clause models. Flood and Marion (1998a) consider that there may be three equilibria, but this does not really influence the conclusions of their study.
6. See Chapter 6, section 3, Theoretical and empirical problems with multiple equilibria.

5. Self-fulfilling Expectations and Currency Crisis Contagion

Pure contagion theory relies on specific aspects of investors' behaviour. Crises are said to be conveyed across markets as a result of decisions that are optimal and rational on an individual basis, though no deteriorated fundamental warrants contagion. This kind of behaviour may be explained by institutional liquidity constraints, informational asymmetry on foreign exchange markets, or by speculators who engage in mimetic behaviour because of informational cascades.

By building on these studies, models of pure contagion attempt to explain how speculative attacks are propagated, although fundamentals are still compatible with a fixed exchange rate regime.

1. MAIN ASSUMPTIONS OF PURE CONTAGION MODELS

Following Masson (1998), pure contagion characterises the transmission of speculative attacks that cannot be explained by the evolution of macroeconomic fundamentals. Currency crises result from market participants' self-fulfilling expectations. Pure contagion models are thus based on the destabilising nature of speculation.[1]

This section surveys potential cases of market participants' behaviour conveying crises from one country to another, even though no fundamental disequilibrium justifies such a spread.

1.1. Institutional Constraints of Liquidity

Institutional constraints of liquidity are likely to convey speculative attacks between countries. Claessens, Dornbusch and Park (2000) suggest that investors who sustain losses on a market may close their positions on one or several other markets because they expect that the bulk of investors is likely to do the same. Garber (1998) considers that crises may be transmitted between emerging countries as a result of speculators using financial derivatives. Schinasi and Smith (2000) state that Value at Risk models provide investors with incentives to sell their most risky assets when only the value of one of them decreases.

Calvo and Mendoza (2000) state that the globalisation of financial markets fosters pure contagion. Globalisation provides incentives to market participants to develop similar portfolio allocations by reducing their incentives to acquire information that can be quite costly. The authors consider n international assets with J countries with J=2,3,.... There is a large number of identical speculators who allocate their wealth between J-1 identical countries and country i, whose asset return features are different. All countries but country i pay returns following an i.i.d. process with mean ρ and variance σ_j^2. Country i pays expected returns z' and variance σ_i^2 that are correlated with other countries by a correlation coefficient η. In this framework, each one of the J-1 countries gets an identical portfolio share $v/(J-1)$, with v being the share of the portfolio invested in all these countries.

Investors have preferences expressed by the indirect expected utility function:

$$EU(v) = \mu(v) - \frac{\gamma}{2}\sigma(v)^2 - \kappa - \lambda(\mu(V) - \mu(v)) \tag{5.1}$$

where γ is the strictly positive coefficient of absolute risk-aversion, μ and σ the mean and standard deviation of the portfolio as a function of v, κ the strictly positive fixed cost of acquiring country-specific information, and $\lambda(\mu(V)-\mu(v))$ the variable performance cost (benefit) of obtaining a mean portfolio return lower (higher) than the mean return of an arbitrary portfolio V. The cost function $\lambda(\mu(V)-\mu(v))$ satisfies the following properties:

- $\lambda > 0$ if $\mu(V)-\mu(v)$, $\lambda \leq 0$ if $\mu(V)-\mu(v)$, $\lambda(0)=0$;
- $\lambda' \geq 0$ with $\lambda'(x) > \lambda'(-x)$ and $x=\mu(V)-\mu(v)>0$;
- $\lambda' \leq 0$.

It is initially assumed that country i does not differ from the rest of the world. Asset returns are the same in all countries and are not correlated, so that:

$$z' = \rho$$
$$\sigma_i^2 = \sigma_j^2$$
$$\eta = 0$$

In this case, speculators allocate the same amount of wealth across all countries. If speculators' wealth is normalised to 1, the portfolio share invested in each country is $1/J$; the portfolio mean return and variance are respectively ρ and σ^2/J.

Then there is a 'credible rumour' on foreign exchange markets in which each investor starts to believe. It is said that country i's mean return is $z \leq z'$, but its variance is still σ^2. If agents pay the fixed cost κ, they acquire country-specific information. They then allocate their wealth between the J countries, with same variance σ^2 but the expected return of country i is z while it is ρ in the J-1 other markets. For simplicity paying κ implies that speculators know the exact return of country i, denoted z_i with zero variance. If they do not pay κ, return z_i is a random variable.[2]

Let v_{UI} and v_I be the portfolio shares chosen by the investor if he decides to be uninformed and informed, respectively. The speculator chooses v_{UI} so as to maximise:

$$EU_{UI} = v_{UI}\rho + (1 - v_{UI})z - \frac{\gamma}{2}\left[\frac{(v_{UI})^2}{J-1} + (1 - v_{UI})^2\right]\sigma^2 \tag{5.2}$$

with EU_{UI} being the speculator's expected utility conditional on free information, i.e., when the speculator does not pay κ.

If it is assumed that there is a corner solution, the corresponding first-order conditions imply that the optimal portfolio is:

$$v_{UI} = \left(\frac{J-1}{J}\right)\left(1 + \frac{\rho - z}{\gamma\sigma^2}\right) \tag{5.3}$$

Such a corner solution may be optimal as a result of short-selling constraints.

Let a and b be constants such that $a \in [0;+\infty[$, $b \in [1;+\infty[$ and:[3]

$$-a \leq v_{UI} \leq b \tag{5.4}$$

Short selling constraints are such that:

$v_{UI} = b$ for $z^{\min} \geq z$
$v_{UI} = -a$ for $z \geq z^{\max}$

with:

$z^{min} = \rho - [\gamma\sigma^2(J(b-1)+1]/(J-1)$
$z^{max} = \rho + [\gamma\sigma^2(J(1+a)+1]/(J-1)$

As the number of markets grows, i.e., as $J \rightarrow +\infty$, the interval of returns with corner solutions for v_{UI} converges to:

$$z^{max} - z^{min} = \gamma\sigma^2(b+a) \tag{5.5}$$

If z is such that the uninformed speculator's portfolio allocation has corner solutions, then it may be assumed that z belongs to the interval $]z^{min};z^{max}[$. In that case, the maximum value of EU_{UI} is:

$$EU_{UI} = \left(z - \frac{\gamma}{2}\frac{\sigma^2}{J} + \frac{\rho - z}{2} \times \frac{J-1}{J}\left(2 + \frac{\rho - z}{\gamma\sigma^2}\right)\right) \tag{5.6}$$

If speculators pay κ to learn z_i, their state-contingent utility $U_I(z_i)$ is:

$$U_I(z_i) = v_I\rho + (1 - v_I)z_i - \frac{\gamma}{2}\left(\frac{(v_I)^2}{J-1}\right)\sigma^2 - \kappa \tag{5.7}$$

When a corner solution is assumed, the optimal state-contingent portfolio allocation is:

$$v_I(z_i) = (J-1)\left(\frac{\rho - z_i}{\gamma\sigma^2}\right) \tag{5.8}$$

Short-selling constraints imply that:

$v_I(z_i) = a$ if $z_i \geq z_i^{max}$
$v_I(z_i) = b$ if $z_i \geq z_i^{min}$

with:

$z_i^{min} = \rho - (b\gamma\sigma^2)/(J-1)$
$z_i^{max} = \rho + (a\gamma\sigma^2)/(J-1)$

Let $F(z_i)$ and $f(z_i)$ denote the cumulative distribution function (c.d.f.) and probability density function (p.d.f.) of z_I. Let EU_I be the speculator's expected utility conditional on costly information:

$$EU_I = \int_{-\infty}^{+\infty} \left(v_I(z_i)\rho + (1 - v_I(z_i))v_I - \frac{\gamma}{2}\left(\frac{(v_I(z_i))^2}{J-1}\right)\sigma^2 \right) f(z_i)dz_i - \kappa \quad (5.9)$$

Such results imply that the interval of returns for the informed speculators' optimal portfolio allocations diminishes when J tends to infinity. In this framework, Calvo and Mendoza (2000) show that:

- short-selling constraints are not binding for the portfolio of an uninformed investor, that is $z^{min} < z < z^{max}$;
- if the speculator believes the return in country i is lower or equal to asset returns in the rest of the world, then the gain from costly information E_{UI}-EU_{UI} may be shown to converge to a constant level independent of J as J grows towards infinity[4]. This constant utility level is either positive or negative, and hinges on the values of κ and ρ.

The analysis of Calvo and Mendoza (2000) shows that, in the presence of information and short-selling constraints, the incentives to gather information are diminished. They also point out that informational asymmetry between speculators may be a source of crisis propagation.

1.2. Informational Asymmetry

For King and Wadhwani (1990), Caplin and Leahy (1994), Levy-Yeyati and Ubide (1998), Calvo (1999), Frankel and Schmukler (2000), Kodres and Pritsker (2002), informational asymmetry plays a major role in the occurrence of pure contagion by conveying speculators' self-fulfilling expectations. These studies consider that the cost of acquiring information creates on financial markets well- and poorly-informed investors. The latter are likely to transmit shocks between markets independently of fundamentals, since their portfolio allocations do not take into account economic fundamentals as a result of a lack of information.

Drawing on Kodres and Pritsker (2002), it is possible to model various channels of financial contagion stemming from informational asymmetry between market participants. In an economy with N risky assets, it is assumed that the liquidation value of assets is represented by a random vector v such that:

$$v = \theta + u \quad (5.10)$$

with θ the expected value of v conditional on the information of informed investors, and u the residual component unexplained by information.

It is also assumed that the unconditional joint distribution of θ and u is normal with probability distribution:

$$\begin{pmatrix}\theta \\ u\end{pmatrix} - N\left[\begin{pmatrix}\overline{\theta} \\ 0\end{pmatrix}, \begin{pmatrix}\Sigma_\theta & 0 \\ 0 & \Sigma_u\end{pmatrix}\right] \tag{5.11}$$

Since u is a residual, it is not correlated with θ, and its mean is zero.

Kodres and Pritsker (2002) distinguish between three categories of market participants – informed investors, uninformed investors and noise traders:

- It is assumed that informed investors have Constant Absolute Risk Aversion[5] (CARA) with risk tolerance parameter τ and fixed net supply X_I. Each one chooses his positions in the market $X_I(P, \theta)$, with P the price vector, so as to maximise their expected utility denoted EU_I:

$$EU_I = \left[-\exp\left(\frac{-W_2}{\tau}\right)\middle|\theta\right] \tag{5.12}$$

under the constraint:

$$W_2 = W_1 + X_I(v - P) \tag{5.13}$$

with W_t the trader's wealth at time t.

The informed investor's optimal portfolio allocation $X_I(P, \theta)$ is:

$$X_I(P,\theta) = \tau \mathrm{Var}(v|\theta)^{-1}(E(v|\theta) - P) \tag{5.14}$$

Since $\mathrm{Var}(v|\theta) = \Sigma_u$ and $E(v|\theta) = \theta$, equation (5.14) may be rewritten as:

$$X_I(P,\theta) = \tau \Sigma_u^{-1}(\theta - P) \tag{5.15}$$

- Uninformed investors choose their portfolio allocations without knowing θ. It is however assumed they are knowledgeable about the unconditional distribution of θ and u as given by equation (5.10), and observe the price vector P. They choose their positions in the risky market $X_{UI}(P)$ conditional on P so as to maximise their expected utility denoted EU_{UI}:

$$EU_{UI}\left[-\exp\left(\frac{-W_2}{\tau}\right)\middle|P\right] \quad (5.16)$$

under the constraint:

$$W_2 = W_1 + X_{UI}(v-P) \quad (5.17)$$

The uninformed investor's optimal choice of $X_{UI}(P)$ is:

$$X_{UI}(P) = \tau \operatorname{Var}(v|P)^{-1}(E(v|P)-P) \quad (5.18)$$

Equation (5.18) shows that $X_{UI}(P)$ depends on the degree of information included in P for v. Kodres and Pritsker (2002) however consider that P can only be determined as a solution to the general equilibrium of this model. Hence noise traders are introduced in the model.

- Noise traders buy and sell assets on the basis of information that is not connected to the state of the market.[6] Their portfolio choices are not related either to the fundamental value of assets or to other market participants' objectives. Noise traders however prevent the equilibrium in process from fully revealing the information of informed investors. The net demand of noise traders is denoted by ε, whose distribution is $N(0,\Sigma_\varepsilon)$.

Since market participants have been dealt with, the equilibrium value of P may be determined. Prices P and beliefs $\operatorname{Var}(v|P)$ and $E(v|P)$ must be such that the following market clearing conditions hold, i.e., supply must equal demand:

$$X_T = n_{UI} X_{UI}(P) + n_I X_I(\theta,P) + \varepsilon \quad (5.19)$$

which can be rewritten as:

$$X_T = n_{UI}\tau \operatorname{Var}(v|P)^{-1}(E(v|P)-P) + n_I \tau \Sigma_u^{-1}(\theta\text{-}P) + \varepsilon \quad (5.20)$$

with n_{UI} and n_I the numbers of uninformed and informed speculators and X_T the fixed net supply in the economy.

From equation (5.20), the uninformed speculators' knowledge may be expressed as a noisy signal of θ:

$$K_{UI}(P) = \theta + \frac{\Sigma_u \varepsilon}{\tau n_I} \tag{5.21}$$

so that:

$$K_{UI}(P) = \frac{1}{\tau n_I} \Sigma_u \left[n_{UI}\ \tau \mathrm{Var}(v|P)^{-1} \left(E(v|P) - P \right) - n_I \tau \Sigma_u^{-1} P - X_T \right] \tag{5.22}$$

Given their beliefs and knowledge of the economic structure, uninformed speculators learn information from prices as shown by equation (5.22). If beliefs are to be consistent with the information revealed by prices, the following conditions must be satisfied:

$$E(v|P) = E[v|K_{UI}(P)] \tag{5.23}$$

and:

$$\mathrm{Var}(v|P) = \mathrm{Var}[v|K_{UI}(P)] \tag{5.24}$$

Equilibrium price conditions are found by rewriting market clearing conditions, i.e equation (5.19), using $E(v|P)$ and $Var(v|P)$. Computations yield:

$$P = M_0 + M_1 E(v|P) + M_2 \theta + M_3 \varepsilon \tag{5.25}$$

with:

$M_0 = -\Psi^1 X_T$
$M_1 = \Psi^1 n_{UI}\ \tau[\mathrm{Var}(v|P)]^{-1}$
$M_2 = \Psi^1 n_{UI}\ \tau.\Sigma_u^{-1}$
$M_3 = \Psi^{-1}$
$\Psi = n_{UI}\ \tau[\mathrm{Var}(v|P)]^{-1} + n_I\ \tau.\Sigma_u^{-1}$

Differentiating P in relation to ε, the price variation resulting from liquidity shocks, that is from noise trading, is:

$$\frac{\partial P}{\partial \varepsilon} = M_1 \frac{\partial E(v|P)}{\partial \varepsilon} + M_3 \tag{5.26}$$

Differentiating P in relation to θ, the price variation resulting from information shocks is:

$$\frac{\partial P}{\partial \theta} = M_1 \frac{\partial E(v|P)}{\partial \theta} + M_2 \qquad (5.27)$$

In such a framework, there are three channels of financial contagion:

- If Σ_θ is a nondiagonal matrix, information on assets is correlated across markets. This type of contagion has been investigated by King and Wadhwani (1990). They show that crises spread between markets as a result of rational investors trying to infer information from price variations. In a non fully revealing price equilibrium, price changes in one market depend on price changes in other markets. King and Wadhwani (1990) consider that mistakes and idiosyncratic shocks may be transmitted from one market to another, thus increasing volatility and the likelihood of currency crises.
- If Σ_ε is a nondiagonal matrix, a liquidity shock in one market is correlated with liquidity shocks in other markets. This type of contagion has been investigated by Calvo (1999). In his framework, the cost of information acquisition creates well- and poorly-informed investors. The latter are likely to transmit shocks between markets independently of fundamentals. Indeed they do not take fundamentals into account when diversifying their portfolio allocations. Instead they rely on their observations of well-informed investors' transactions. If these well-informed speculators are compelled to sell their assets in an emerging market because they face margin call-ups in other financial markets, these sales may be misinterpreted by poorly-informed investors. The latter consider that they signal that returns on these markets are to decrease shortly. Thus poorly-informed investors spread currency crises in emerging markets.
- If Σ_u is a nondiagonal matrix (or if Var($v|P$) is nondiagonal, or both), there is contagion through cross-rebalancing. Price changes in one market provoke variations in asset demands in other markets. Kodres and Pritsker (2002) consider that speculators' portfolio exposure to macroeconomic risks explains why idiosyncratic shocks are spread across markets. The pattern and severity of the contagion hinges on markets' sensitivities to shared macroeconomic risk factors, and on the level of informational asymmetry in each market. Currency crisis contagion may thus occur in the absence of news, as well as between markets that do not directly share any macroeconomic links.

Hence studies on informational asymmetry show how speculative attacks may be spread across countries without any relation to the state of macroeconomic fundamentals.

1.3. Informational Cascades

Studies on informational cascades show that, under some circumstances, agents' decisions do not reflect the information they hold privately, but the decisions of individuals who acted before them. Three strands of research in informational cascade theory may be distinguished. They share similarities but nevertheless reflect differences in the principles governing behaviour.

The first strand of literature focuses on the nature of the decision-making institutions and environment. It investigates the underlying reasons for the observed patterns of behaviour. Social psychologists have been at the forefront in observing this type of demeanour, as documented by Aronson, Wilson and Akert (1997). Still they do not call these types of behaviour cascades but distinguish between 'informational social influence' and 'normative social influence'. The former describes conformity resulting from the integration of private information with information inferred from others' behaviour. The latter focuses on conformity stemming from an internal motivation to adopt the perceived norms of the group. In this framework, individuals are sometimes punished by the group if they do not conform. Conformity may be rewarding, whatever the existing information.

The second strand of research on informational cascades emphasises information aggregation. A cascade is viewed as a Pareto improvement over a situation in which individuals base their decisions only on their private information. It comprises more private information than any single individual may have. Still a cascade does not include all information. It is a pattern of decisions that does not sum up and reveal private information as prices do on markets. This strand of research, which includes studies by Karni and Levine (1994) and Plott and Smith (1999), raises questions about the role of institutions and the efficiency of cascades as regards to their allocation and information properties.

The third strand of research originates in studies by Scharfstein and Stein (1990), Banerjee (1992), and Bikhchandani, Hirshleifer and Welch (1992). It has been applied to financial markets by Lux (1995), Chari and Kehoe (1997) and Bikchandani, Hirshleifer and Welch (1998).[7] These studies focus on similarities in individual choices, or interdependencies of preferences through conformity or 'herding'. Such a phenomenon is also known as 'herds', 'fads' or 'conformity'. It is explained that the mimetic behaviour of individuals stems from a lack of common knowledge (on common knowledge, see Chapter 6, section 3.3, Common knowledge between speculators and currency crisis with multiple equilibria). Agents are supposed to acquire information in a sequential manner by observing other individuals' past actions.[8] Assuming the first agent acts according to his own signal, i.e., according to his private information, individuals who act after him may decide to rationally ignore their own signals, which they believe to be dominated by the information revealed by the first agent's choices. The agents' decisions which are optimal at the individual level may then provoke cascades, that is a set of actions that is socially under-optimal.

A simple framework for this type of research can be found in Bikhchandani, Hirshleifer and Welch (1992). It is assumed that a sequence of individuals have to decide whether they adopt or reject a certain behaviour. All individuals have the same cost (equal to 0.5) of adopting the behaviour. The variable G denotes the gain of adopting the behaviour: it is either equal to zero or one, with equal prior probability equal to 0.5.

Each agent privately observes a conditionally independent signal about the value. The signal S_i of agent i is either A or B, where A is observed with probability p_i >0.5 if the true value is 1, and with probability $1-p_i$ if the true value is 0. Table 5.1 describes the agents' behaviour in the 'binary signal case'.

Table 5.1 Agents' behaviour in the 'binary signal case'

	$Prob(S_i=A\|G)$	$Prob(S_i=B\|G)$
$G=1$	p_i	$1-p_i$
$G=0$	$1-p_i$	p_i

For simplicity, it is assumed that signals are identically distributed: for all i, so that $p_i=p$. In that case, the expected value of adoption is just:

$$E(G)=\gamma.1+(1-\gamma).0=\gamma \tag{5.28}$$

where γ is the posterior probability that the true value is 1.

In such a framework, three situations are possible:

- an 'up' cascade: agents follow the first agent who chooses A;
- no cascade: the first agent chooses A and the second agent chooses B, or vice versa so that the third agent is in the same situation as the first agent and follows his own signal;
- a 'down' cascade: agents follow the first agent who chooses B.

It is possible to determine the unconditional *ex ante* probabilities of these three phenomena for two agents:

$$0.5(1-p+p^2)\ ;\ p-p^2\ ;\ 0.5(1-p+p^2) \tag{5.29}$$

and for an even n-number of individuals:

$$\frac{1-(p-p^2)^{\frac{n}{2}}}{2};p-p^2;\frac{1-(p-p^2)^{\frac{n}{2}}}{2} \tag{5.30}$$

Relation (5.30) shows that a cascade is unlikely to start when p is close to 0.5. A decrease in p towards 0.5 increases the likelihood of a cascade by adding noise to the signal. When p=0.5, the signal is uninformative. Besides it must be noted that the probability of a cascade falls exponentially with the number of individuals.

It is now assumed that the true value is 1. The probability of ending up in the correct cascade may be determined. After two individuals, the probabilities of an 'up' cascade, no cascade, and a 'down' cascade are:

$$0.5[p(p+1)]\ ;\ p(1-p)\ ;\ 0.5\ [(p-2)(p-1)] \tag{5.31}$$

and after an even n-number of individuals:

$$\frac{p(p+1)\left[1-(p-p^2)^{\frac{n}{2}}\right]}{2(1-p+p^2)};\ (p-p^2)^{\frac{n}{2}};\ \frac{(p-2)(p-1)\left[1-(p-p^2)^{\frac{n}{2}}\right]}{2(1-p+p^2)} \tag{5.32}$$

The first expression is the probability of finding the correct cascade. It is increasing in p and n. Yet even for very informative signals when p is far from 0.5, the probability of the wrong cascade is high. It is hence likely that shocks may be conveyed by agents across financial markets as a result of lack of common knowledge, and without fundamentals being deteriorated.

Informational cascades theory may seem to provide a relevant explanation of investors' mimetic behaviour on foreign exchange markets. Shiller (1995) however believes that individual behaviour is usually determined by the information at one's disposal, not by the observations of other agents' actions. Thus the lack of common knowledge is of lesser importance. As may be seen in Chapter 6, section 3.3, Common knowledge between speculators and currency crisis with multiple equilibria, Morris and Shin (1998a, 1998b) show that lack of common knowledge does not legitimise the disconnection between economic fundamentals and currency crisis transmission. Besides Masson (1998, 1999) considers that the possible microeconomic problems that pure contagion raises should not overshadow its macroeconomic perspectives which provide a relevant account of the 1997 spread of speculative attacks in East Asia.

2. PURE CONTAGION OF CURRENCY CRISES

Studies by Masson (1998, 1999) relate pure contagion to multiple equilibria. A country whose macroeconomic situation is stable, is likely to be subjected to a speculative attack triggered by the speculators' self-fulfilling expectations following a foreign government's decision to devalue its currency.

As in the 'late' escape clause models of Davies and Vines (1995), Cole and Kehoe (1996) and Obstfeld (1996), Masson (1998, 1999) considers that multiple equilibria appear in a single interval of fundamentals (see Chapter 4, section 2.2, 'Late' escape clause models). 'Jumps' between multiple equilibria occur if specific conditions regarding the debt level and the amount of reserves are satisfied. These 'jumps' follow a stochastic process represented by random shocks on emerging countries' trade balance.

The author considers two emerging countries called *A* and *B*, the United States of America and the rest of the world. By assumption the risks of borrowing default and of a currency crisis are related to public and private sectors' debts held by private foreign institutions. The amount of the expected devaluation and the size of the repayment default are identical and equal to φ, so that borrowing rates on domestic- and foreign-currency denominated debts evolve in a similar way:

$$E_t[(1+i_t)-(s_{t+1}-s_t)] = i_t - \pi_t\varphi \tag{5.33}$$

and:

$$E_t[(1+i_t)-(v_{t+1}-v_t)] = i_t - \pi_t\varphi \tag{5.34}$$

where E_t is an expectations operator, i_t the domestic interest rate, s_t the spot exchange rate at time t and v_t the value at time t of foreign-currency denominated bonds; π_t is at the same time the devaluation probability and the repayment default probability.

In this framework, investors who are risk-neutral demand a compensation to invest in emerging markets. It is the sum of the constant risk-free interest rate i^*, which is assumed to hold in the USA and in the rest of the world, and of the size φ of the expected devaluation. In that case, the variation in reserves equals:

$$r_{t+1} - r_t = TB_{t+1} - (i^* + \pi_t \varphi)ED \tag{5.35}$$

where r_t is the amount of reserves at time t, TB_{t+1} the trade balance disequilibrium at time $t+1$, ED the domestic- and foreign-currency external debt.

An attack occurs at time $t+1$ if:

$$r_{t+1} - \underline{r} < 0 \tag{5.36}$$

where $\underline{r}$ is the amount of reserves where the policymaker decides to let the exchange rate go.

The likelihood in t that a currency crisis and a repayment default happen in $t+1$ is:

$$\pi_t = \text{Prob}[TB_{t+1} - (i^* + \pi_t \varphi)ED + r_t - \underline{r} < 0] \tag{5.37}$$

Let:

$b_t \equiv TB_t - i^* ED + r_{t-1} - \underline{r}$
$\alpha \equiv \varphi ED$
$\phi_t = E_t(b_{t+1})$.

Equation (5.37) becomes:

$$\pi_t = Prob[TB_{t+1} - i^* ED + r_t - \underline{r} < \pi_t \varphi ED] \tag{5.38}$$

whence:

$$\pi_t = \text{Prob}[b_{t+1} < \alpha \pi_t] \tag{5.39}$$

Equation (5.40) shows the relationship between the outbreak of a crisis and the values of α and ϕ_t. In order to express π_t as a function of these two variables, it is assumed that the innovation ε_t in the variable b_t, $\varepsilon_t \equiv b_t - \phi_{t-1}$, follows a normal law with null mean and σ^2-variance and has the following cumulative distribution function (c.d.f.) F:

$$\pi_t = F[\alpha \pi_t - \phi_t] \tag{5.40}$$

Equation (5.41) defines investors' rational expectations of a devaluation. It may have several solutions, since both right- and left-hand sides of this equation hinge positively on π_t. The whole consistency of the model implies that the following necessary condition is satisfied:

$$z \equiv \frac{\alpha}{\sqrt{2\Pi}\sigma} > 1 \quad (5.41)$$

Equation (5.40) states that the density function derived from the c.d.f must have at least a value that is superior to 1. It defines values of fundamentals in relation to the size of the debt and shocks on the trade balance that must be reached if currency crisis contagion is to happen. It is not however a sufficient condition for the occurrence of a currency crisis with multiple equilibria; an additional condition must be met about $\phi_t = E_t(b_{t+1})$. The crisis only occurs in the interval $[\phi_{min}; \phi_{max}]$ where ϕ_{min} and ϕ_{max} correspond to values of ϕ_t where the probability density function derived from F equals 1:

$$\alpha F[-\sqrt{2 \log z}] + \sigma\sqrt{2 \log z} < \phi_t < \alpha F[-\sqrt{2 \log z}] - \sigma\sqrt{2 \log z} \quad (5.42)$$

From equation (5.37), one can obtain the level of reserves r_{min} and r_{max} corresponding to ϕ_{min} and ϕ_{max} where crises with multiple equilibria occur:

$$r_{min} \equiv \phi_{min} - E_t(TB_{t+1}) + i^* ED + \underline{r} \quad (5.43)$$

and:

$$r_{max} = \phi_{max} - E_t(TB_{t+1}) + i^* ED + \underline{r} \quad (5.44)$$

Thus Masson (1999) formalises a model in which currency crisis propagation results from speculators' self-fulfilling expectations. Contagion may only occur if some conditions are satisfied, for example if the country:

- is highly indebted;
- runs a large trade deficit;
- has few foreign exchange reserves.

In the framework of Masson (1999), just like in the 'late' escape clause models of Cole and Kehoe (1996), Davies and Vines (1995), Obstfeld (1996), fundamentals are at the same time compatible with keeping or abandoning the fixed exchange rate regime. In all of these papers, the 'jump' from the good to the bad equilibrium is stochastic by nature. These strong assumptions shed some doubts on the relevance of these analyses, and, more generally, the pertinence of second-generation models.

3. CHAPTER SUMMARY

Studies concerning currency crisis contagion seek to explain how one or several countries may be successively compelled to let their exchange rate go. Some of this research emphasises the role of fundamentals during crisis propagation. Other studies develop a theory of 'pure contagion' where only speculators' self-fulfilling expectations propagate speculative attacks across countries.

'Pure contagion' does not result from changes in economic fundamentals, but from private agents' behaviour. It implies that a crisis in a given country may lead market participants to sell currencies from other economically- or geographically-related nations without distinguishing between domestic fundamentals. Masson (1998, 1999) thus formalises a currency crisis model where pure contagion is linked to the existence of multiple equilibria. In his framework, countries may suffer from self-fulfilling speculative attacks, provided the macroeconomic situation is sufficiently deteriorated.

This kind of contagion is often associated with irrational market behaviour, such as financial panics, confidence loss and herd movements. However, such phenomena may be a consequence of individual and rational behaviours. Studies on informational cascades, e.g., Scharfstein and Stein (1990), Banerjee (1992), and Bikhchandani, Hirshleifer and Welch (1992, 1998), show that agents follow the herd and bring about crises as a result of optimal decisions that are rational at the individual level. Other research emphasises informational asymmetry and institutional constraints of liquidity, e.g., Calvo and Mendoza (2000), Kodres and Pritsker (2002).

NOTES

1. It is often discussed whether speculation stabilizes or destabilizes financial markets. The analyses of Marshall (1923) and Williams (1936) were criticized by Keynes (1937) and Kaldor (1939). The rationale of Friedman (1953) favouring speculation was attacked by Baumol (1957). The views of Hirshleifer (1975) and Tirole (1982) are also opposed. Black (1986) argued that some investors, called noise traders, buy and sell assets using information that is inconsistent with the state of the market
2. The speculator only pays if his priors are such that his expected utility conditional on costly information is higher than his expected utility conditional on free information. Formally it

may be said that the potential update of the return z_i is drawn from a known probability distribution function (p.d.f) that represents the investor's priors.

3. If a=0 and b=1, short positions are not allowed in country i, as well as in the rest of the world.
4. This result holds if the number J of countries is superior to $1/\{1-[F(\rho)(b^2-a^2)+a^2]^{1/2}\}$.
5. Investors with Constant Absolute Risk Aversion hold the same amount of risky assets as their wealth increases.
6. On the behaviour of noise traders, see among others Black (1986), DeLong, Shleifer, Summers and Waldmann (1990), Froot, Sharfstein and Stein (1992) and Madrigal (1996). See Vitale (2000) for a study on noise trading on foreign exchange markets.
7. Bikhchandani and Sharma (2000) provide a survey of herd behaviour on financial markets with a perspective that differs from ours.
8. On information acquisition in financial markets, see amongst others, Grossman (1976), Grossman and Stiglitz (1980), Hellwig (1980), Verrechia (1982), Admati (1985), Wang (1993, 1994), and Barlevy and Veronesi (2000).

6. The Relevance of Second-generation Models

Second-generation models rest on the idea that fundamentals do not account, or account only partially, for speculative attacks. They emphasise multiple equilibria and the speculators' self-fulfilling expectations. This chapter examines the validity of their regulatory implications, their empirical relevance, and discusses the theoretical and empirical problems raised by multiple equilibria.

Since second-generation models consider that crises are triggered by speculators' self-fulfilling expectations, it has been suggested that regulations should be established to avoid speculative attacks. Some favour the establishment of capital controls, others prefer taxes on financial transactions.

The central assumption of second-generation models, i.e., attacks occur independently of the state of fundamentals, is discussed more or less explicitly by empirical studies on currency crises. They use different methods to assess whether speculators' expectations about a forthcoming crisis are warranted by deteriorated fundamentals.

Finally this chapter analyses the problems that multiple equilibria raise. Their validity in currency crisis is discussed under a perspective that is both theoretical and empirical.

1. REGULATORY IMPLICATIONS OF SECOND-GENERATION MODELS

Second-generation models describe the policymaker as powerless against speculative attacks and consider that speculators are solely responsible for currency crises. This is why they are often used to advocate financial market regulations. They are said to stabilise financial markets by convincing private agents of the policymaker's capacity to keep the exchange rate fixed. Second-generation models thus revive discussions on capital controls and on financial taxes on international capital transactions.

As was seen in Chapter 2, section 1.1, Capital controls, there is no agreement on the effects of capital controls in first-generation models. The same statement holds in second-generation models. Ozkan and Sutherland (1995) consider that a fixed exchange rate regime is less vulnerable to shocks when capital controls are brought in. Dellas and Stockman (1993) assert the opposite and consider that agents' expectations about the establishment of capital controls may trigger speculative attacks. In their opinion, introducing capital controls entails a risk premium and provokes the appreciation of the domestic interest rate, and this is precisely what it is meant to avoid. Thus the uncertain effects of capital controls lead some authors to suggest a tax on international speculative transactions.

This kind of regulation has first been suggested by Tobin (1978) – the 'Tobin tax'. It aims at lengthening the investors' temporal horizon in order to avoid crises. Eichengreen, Tobin and Wyplosz (1995) and Eichengreen and Wyplosz (1996) assert that it is also likely to increase market participants' trust in the policymaker's ability to maintain a fixed exchange rate regime. Similar arguments are made by Bensaïd and Jeanne (1996) and Jeanne (1996b).

Several criticisms are levelled against the Tobin tax by Dooley (1996), Frankel (1996), Garber (1996b), Garber and Taylor (1995) and Kenen (1995, 1996). The tax rests on the assumption that short-term speculation is always destabilising, which may not be the case. Moreover such a tax may create distortions in fund allocations and market inefficiencies. Market participants are also likely to circumvent regulation, assert the opponents. To be effective, the tax must be enforced in all financial markets. Agents would also have to be prevented from transferring their speculative transactions from the currency market to the asset and derivative markets.

Another financial tax, suggested by Eichengreen, Tobin and Wyplosz (1995), is less subjected to criticism. They suggest introducing a tax on domestic-currency lending from residents to non-residents. Such a regulation could be easily enacted by a domestic policymaker, without concern for foreign governments. Yet this tax would have less impact than the Tobin tax. It is only aimed at non-resident speculators who borrow from residents in domestic currency, invest in foreign assets, and expect a devaluation that will help them make a profit when repaying their loans. The authors consider that this phenomenon accounts for a large part of the 1992 and 1993 speculative attacks against the European Monetary System. Miller (1999) provides similar arguments and asserts that restrictions, and even interdictions, against domestic-currency denominated bank lending would prevent speculative attacks from foreign investors. This is a questionable conclusion. All in all it remains uncertain whether regulations or financial taxes may really prevent the outbreak or propagation of currency crises.

2. EMPIRICAL ASSESSMENTS OF CURRENCY CRISES

Empirical research provides a more or less explicit assessment of the relevance of second-generation models. They seek empirical relations between the evolution of macroeconomic fundamentals and the outbreak of currency crises.[1] Two approaches may be distinguished: some studies attempt to estimate market participants' devaluation expectations while others develop early-warning systems of currency crises. In addition, if these models are able to determine the fundamentals that cause currency crises, they may be helpful in predicting speculative attacks.

2.1. The Estimation of Market Participants' Devaluation Expectations

Several studies seek to determine the fundamental or self-fulfilling nature of currency crises by assessing speculators' expectations of future parity realignments between currencies. They assume that stock exchange prices reflect the information that agents possess. If a sharp change in stock prices occurs before a speculative attack, the currency crisis may be said to be anticipated. It results from market participants observing the deterioration of macroeconomic fundamentals on foreign exchange markets. If stock prices do not vary, the currency crisis must be attributed to market participants' self-fulfilling expectations.

Different methods are used to estimate realignment expectations. This sub-section focuses on two approaches: one uses the 'drift correction method' and the other the prices of currency options.

2.1.1. The 'drift correction' method

The 'drift correction' method is based on papers by Bertola and Svensson (1993) and Svensson (1993) that deal with exchange rate target zones.[2] It is used by Caramazza (1993), Rose and Svensson (1994), Thomas (1994) and Chen and Giovannini (1997). This approach rests upon the assumption that the uncovered interest rate parity condition is satisfied. The differential in interest rates between countries for a given maturity is said to reveal the expected variations in the exchange rate during that period. It is thus possible to decompose expected variations in the exchange rate between anticipated movements inside a margin of fluctuation, and expected changes in the central parity, which may be interpreted as realignment expectations.

The realignment expectations may be estimated via the expected movements in the exchange rate inside the fluctuation band:

$$s_t = e_t + z_t \qquad (6.1)$$

with s_t being the exchange rate at time t, z_t the central parity and e_t the deviation from the central parity, all expressed in logarithms.

The expected realignment rate at time t for maturity Δt is then defined as:

$$g_t^{\Delta t} = \frac{E_t(z_{t+\Delta t} - z_t)}{\Delta t} \tag{6.2}$$

When the uncovered interest rate parity holds:

$$\delta_t^{\Delta t} = i_t^{\Delta t} - i_t^{\Delta t*} \tag{6.3}$$

where $i_t^{\Delta t}$ and $i_t^{\Delta t*}$ are respectively the domestic and foreign interest rates at time t for maturity Δt, and $\delta_t^{\Delta t}$ the deviation from the corresponding rate. Equation (6.3) may be rewritten as:

$$\delta_t^{\Delta t} = \frac{E_t(s_{t+\Delta t} - s_t)}{\Delta t} \tag{6.4}$$

The expected realignment rate at time t for maturity Δt is equal to :

$$g_t^{\Delta t} = \delta_t^{\Delta t} - \frac{E_t(e_{t+\Delta t} - e_t)}{\Delta t} \tag{6.5}$$

The expected realignment rate represents the anticipated variations in the central parity weighted by the corresponding maturity. It is interpreted as the product of the anticipated frequency of realignments and the expected size of each realignment.

As can be seen, the 'drift correction' method provides a simple estimation of expected variations in the exchange rate inside a fluctuation band. It is however criticised by Branson (1994) on two grounds. It rests upon the uncovered interest parity condition which is seldom verified empirically. Moreover the explicative power of the undertaken econometric regressions is often disappointing. Such observations lead some authors to investigate another method for retrieving speculators' expectations in times of speculative pressure.

2.1.2. Retrieving speculators' expectations with currency options

In order to retrieve speculators' expectations before currency crises, Söderlind and Svensson (1997) and Söderlind (2000) use currency options. They consider that option prices reflect the perceived likelihood of a realignment. They try to rebuild the subjective probability distribution of the market by combining the information included in several options with different strike prices.

Söderlind (2000) shows how to retrieve the distribution of speculators' expectations from the prices of options and forward contracts. A foreign exchange market where the law of one price holds is considered.[3] The call price C of a European option that gives at time t the right but not the obligation of buying an asset for the strike price X at the expiry date τ is:

$$C(t,\tau,\tau) = E_t[D(t,\tau).\max(0, Q(\tau) - X)] \tag{6.6}$$

where $Q(\tau)$ is the price of the asset and $D(t,\tau)$ the nominal discount factor.

The distribution of the logarithms of $Q(\tau)$ and $D(t,\tau)$ is conditional on information available at time t and is assumed to be a mixture of n bivariate normal distributions. Let $\varphi(x,\mu,\Omega)$ denote a normal multivariate density function over x with mean vector μ and covariance matrix Ω. Let the weight of the jth normal distribution be $\alpha^{(j)}$. Thus the probability density function (p.d.f.) of $ln[D(t,\tau)]$ and $ln[Q(\tau)]$ is assumed to be:

$$p.d.f.\left(\begin{bmatrix} ln\ D(t,\tau) \\ ln\ Q(\tau) \end{bmatrix}\right) = \sum_{j=1}^{n} \alpha^{(j)} \varphi\left(\begin{bmatrix} ln\ D(t,\tau) \\ ln\ Q(\tau) \end{bmatrix} \begin{bmatrix} \bar{d}^{(j)} \\ \bar{q}^{(j)} \end{bmatrix} \begin{bmatrix} \sigma_{dd}^{(j)} \sigma_{dq}^{(j)} \\ \sigma_{dq}^{(j)} \sigma_{qq}^{(j)} \end{bmatrix}\right) \tag{6.7}$$

with:

$$\sum_{j=1}^{n} \alpha^{(j)} = 1 \tag{6.8}$$

and:

$$\alpha^{(j)} \geq 0 \tag{6.9}$$

Soderlind (2000) interprets this mix of normal distributions as a representation of each different macroeconomic state. Each weight describes the likelihood of the probability of state j.

Let $i(t,\tau)$ be the spot interest rate on a bill with maturity date τ, and $\Phi(.)$ be the standardised normal distribution function. If:

$$\bar{d}^{(j)} = \bar{d}$$
$$\sigma_{dd}^{(j)} = \sigma_{dd}$$

in equation (6.7), then equation (6.6) has a closed-form solution in terms of the spot interest rate, the strike price and the parameters of the bivariate distribution. The price of the European call option may be rewritten as:

$$C(X) = \exp[-i(t,\tau)(\tau - t)]\sum_{j=1}^{n} \alpha^{j} \cdot$$

$$\left[\exp\left(\overline{q}^{(j)} + \frac{1}{2}\sigma_{qq}^{(j)} + \sigma_{dq}^{(j)}\right)\Phi\left(\frac{\overline{q}^{(j)} + \sigma_{qq}^{(j)} + \sigma_{dq}^{(j)} - \ln X}{\sqrt{\sigma_{qq}^{(j)}}}\right)\right.$$

$$\left. - X\Phi\left(\frac{\overline{q}^{(j)} + \sigma_{dq}^{(j)} - \ln X}{\sqrt{\sigma_{qq}^{(j)}}}\right)\right] \qquad (6.10)$$

A forward contract written in t stipulates that, in period τ, the holder of the contract gets one asset and pays $F(t, \tau)$.[4] Given equation (6.10), the price of the forward contract is:

$$F(t,\tau) = \sum_{j=1}^{n} \alpha^{(j)} exp\left(\overline{q}^{(j)} + \sigma_{dq}^{(j)} + \frac{\sigma_{qq}^{(j)}}{2}\right) \qquad (6.11)$$

To assess the possibility of a realignment, the marginal distribution of the log future asset price $ln[Q(\tau)]$ in equation (6.7) should be estimated, using the option and forward prices in equations (6.10) and (6.11). This requires information about risk premia that is seldom available. To simplify the estimation, it is assumed that risk premia are null, that is $\sigma_{dd}^{(j)}=0$. This is why the estimated distributions are called 'risk neutral distribution'. Forward prices measure the risk neutral mean of a future asset price while option prices provide an estimate of the entire risk neutral distribution.

Such a technique provides quantitative answers on speculators' expectations of a future realignment. This method also provides an assessment on the evolution of interest rates. Its results are however questionable since they rely on a strong assumption, that is risk premia equal zero. This is why other methods for estimating speculators' expectations are investigated.

Coeuré and Magnier (1996) examine the long-term relations between the evolution of fundamentals and the devaluation expectations, by seeking a Granger-type causality using the sequential strategy suggested by Toda and Phillips (1993, 1994). Weber (1991) suggests a model with unobservable components estimated by a Kalman filter with Bayesian learning. Garretsen, Knot and Nijsse (1998) also use a Bayesian learning process to develop a discrete-time model of exchange rate determination. Campa and Chang (1996) and Campa, Chang and Refalo (2002) estimate a 'minimal realignment intensity' by using different arbitrage techniques. It should however be discussed whether any of these methods provide an efficient assessment of speculators' self-fulfilling expectations before the outbreak of speculative attacks.

2.1.3. Speculators' devaluation expectations and the causes of speculative attacks

Except for the study by Campa, Chang and Refalo (2002), which deals with the Brazilian currency stabilisation plan between 1994 and 1999, research on devaluation expectations analyses the causes of the speculative attacks in the European Monetary System in 1992 and 1993. Some studies, such as Eichengreen and Wyplosz (1993), Jeanne (1996b) and Bensaïd and Jeanne (1996), consider that self-fulfilling expectations played a major role in explaining these crises. Rose and Svensson (1994) state that, among all the fundamentals taken into account in their study, only inflation influences devaluation expectations in a significant manner. Their results are compatible with first-generation models. Chen and Giovannini (1997) state that various fundamentals seem to influence some parities for short maturities but find it difficult to generalise these empirical correlations. Caramazza (1993) and Thomas (1994) also assert that fundamentals are weakly correlated to devaluation expectations. Many macroeconomic variables other than domestic credit may however influence market participants' devaluation expectations. Moreover the various econometric methods used by Coeuré and Magnier (1996) confirm the idea that it is difficult to establish robust links between the agents' expectations and fundamentals. They suggest that this lack of empirical relations implies that the European Monetary System crises mainly resulted from market participants' self-fulfilling expectations.

Studies using currency options state the exact opposite, but without providing any convincing evidence. For instance Söderlind (2000) asserts that his estimation methods show that speculators anticipated a realignment in the German mark / British pound exchange rate, although this expected realignment was of lesser importance than the actual realignment.

From this empirical evidence, it is difficult to determine the real influence of self-fulfilling expectations and of fundamentals when assessing devaluation expectations. That is why some studies do not attempt to retrieve speculators' expectations and take a different approach in order to explain the causes of currency crises.

2.2. Early Warning Systems of Currency Crises

To assess the likelihood of currency crises, some empirical studies attempt to determine the macroeconomic variables that are deteriorated when speculative attacks happen and influence the collapse of fixed exchange rate regimes.

Since these empirical analyses do not use a structural model, they do not use the same currency crisis definition.[5] Edwards (1989), Edwards and Montiel (1989) and Frankel and Rose (1996) only take into account major devaluations, while Klein and Marion (1997) consider small-sized devaluations. Eichengreen, Rose and Wyplosz (1996b), Kaminsky, Lizondo and Reinhart (1997), Kaminsky (1999), Kaminsky and Reinhart (1999), Sachs, Tornell and Velasco (1996a), and Tornell (1999) aim at building an indicator based on the study by Girton and Roper (1977) in order to determine speculative pressure periods. This approach allows the influence of various macroeconomic fundamentals in times of market instability to be assessed, even if the policymaker is eventually not compelled to let the exchange rate go.

Eichengreen, Rose and Wyplosz (1996b) determine speculative pressure periods by defining the speculative pressure index K_t:

$$K_t=\omega_1\Delta s_t+\omega_2(-\Delta r_t)+\omega_3\Delta i_t \tag{6.12}$$

where ω_1, ω_2, and ω_3 are the weights respectively assigned to the exchange rate, reserves and the interest rate.

Let J be defined as $J=m+2\sigma$, where m and σ are the mean and the standard deviation of the data in the study. If:

$$K_t>J_t \tag{6.13}$$

then time period t is a speculative pressure period.

The weights ω_1, ω_2, and ω_3, just like the threshold J used to identify speculative attacks, are arbitrary. Hence it is likely that the index of Eichengreen, Rose and Wyplosz (1996b) misses speculative pressure periods.

There are other methods for determining speculative pressure periods.[6] Edwards (1989), Funke (1996), Frankel and Rose (1996), Goldfajn and Valdès (1996, 1998), Klein and Marion (1997), Otker and Pazarbasioglu (1997a, 1997b) use logit and probit models to distinguish times of tranquillity and periods of speculative pressure on the foreign exchange markets. For instance the predicted value of the dependent variable in a probit model may be interpreted as the probability of a regime change:

$$\pi_t=\text{Prob}(Y=1)=\pi[(i_t- i_t^*),r_t, \dot{r},e_t] \quad (6.14)$$

where i_t is the domestic interest rate, i_t^* the interest rate in the anchor country, r_t the foreign exchange reserves, $\dot{r}$ the variation rate of reserves, and e_t the deviation from the central parity.

Other studies by Kaminsky, Lizondo and Reinhart (1997), Kaminsky (1999), Kaminsky and Reinhart (1998, 1999) use a method similar to Eichengreen, Rose and Wyplosz (1996b). They assess the respective influence of various fundamentals during periods preceding speculative attacks by building currency crises indicators. They then compare the evolution of various variables in relation to vulnerability thresholds that are defined a priori.

Despite some diverging views, these studies agree on the role of fundamentals during the outbreak and propagation of currency crises. Table 6.1 sums up their main results.

Table 6.1 Empirical findings on the causes of speculative attacks

Speculative attacks triggered by budgetary problems	Speculative attacks triggered by the real sector and external situation	Speculative attacks triggered by the weakness of the financial and banking sector
Budgetary deficit Public spending Bank loans to the public sector	Current account Real exchange rate Evolution of the trade balance Gap between the domestic interest rate and the national interest rate Changes in the nature of capital inflows and outflows Growth rate Unemployment rate Political regime and institutional structures	Credit growth to the private sector Measures in financial liberalisation Short-term debt level held by private financial institutions Structure in interest rates Changes in financial assets prices Quality of banking bonds

2.3. Currency Crisis Prediction

Studies on speculators' devaluation expectations and on early-warning systems provide an a posteriori explanation of speculative attacks. They consider that they are able to determine whether currency crises result from market participants' self-fulfilling expectations or from deteriorated fundamentals. Thus they assume that they may identify the macroeconomic causes of speculative attacks. If the macroeconomic causes are similar from one currency crisis to another, such studies should be successful in predicting collapses of fixed exchange rate regimes.

Of course currency crisis prediction is very difficult. If it is possible to identify the causes of currency crises, and even to state that a country will be compelled to let its exchange rate go in the near future, the timing of speculative attacks cannot be determined. Several reasons are given for that. For instance some variables in the prediction process may be omitted. It may also be said that the implicit assumption that past and future behaviours of markets are the same is not true.

Nevertheless some studies, e.g., Goldfajn and Valdès (1998), Berg and Patillo (1999a), Reagle and Salvatore (2000), ask whether it is possible to predict currency crises. Goldfajn and Valdès (1998) investigate whether exchange rate expectations and overvaluations are indicators of future currency crises. They find that distortions on the real exchange rate, in relation to the exchange rate in equilibrium, are a major empirical feature of crises that occurred in emerging countries in the 1990s. They still admit that market participants do not seem to anticipate currency crises. They conclude that their empirical study does not support the claims of first- or second-generation models. Fiscal and monetary policies would not be so crucial in the outbreak of currency crises that may however be related to deteriorated fundamentals. Goldfajn and Valdès (1998) concede that they find it difficult to single out self-fulfilling currency crises.

Berg and Patillo (1999a) analyse the prediction capacity of studies by Frankel and Rose (1996), Kaminsky, Lizondo and Reinhart (1997) and Sachs, Tornell and Velasco (1996a) through out-of-sample testing. They find that the predictive capacity of these three studies is weak. They miss most speculative attacks while giving false warnings of currency crises. This is not surprising. Predictions can only be successful if the relative influence of each variable in times of currency crisis outbreak and contagion does not vary between countries and throughout time.

All in all if these studies do not define satisfactory indicators, they cast a new light on theoretical models of currency crises. They suggest that attacks occur when fundamentals are deteriorated. Fundamentals should not however be limited to fiscal and monetary policies, but should also include variables such as the real exchange rate or aggregate demand. The conclusions of second-generation models whereby only speculators' self-fulfilling expectations would trigger crises also seem questionable. This calls into question the assumption on which second-generation models rest, that is the existence of multiple equilibria.

3. THEORETICAL AND EMPIRICAL PROBLEMS WITH MULTIPLE EQUILIBRIA

The relevance of second-generation models (and even of third-generation models, see below Part 3) is disputable as far as they rely on the existence of multiple equilibria. Both theoretical and empirical criticisms are levelled against multiple equilibria.

3.1. Theoretical Grounds for Multiple Equilibria

Two strands of research justify the use of multiple equilibria. The first one is based on the stochastic model of monetary policy of Obstfeld (1986b) (see Chapter 4, section 1, Self-fulfilling speculative attacks). It is also used by Obstfeld (1991, 1994) and Ozkan and Sutherland (1994, 1995, 1998) in the framework of early escape clause models (see Chapter 4, section 2.1 'Early' escape clause models). These studies assert that multiple equilibria result from speculators' self-fulfilling expectations and that currency crises occur independently of macroeconomic fundamentals.

The second framework is shared by late escape clause and pure contagion models. It is developed by Davies and Vines (1995), Cole and Kehoe (1996) and Obstfeld (1996). These approaches assume that multiple equilibria appear for some specific values of fundamentals.[7] They intuitively seem more grounded than the case in which multiple equilibria are not related to fundamentals. Yet this strand of research is somehow paradoxical. The domestic macroeconomic situation is both compatible with a fixed exchange rate and a float: the speculators' self-fulfilling expectations determine whether or not there is a currency crisis.

This framework is criticised by Krugman (1996)[8], Morris and Shin (1998a) and Garber (1996a, 2000). They consider that the likelihood of multiple equilibria is smaller when fundamentals are deteriorated. If speculators judge that fundamentals are not in line with the fixed exchange rate system, a unique equilibrium where the currency is devalued will emerge. On the other hand, if fundamentals permit the exchange rate to remain fixed, multiple equilibria are likely to appear. In that case, speculators' self-fulfilling expectations compel the policymaker to let the exchange rate go, even though the macroeconomic situation would allow the fixed exchange rate to be maintained. Krugman (1996) also states that speculative attacks may occur without fundamentals being deteriorated, and without the occurrence of multiple equilibria. Speculators launch attacks in order to find out the policymaker's preferences for a fixed exchange rate, even though they know that these attacks are bound to fail.

Krugman (1996) and Garber (1996a, 2000) go as far as to assert that the theoretical existence of multiple equilibria is not really grounded. Even if multiple equilibria existed, no explanation justifies the shift from a fixed-exchange-rate equilibrium to a crisis-equilibrium. This 'jump between equilibria' is never formalised and its causes remain unknown.[9]

However, a theoretical justification of the multiple equilibria may be found in the studies of Kareken and Wallace (1981) and Wallace (1990). They argue that exchange rates are indeterminate in a world of flat currencies. The studies may hence provide a theoretical basis for studies relying on multiple equilibria.[10]

Still the foundations of multiple equilibria are fragile. And their empirical validity questionable.

3.2. Empirical Relevance of Multiple Equilibria

Several empirical studies attempt to assess the influence of multiple equilibria on the outbreak of currency crises. They take two distinct approaches: some devise a specific framework to test multiple equilibria in escape clause models, others rely on Markov-switching regimes.

3.2.1. Testing for multiple equilibria in escape clause models

The test of structural escape clause models with equilibria *à la* Obstfeld (1991, 1994) is rather difficult. Jeanne (1997) undertakes such an estimation for the 1993 French franc crisis. His method is also applied by Masson (1999) to the 1994 Mexican and 1997 Thai crises, and by Lyrio and Dewachter (2000) to the credibility of the Brazilian crawling peg between 1995 and 1998.

Drawing on Lyrio and Dewachter (2000), the equations to be estimated using a maximum likelihood method are:

$$\pi_t = F[\alpha\pi_t - \phi_t] \tag{5.40}$$

with:

$b_t \equiv TB_t - i^* ED + r_{t-1} - \underline{r}$
$\alpha \equiv \varphi ED$
$\phi_t = E_t(b_{t+1}).$

where E_t is an expectations operator, i_t the domestic interest rate, i^* the risk-free interest rate, s_t the spot exchange rate at time t, and v_t the value at time t of foreign-currency denominated bonds; π_t is at the same time the devaluation probability and the repayment default probability; φ the size of the expected devaluation; TB_{t+1} the trade balance disequilibrium at time $t+1$; ED the domestic- and foreign-currency denominated external debt.

It has been explained in Chapter 5, section 2, Pure contagion of currency crises, how equation (5.40) is obtained. It shows the relationship between the outbreak of a crisis and the values of α and ϕ_t. In order to express π_t as a function of these two variables, it is assumed that the innovation ε_t in the variable b_t, $\varepsilon_t \equiv b_t - \phi_{t-1}$, follows a normal law with null mean and σ^2-variance and has a cumulative distribution function (c.d.f.) F.

The size of the expected devaluation φ is computed following the 'drift adjustment' method of Bertola and Svensson (1993) and Svensson (1993) that was presented above in this chapter, section 2.1.1, The 'drift correction' method. The expected depreciation within the band is estimated, then subtracted from the interest rate differential.

The studies that test the role of multiple equilibria in the outbreak of currency crises do not have clear-cut conclusions. In his research on the 1993 French franc crisis, Jeanne (1997) considers that some periods of speculative pressure before the crisis may be related to deteriorated fundamentals, but that several attacks seem to result from speculators' self-fulfilling expectations. The same approach is used by Lyrio and Dewachter (2000) who analyse the credibility of the Brazilian crawling peg between 1995 and 1998. They believe that the crisis that took place in early January 1999 resulted from the deterioration of the macroeconomic situation in Brazil, and not from market participants' self-fulfilling expectations.

3.2.2. Testing for multiple equilibria with Markov-switching regimes

Unlike Jeanne (1997), Masson (1999) and Lyrio and Dewachter (2000), some studies that try to assess the influence of multiple equilibria in the outbreak of speculative attacks do not seek to test escape clause models. Weber (1998), Martinez Peria (1999), Jeanne and Masson (2000), Kajanoja (2001), Tronzano (2001) use Markov-switching methods in order to establish the extent to which speculators' self-fulfilling expectations may explain crises. These studies aim at providing evidence of the existence of multiple equilibria on foreign exchange markets before speculative attacks are launched. All these analyses deal with the 1993 French franc devaluation; they consider that this devaluation resulted more from market participants' self-fulfilling prophecies rather than from the deterioration of fundamentals. But are these unanimous conclusions not the consequence of the method that these studies share?

These studies use Markov switching regime models developed by Hamilton (1990, 1994, 1996), and interpret switches in regime as jumps between multiple equilibria.

In a framework with time-invariant transition probabilities, the following equation is tested:

$$\pi_t = \alpha_s + \beta\theta_t + \varepsilon_t \tag{6.15}$$

with π_t being a measure of the realignment expectations, α_s the constant term of the regression which is conditional on the state of the economy s, θ_t the vector of explanatory macroeconomic variables, β the coefficient vector, ε_t the normally distributed error term.

The economy is allowed to jump between two different states s_t=1 or s_t =2 following the Markov matrix P:

$$P = \begin{bmatrix} p_{11} & 1-p_{11} \\ 1-p_{22} & p_{22} \end{bmatrix} \tag{6.16}$$

with $p_{11} \in [0;1]$ and $p_{22} \in [0;1]$.

If the economy is in state 1 (respectively state 2) at time t, then the probability that it will remain in the same state in t+1 is p_{11} (respectively p_{22}). The probability of transition from state 1 to state 2 (respectively from state 2 to state 1) is 1-p_{11} (respectively 1-p_{22}).

The maximum likelihood estimation of the regime switching model requires values to be found for the following parameters: α_1, α_2, β, p_{11} and p_{22}. The likelihood function of the model must be maximised, assuming the error term is normally distributed.

A framework with time-varying transition probabilities estimates the same parameters by assuming that p_{11} and p_{22} depend on observable economic variables. This approach is a variant of Hamilton (1990, 1994, 1996) as put forward by Diebold, Lee and Weinbach (1994). It allows an assessment of the influence of exogenous macroeconomic variables one at a time. It is possible to tell whether some fundamentals significantly affect the probability of remaining in a fixed exchange regime or of a shift to a flexible exchange rate system. In this framework, p_{11} and p_{22} are worth:

$$p_{11} = \frac{\exp(a_1 + \beta_1 x_{t-1})}{1 + \exp(a_1 + \beta_1 x_{t-1})} \tag{6.17}$$

and

$$p_{22} = \frac{\exp(a_2 + \beta_2 x_{t-1})}{1 + \exp(a_2 + \beta_2 x_{t-1})} \tag{6.18}$$

where a_1 and a_2 are constant terms, β_1 and β_2 parameters governing transition probabilities and x_{t-1} an exogenous macroeconomic variable at time t-1.

The Markov-switching regime approach is not flawless. Such a method asserts that speculators' self-fulfilling expectations entail a high and arbitrary number of multiple equilibria – at least six or seven. Needless to say, this assertion takes us far from the general framework of models with self-fulfilling expectations.

To sum up, these empirical studies do not provide a convincing estimate of multiple equilibria in times of speculative attacks. They suppose their existence but do not prove it. Only Morris and Shin (1998a, 1998b) provide a convincing theory of multiple equilibria in times of currency crises.

3.3. Common Knowledge between Speculators and Currency Crisis with Multiple Equilibria

Morris and Shin (1998a, 1998b) develop a currency crisis model where speculators' expectations and the deterioration of macroeconomic fundamentals foster speculative attacks. The novelty in their analysis lies in the introduction of heterogeneous information among speculators. This justifies the existence of self-fulfilling currency crises under a unique equilibrium on foreign exchange markets.[11]

The authors consider that multiple equilibria are theoretically possible, but unlikely to occur. Multiple equilibria only appear when there is sufficient common knowledge among market participants, i.e., when each agent knows the actions of other speculators under equilibrium.[12] But such a situation is unlikely: market participants only possess incomplete information on fundamentals. And the quantity of information that speculators possess matters less than its transparency and its degree of circulation among agents. If they observe macroeconomic and microeconomic data with noise, they ignore some private or public information. The equilibrium on foreign exchange markets is unique.

This section presents the main elements of both analyses of Morris and Shin (1998a, 1998b). They develop a unique equilibrium currency crisis model with self-fulfilling expectations. They assume that θ represents the perception that the authorities have of fundamentals, with $\theta \in \Re$. The share of market participants on the foreign exchange market that is necessary for a speculative attack to be successful when the state of fundamentals is θ, is denoted $a(\theta)$. Thus θ may be seen as an assessment of the policymaker's capacity to resist an attack, and $a(\theta)$ as the size of this attack. In order to determine the different equilibria, assumptions need to be made about the $a(.)$ function as well as about the values of θ in $\Re$:

- $\underline{\theta}$ is such that $\forall\,\theta\in\Re,\ \theta\leq\underline{\theta},\ a(\theta)=0$;
- $\overline{\theta}$ is such that $\forall\,\theta\in\Re,\overline{\theta}<\theta,\ a(\theta)$ is undefined;
- when $a(\theta)\in[0;1]$, $a'(\theta)>0$;
- there exists a lower bound b on the first derivative of function a so that $0<b\leq a'(\theta)$.

There are three intervals of fundamentals corresponding to different equilibria:

- In the interval $]-\infty;\ \underline{\theta}]$, the defence costs of the fixed exchange system exceeds the benefits to the policymaker. There is a unique equilibrium where the policymaker lets the exchange rate go, whatever speculators' actions.
- In the interval $]\underline{\theta}\ ;\overline{\theta}\ ]$, the currency is 'ripe for an attack': the macroeconomic conditions are such that a crisis occurs if a share $a(\theta)$ of speculators triggers a self-fulfilling attack. The appendix to this chapter shows that, when common knowledge is lacking, this interval has a unique currency crisis equilibrium which is not necessarily realised. But if there is common knowledge, the interval has two equilibria: one where the exchange rate remains fixed, the other where there is a shift to a flexible exchange rate.
- In the interval $]\overline{\theta}\ ;+\infty[$, the cost of an attack, for speculators, is superior to the profit they can make out of it. There is a unique equilibrium where the fixed exchange rate is maintained until the following period.

The evolution of fundamentals as perceived by the policymaker, i.e., the variable θ, is analysed in a discrete-time framework. At time t, $\theta=\theta_t$. Assume that increments in time equal $\Delta>0$. The value of θ at time $t+\Delta$ is denoted $\theta_{t+\Delta}$: it is conditional to the information in θ_t and follows a normal law distribution, with mean θ_t and variance Δ. The variable θ follows a Brownian motion process $d\theta=z(\Delta)^{0.5}dt$, where z is a standard normal random law $N(0;1)$.

By assumption the policymaker has the knowledge of θ since this variable represents his perception of the state of fundamentals. At time t, he thus possesses the information $\{\theta_t;a(\theta)\}$ and forsakes the fixed exchange rate system when $s\geq a(\theta)$. Market participants however observe θ_t after a Δ–delay in time. At time t, they observe θ_t with a noisy signal. Speculator i observes the random variable $x_{i,t}$ such that $x_{i,t}=\theta_t+\eta_i$, where η_i is a random variable independent of θ and normally distributed with zero mean and variance $\varepsilon\Delta$, where ε is a small strictly positive number such that for every $i \neq j$, $\eta_i \neq \eta_j$. Therefore speculator i possesses information $\{\theta_{t-\Delta}; x_{i,t}\}$ at time t.

During each time period, speculators either attack or refrain from attacking the currency based on the information they possess.[13] Some agents receive informational signals such that they believe the policymaker may keep the exchange rate fixed. Therefore they do not launch an attack. It must be noticed that the uniqueness of the equilibrium in this currency crisis model is compatible with the multiplicity of speculators' actions.

Speculators bear a transaction cost when they attack the currency. This cost, denoted *cs*, is a known constant lump sum. The policymaker observes the proportion of agents who take part in the attack. He makes a benefit v from keeping the exchange rate fixed and bears a cost $C[a(\theta)]$ when speculators attack the currency. If the share of agents who attack the fixed exchange rate is superior to $a(\theta)$, he gives up on the fixed exchange rate system. The currency is devalued by an amount equal to 1 by assumption. Then it is never more subjected to speculative pressures. In this framework, the matrices of payoffs are given by Tables 6.2 and 6.3.

Table 6.2 Payoffs of each speculator

	Fixed exchange rate maintained	Fixed exchange rate abandoned
Attack	-*cs*	1-*cs*
No attack	0	0

Table 6.3 The policymaker's payoffs

	Fixed exchange rate maintained	Fixed exchange rate abandoned
Attack	$v-C[a(\theta)]$	$v-C[a(\theta)]-1$
No attack	0	0

The analyses of Morris and Shin (1998a, 1998b) provide a new interpretation of crises. When information is noisy, agents learn about fundamentals without much error, but interpret their level differently. The outbreak of a currency crisis may result from the arrival of noisy information on the foreign exchange market that all agents interpret in the same way. Each agent expects all the others will launch an attack on the peg, though each agent knows that the state of fundamentals in itself would not lead to an exchange rate crisis. But crises are not triggered by extreme or median views. They stem from high order beliefs[14] of speculators who try to discover the opinions of market participants concerning other agents' crisis expectations. A crisis happens when a rumour provokes the disappearance of lack of common knowledge on the market, while θ_t is in the interval $]\underline{\theta}\,;\overline{\theta}\,]$.

The framework of Morris and Shin (1998a, 1998b) is however criticized by Sbracia and Zhagini (2001), Chan and Chiu (2002) and Femminis (2002). They consider that multiple equilibria cannot be ruled out because of a lack of common knowledge. Furthermore they believe noisy private observations are not usually sufficient to prevent the multiplicity of equilibria. Their conclusions are however criticized by Heinemann and Illing (2002) who consider that a decrease in the dispersion of private signal noise reduces the critical situation where a crisis is triggered. Heinemann and Illing (2002) also find support for the uniqueness of the equilibrium in the manner of Morris and Shin (1998a).[15]

The framework of Morris and Shin (1998a, 1998b) also has policy implications. In their view, the policymaker may try to prevent crises by increasing transactions costs. This increase shortens the interval where self-fulfilling currency crises are likely to happen. Establishing capital controls is also efficient when there exists a great deal of uncertainty on the fundamentals since speculators do not interpret the macroeconomic situation in the same way. Yet capital controls are likely to change aggregate wealth. They decrease the value of $a(\theta)$ – the proportion of speculators necessary for an attack to occur – and may increase the likelihood of currency crises.

This observation leads Corsetti, Dasgupta, Morris and Shin (2000) to investigate the role of speculators with significant financial means.[16] They consider that these speculators influence the stability of fixed exchange rate systems. They affect the behaviour of 'small' speculators who supposedly imitate their portfolio allocations on financial markets. This influence is strengthened when 'small' speculators are less informed than 'large' ones on foreign exchange markets.

All in all Morris and Shin (1998a, 1998b) consider that currency crises may be prevented if common knowledge exists on the foreign exchange markets. This implies that the policymaker conducts his economic policies in a transparent fashion and disseminates information among all relevant agents. For both authors, policy announcements may prevent speculative attacks. But they do not demonstrate it. They insist on the quality of information the policymaker provides agents with. Yet the policymaker's reputation must be good, as his communication skills and the content of the information should be, in order to prevent a speculative attack. In any case, Morris and Shin (1998a, 1998b) provide a new perspective on currency crisis theory and pave the way for third-generation models focusing on the interactions between public policies, fundamentals and speculators' self-fulfilling expectations.

4. CHAPTER SUMMARY

Second-generation models, and especially escape clause models, describe a powerless policymaker and hold speculators responsible for the outbreak of currency crises. These models are usually used to promote regulations on financial markets, e.g., capital controls and taxes on international financial transactions. These regulations are said to help the policymaker keep the exchange rate fixed by convincing speculators that he is committed to a fixed peg.

Second-generation models of currency crises assume that a lack of deteriorated fundamentals characterises speculative attacks and multiple equilibria. In this respect, an assessment of empirical studies analysing the influence of fundamentals on currency crises must be conducted, while theoretical and empirical problems concerning multiple equilibria must be dealt with.

Empirical studies on currency crises assess the existence of stable relationships between fundamentals and the outbreak of speculative attacks. Different kinds of analyses may be distinguished: those seeking to establish a relationship between the dynamic of fundamentals and market participants' devaluation expectations, e.g., Rose and Svensson, (1994), Thomas (1994), Coeuré and Magnier (1996), Chen and Giovannini (1997) Söderlind (2000); and those using vulnerability indicators, e.g., Eichengreen, Rose and Wyplosz (1996b), Kaminsky and Reinhart (1998, 1999). On the whole, empirical research on currency crises shows that speculative attacks occur when fundamentals are deteriorated, unlike the situation described by second-generation models. These models are therefore questionable, as the very existence of multiple equilibria is uncertain.

Critics of multiple equilibria such as Garber (1996a, 2000) and Krugman (1996) argue that there is no theoretical justification for the existence of more than a single equilibrium under the same market conditions. They also consider that a convincing theory of shifts between equilibria is lacking. But such criticisms do not reflect the fact that multiple equilibria are a theoretical construct describing a very peculiar situation, that is a macroeconomic situation where a currency crisis may or may not happen, depending on market participants' self-fulfilling expectations. An uncommon case indeed. Morris and Shin (1998a, 1998b) demonstrate that there must be sufficient common knowledge among market participants for multiple equilibria to appear. Without common knowledge, agents get an independent noisy signal on the economy. There is a unique macroeconomic equilibrium that may bring about a self-fulfilling currency crisis.

5. APPENDIX

This appendix provides a sketch of the demonstration on the uniqueness of the equilibrium when there is no common knowledge, as shown by Morris and Shin (1998a, 1998b) (see Chapter 6, section 3.3, Common knowledge between speculators and currency crisis with multiple equilibria).

In order to demonstrate the uniqueness of the equilibrium in the interval of fundamentals $]\underline{\theta}; \overline{\theta}]$, the limits of the speculators' strategies under equilibrium must be determined. Let $p(x, \theta_{t-\Delta})$ be the share of speculators who attack the peg given $(x, \theta_{t-\Delta})$, where x is the value of the fundamental at time t observed with noise, and $\theta_{t-\Delta}$ the fundamental observed without uncertainty at time t. Denote E the set of values of p that may occur in the equilibrium of the game. In other words, $p \in E$ if and only if there is an equilibrium in which the share of speculators taking part in a speculative attack is $p(x, \theta_{t-\Delta})$, given $(x, \theta_{t-\Delta})$. Then define:

$$\underline{x}(\theta_{t-\Delta}) = \inf\{x | p(x, \theta_{t-\Delta}) < 1 \text{ and } p \in A\} \tag{6.19}$$

and

$$\overline{x}(\theta_{t-\Delta}) = \sup\{x | p(x, \theta_{t-\Delta}) > 0 \text{ and } p \in A\} \tag{6.20}$$

Given $(x, \theta_{t-\Delta})$, a speculator attacks the currency for each equilibrium of the model if $x < (x, \theta_{t-\Delta})$. Conversely if $x > (x, \theta_{t-\Delta})$, a speculator does not take part in any attack for each equilibrium of the model, given $(x, \theta_{t-\Delta})$. The limits $\underline{x}(\theta_{t-\Delta})$ and $\overline{x}(\theta_{t-\Delta})$ may be determined by using a continuous function $U(x, \theta_{t-\Delta})$ such that:

- $\lim_{x \to -\infty} U(x) = 1 - cs$;
- $\lim_{x \to +\infty} U(x) = -cs$;
- $\overline{x}(\theta_{t-\Delta}) = \max\{x | U(x, \theta_{t-\Delta}) = 0\}$;
- $\underline{x}(\theta_{t-\Delta}) = \min\{x | U(x, \theta_{t-\Delta}) = 0\}$;
- $\dfrac{\partial U(x, \theta_{t-\Delta})}{\partial \theta_{t-\Delta}} < 0$ and for sufficiently low values of ε, $\dfrac{\partial U(x, \theta_{t-\Delta})}{\partial x} < 0$.

Function U is continuous, positive for small values of x and negative when x takes large values. It intersects the horizontal axis at least once. It may be demonstrated that the smallest value of x such that U intersects the horizontal axis is $\underline{x}(\theta_{t-\Delta})$, while the largest is $\overline{x}(\theta_{t-\Delta})$. Once function U is determined, describing the speculators' actions under equilibrium comes down to determining the value of x such that $U(x, \theta_{t-\Delta})$ intersects the horizontal axis. Given conditions (6.19) and (6.20), U only intersects the horizontal axis once. Thus:

$$\underline{x}(\theta_{t-\Delta}) = \bar{x}(\theta_{t-\Delta}) \tag{6.21}$$

Equality (6.21) implies the existence of a unique equilibrium when there is no common knowledge of fundamentals. If ε is sufficiently small, there is a unique equilibrium θ^* for each $\theta_{t-\Delta}$ such that, for any equilibrium, the policymaker forsakes the fixed exchange rate system if and only if $\theta \leq \theta^*$.

Define the hurdle process $g(t)$ of a speculative attack outbreak: it allows the value of θ^* that is associated with the realisation of $\theta_{t-\Delta}$, to be determined, and thus, the moment when the speculative attack happens. Given process $g(t)$ and conditions (6.19) and (6.20), a first theorem is presented:

> For sufficiently small values of ε, there is a stochastic process $g(t)$ such that the fixed exchange rate is maintained as long as $\theta_t > g(t)$, but abandoned as soon as $\theta_t < g(t)$ (Theorem 1).

This theorem asserts that a stochastic process of a speculative attack outbreak exists when speculators possess sufficiently accurate information on the state of fundamentals. The outbreak of crises is therefore a random process where the date of the attack is related to the 'fall' of fundamentals on a 'hurdle'. A second theorem follows:

> $g(t) \geq g(t-\Delta)$ if and only if $\theta_{t-\Delta} \leq \theta_{t-\Delta}$ (Theorem 2).

Theorem 2 asserts that the hurdle moves in an opposite way to the fundamentals. When the state of the fundamentals improves, the hurdle decreases. The reverse occurs when fundamentals deteriorate. This implies that the likelihood of a crisis increases more than proportionally to the deterioration of the fundamentals.

NOTES

1. These studies differentiate from researches by Blanco and Garber (1986), Cumby and Van Wijnbergen (1989), Goldberg (1994) and Melick (1996) that test the hypotheses of first-generation models.
2. See also Svensson (1992a, 1992b) for a more general perspective.
3. The law of one price states that assets with the same payoff structure have the same price.
4. This can be thought of as an option with a zero strike price and no discounting.
5. For a discussion on the main empirical definitions of currency crises, see Berg and Patillo (1999a, 1999b, 1999c) and Glick and Hutchinson (1999).

6. On the methodologies used by empirical studies dealing with currency crises, see Kaminsky, Lizondo and Reinhart (1997), Berg, Borensztein, Milesi-Ferretti, and Patillo (1999) and Berg and Patillo (1999a, 1999b, 1999c).
7. See Chapter 4, section 2.2, 'Late' escape clause models.
8. Krugman (2000) has a different opinion on multiple equilibria. He believes that they explain the propagation of the East Asian crisis to Russia, since there are few, if any, fundamental macroeconomic links between East Asian countries and Russia.
9. Jeanne (1997, 2000), Masson (1998, 1999) and Jeanne and Masson (2000) consider that the jump between equilibria results from the existence of sunspots. This comes down to explaining one stochastic phenomenon by another stochastic phenomenon.
10. We owe this point to a referee.
11. Morris and Shin (1998a, 1998b) build on the global game analysis developed by Carlson and Van Damme (1993).
12. Aumann (1976) provides a formal definition of common knowledge. Geanakoplos (1992) presents its main implications.
13. Each speculator chooses his action conditional to the history of θ. Speculator i's strategy may be assumed to be restrained to a Markovian form of the type $\{\theta_{t-\Delta}; x_{i,t}\} \rightarrow$ {Attack; No attack}, since the value of θ at a given date does not reveal more information that its previous realisation.
14. The term 'high order beliefs' designates a situation where the chain of reasoning around common knowledge proceeds from a great number of recurrences.
15. The analysis of Heinemann and Illing (2002) relies on the iterated technique of dominated strategies and the concept of rationalizable equilibrium that were surveyed by Brandenburger (1992).
16. Corsetti, Pesenti and Roubini (2002) also deal with the role of 'large' speculators in times of currency crises.

PART THREE

Third-generation Models of Currency Crises

Third-generation models of currency crises build upon first– and second–generation models. They have constituted the basis of many studies since the East Asian crisis of 1997 and the subsequent events in Russia and Brazil in 1998 and 1999. Market participants' expectations seem to have played a crucial role, especially in East Asia where capital inflows were important during the two years before the crisis, though macroeconomic fundamentals were already quite deteriorated at that time. As studies on the East Asian crises note, e.g., Radelet and Sachs (1998a, 1998b) and Corsetti, Pesenti and Roubini (1999a, 1999b), it has been said that these capital inflows to East Asia resulted from speculators' loss of confidence in Latin America after the 1994 Mexican crisis.

Third-generation models give a crucial role to fundamentals but do not neglect the potential effects of speculators' self-fulfilling expectations. A common feature of these models is that fundamentals are not limited to fiscal and monetary policies, but also include the level of unemployment, the interest rate, and even the policymaker's reputation.

These models are not flawless. They hardly agree on the nature of the macroeconomic equilibrium. Some restrain fundamentals to the financial sector. Others have difficulties assessing whether increased speculative pressures mainly result from deteriorating fundamentals or from speculators' self-fulfilling expectations.

Despite these limits, third-generation models provide a much more relevant analysis of the 1990s emerging markets' currency crises than first- and second-generation models. They point to what could be the future of currency crisis research.

Chapter 7 analyses the policymaker's optimal commitment to fixed exchange rate stability. This is related to the monetary policy he conducts when he aims at preventing speculative attacks. It also concerns the links between exchange-rate based stabilisation plans and the outbreak of currency crises. This commitment to a fixed exchange rate also implies that the policymaker may have incentives to launch defences of the fixed exchange rate system. In this respect, hikes in the interest rate may avoid speculative attacks, but increases in the policymaker's reputation may not.

Chapter 8 studies how currency crisis contagion is conveyed through the fundamentals link countries have. Different forms of such 'fundamental' contagion are distinguished. Some emphasise 'common shocks', that is crises in developing countries that are triggered by major economic changes in developed countries. Others focus on macroeconomic links of a commercial, financial or political nature, without distinguishing between emerging and developed countries.

Chapter 9 deals with studies that attempt to formalise the relationships between deteriorated fundamentals and speculators' self-fulfilling expectations in times of speculative pressure. In the wake of the East Asian crisis, these works mainly focus on the links between unhealthy banking institutions and the outbreak of speculative attacks. They also provide a different perspective on the occurrence of self-fulfilling crises.

7. Economic Policy Tradeoffs and the Outbreak of Currency Crises

The 'early' escape-clause models of Obstfeld (1991, 1994) and Ozkan and Sutherland (1994, 1995, 1998) consider that the policymaker faces a tradeoff between various economic policy objectives, while he also guarantees that the fixed exchange rate will remain fixed. This commitment is however revocable at any moment. Speculators are aware of the dilemma the policymaker faces. They can trigger a self-fulfilling speculative attack which may lead to a shift to a flexible exchange rate system, even though economic policies are compatible with a fixed exchange rate regime. Escape clause models thus suggest that speculators are responsible for attacks, while the policymaker systematically is not.

This seems an over-simplifying view of the policymaker's arbitrages. He may choose to devalue because he faces fiscal or other economic problems which he hopes to solve by opting for a flexible exchange rate system. This may influence the links between currency crises and exchange-rate based stabilisation plans. The policymaker may also determine the optimal interest rate rise necessary to keep the exchange rate fixed, and decide whether or not it is relevant to invest in his reputation.

1. THE POLICYMAKER'S OPTIMAL COMMITMENT TO EXCHANGE RATE STABILITY

Unlike 'early' escape-clause models, Velasco (1996) asserts that the policymaker may choose to let the exchange rate go, independently of speculative attacks. The policymaker has incentives to opt for a flexible exchange rate when public debt is too high. When abandoning the fixed exchange rate, he creates inflation which is not anticipated by agents. He levies a lump tax on his nominal debts.

The decrease in public debt is not the only reason that may lead the policymaker to devalue. Jeanne (2000) suggests that the fixed exchange rate may be forsaken when the domestic currency is overvalued, the inflation or the unemployment rate is too high, or the trade balance deficit is too important. This framework is formalised by Andersen (1994): the policymaker faces a tradeoff between keeping the exchange rate fixed – and importing deflation or inflation from the foreign country – or shifting to a flexible exchange rate system. The float occurs when the level of foreign prices exceeds a given threshold that hinges on the rate of inflation or deflation tolerated by the policymaker.

Recent studies by Aghion, Bacchetta and Banerjee (2000, 2001) do not only deal with the policymaker's tradeoff in times of speculative pressures. They examine the links between monetary and budgetary policies and currency crises. Aghion, Bacchetta and Banerjee (2000, 2001) develop a model where currency crises result from credit constraints that domestic private firms face, and from nominal price stickiness. In a framework where multiple equilibria are possible, their model suggests that a currency-crisis equilibrium with low national product is possible. Indeed when prices are sticky, domestic firms whose debts rise are less profitable. Their investment capabilities, as well as the national product, decrease. In an economy with credit constraints, Aghion, Bacchetta and Banerjee (2000, 2001) show that a fall in domestic demand occurs: a currency crisis ensues.

In this framework, Aghion, Bacchetta and Banerjee (2001) analyse the optimal monetary policy capable of preventing speculative attacks. They consider that a speculative attack may occur under a fixed as well as under a flexible exchange rate regime as a result of disequilibria in firms' balance sheets. Some aspects of the analyses of Aghion, Bacchetta and Banerjee (2001) may be related to studies on the role of firms and financial institutions in currency crisis models with self-fulfilling expectations (see Chapter 9, section 1, Currency crises and financial crises).

All in all, studies by Andersen (1994), Velasco (1996), and Aghion, Bacchetta and Banerjee (2000, 2001) consider that the policymaker does not aim at keeping the exchange rate fixed per se. His objective is to gain some economic advantages, e.g., protecting the domestic industrial and financial system. This has consequences for the business cycle, and downturns in economic activity may lead to currency crises.

2. EXCHANGE-RATE BASED STABILISATION PLANS AND CURRENCY CRISES

More often than not, exchange-rate based stabilisation plans end up in currency crises[1]. They also seem to produce boom–recession cycles, sharp appreciations of the real exchange rate, increases in the current account and trade balance deficits, and a fall in the velocity of money. Some of these phenomena are considered as signs of forthcoming speculative attacks by studies of early-warning systems of currency crises (see Chapter 6, section 2, Empirical assessments of currency crises). Recent studies by Mendoza and Uribe (1997, 2000), Arellano and Mendoza (2002) and Uribe (2002) have started to investigate how characteristics of business cycles linked to exchange-rate management plans may herald currency crises.

Drawing on Mendoza and Uribe (2000), a two-sector small open economy is considered. There are competitive firms producing traded and non-traded goods with capital and labour. To simplify the analysis, several assumptions are laid out:

- Capital is a tradable factor of production that may be accumulated;
- Factors of production are specific to each industry so that they cannot move across sectors;
- Households and firms have unrestricted access to a perfectly competitive world market, but markets of contingent claims are incomplete;
- Households have an infinite life.

In this framework, households maximise the following expected utility function:

$$E_0 \sum_{t=0}^{\infty} \beta \frac{\left(C_t (1 - L_t^N - L^T)^{\gamma}\right)^{1-\sigma}}{1-\sigma} \tag{7.1}$$

under the two constraints:

$$B_{t+1} - (1+\rho^*)B_t + \left(C_t^T + p_t^N C_t^N\right) + I_t = A_t^T \left(K_t^T\right)^{1-\alpha T} \left(L^T\right)^{\alpha T}$$
$$+ p_t^N A_t^N \left(K^N\right)^{1-\alpha N} - \frac{\varphi}{2}\left(K_{t+1}^T - K_t^T\right)^2 - m_t V_t f(V_t) + \frac{m_{t-1}}{1+s_t} - m_t + H_t \tag{7.2}$$

$$I_t = K_{t+1}^T - (1-\delta)K_t^T \tag{7.3}$$

with:

$$C_t = \left[\omega (C_t^T)^{-\mu} + (1-\omega)(C_t^N)^{-\mu}\right]^{-\frac{1}{\mu}} \tag{7.4}$$

The isoelastic aggregator defined in equation (7.4) represents private consumption of traded goods and non-traded goods that are respectively denoted C_t^T and C_t^N, with $1/(1+\mu)$ being the elasticity of substitution between traded and non-traded goods such that $1/(1+\mu)>0$. Households supply labour to industries producing both goods. Labour is specific to each industry. It is supplied inelastically to the industry that produces traded goods, in an amount equivalent to L^T units of 'raw time'. Labour supplied to the nontraded goods industry, which is denoted L_t^N, and leisure are considered perfect substitutes. Normalising the time constraint, leisure is simply defined as $1-L^T-L_t^N$. Utility from consumption and leisure is represented by a Constant Relative Risk Aversion (CRRA) utility function,[2] with σ measuring both the coefficient of relative risk aversion and the inverse of the intertemporal elasticity of substitution in consumption. The parameter $\beta\in[0;1]$ is the subjective discount factor, while γ governs the steady-state ratio leisure-to-consumption.

It is assumed that world asset trading is limited to one-period bonds B paying the time-invariant real interest ρ^* in units of the traded good. Household income on the left-hand side of equation (7.2) helps buy traded and non-traded goods for consumption C_t and investment I_t and changes in bond holdings net of interest. The relative price of non-tradables is defined as p^N. It is assumed that the purchasing power parity condition holds with respect to tradable goods so that p^N may be said to represent the real exchange rate. Household income (the right-hand side of equation (7.2)) stems from government transfers and from factor incomes from industries producing traded and non-traded goods that are net of capital adjustment costs as well as of transaction costs, and changes in real money demand.

Production functions are of the Cobb-Douglas form. Capital is specific to each industry. It is inelastically supplied to the non-traded sector in the amount K^N and does not depreciate. Capital in the traded sector, K_t^T, is a traded good and depreciates at rate δ. In line with Mendoza (1995), capital adjustment costs distinguish between financial and physical assets to prevent excessive investment variability. Real money balances, denoted m_t, are measured in terms of traded goods and meant to economise transaction costs in this framework. Transaction costs per unit of private absorption are given by $f(.)$ which is a convex function of expenditure velocity denoted V_t:

$$V_t = \left(C_t^T + p_t^N C_t^N + I_t\right)/m_t \tag{7.5}$$

In this framework, purchasing power parity holds and foreign prices are constant. It is assumed that s_t represents both the inflation rate of tradable goods and the currency depreciation rate, while H_t is a lump sum transfer from the government.

Different time periods are distinguished. Before time period t = 0, the policymaker maintains an exchange rate regime with a constant rate of depreciation $s^{\delta}>0$. This regime is said to be sustainable: s^{δ} is consistent with a stationary equilibrium of the model. At t =0, the policymaker fixes the exchange rate, so that s_0=0. At time period t =T, a devaluation occurs. At time T+1, after the collapse of the peg, the exchange rate depreciates again at rate s^{δ}.

When the fixed exchange regime is maintained, the policy reaction function is assumed to follow a logistic stochastic process. Hence the conditional probability of devaluation, denoted π_t, is:

- if $t \geq 0$:

$$\pi_t \equiv \text{Prob}(s_{t+1}>0|s_t=0) \tag{7.6}$$

- if $0 \leq t < T$-1:

$$\pi_t = \exp\left[\Gamma + \frac{B}{\left(\frac{R_{t-1}}{Y_{t-1}}\right) - \underline{R}}\right] \Bigg/ 1 + \exp\left[\Gamma + \frac{B}{\left(\frac{R_{t-1}}{Y_{t-1}}\right) - \underline{R}}\right] \tag{7.7}$$

- if $t \geq T$-1:

$$\pi_t = 1 \tag{7.8}$$

where R_t is the level of foreign exchange reserves, Y the country's output, $\underline{R}$ a threshold level such that the policymaker lets the exchange rate go when the ratio R/Y equals $\underline{R}$, B the exogenous amount of one-period bonds, Γ an exogenous constant.

Equation (7.7) describes the probability of devaluation as a decreasing function of the observed gap between the lagged reserve/GDP ratio and a minimum critical value of this ratio.

The relationship between exchange rate policy and fiscal policy is summed up in the policymaker's simplified intertemporal budget constraint:

$$G_t + H_t + R_{t+1} = m_t - \frac{m_{t-1}}{1+s_t} + m_t V_t f(V_t) + (1+\rho^*)R_t \tag{7.9}$$

with:

$$\lim_{t\to+\infty} (1+\rho^*)^{-t} R_t=0 \tag{7.10}$$

When the peg holds, the dynamics of m_t and V_t reflect the private sector's optimal plans that are accommodated by the policymaker. His fiscal policy choices are G_t and H_t representing unproductive expenditures and transfers, following the rules:

$$G_t = m_t - \frac{m_{t-1}}{1+s_t} + m_t V_t f(V_t) \tag{7.11}$$

and if s_t=0, then:

$$G_t+H_t=\kappa(G_{t-1}+H_{t-1}) \tag{7.12}$$

While the peg is in place, equation (7.9) determines the evolution of reserves so that the policymaker's budget constraint holds. Equations (7.11) and (7.12) imply that government outlays remain constant while the exchange rate is fixed. Lastly the collapse of the peg is followed by adjustments in lump-sum transfers so that the policymaker's intertemporal budget constraint in equation (7.9) holds. This in turn ensures that the present value of transfers as of t =0 equals $(1+\rho^*)R_0$ as long as equations (7.9) and (7.11) are satisfied.

In this model, there are three atemporal and three intertemporal optimality conditions that characterise households' optimal decisions. They are identical to those of Mendoza and Uribe (1997).

The three intertemporal conditions are Euler equations that equate:

- the marginal costs of sacrificing a unit of tradables consumption to
- the marginal benefits of investing a unit of tradables consumption in each of the three assets available in the economy: foreign bonds, real balances and physical capital.

The three atemporal conditions equate:

- the marginal utility of consumption of the numeraire good C^T with the marginal utility of wealth multiplied by the marginal cost of transactions;
- the marginal rate of substitution between C^T and C^N to the corresponding relative price;
- the marginal disutility of labour in the non-tradable sector to its marginal cost of transactions.

Under these optimality conditions, the intertemporal equilibrium allocations and prices, as well as the time path of devaluation probabilities in equations (7.7) and (7.9) may be determined. They define a rational-expectations equilibrium that satisfies:

- the optimality conditions of households and firms;
- the market-clearing conditions for traded and non-traded goods;
- the intertemporal government budget constraint;
- the consistency condition such that the equilibrium dynamics of reserves in equation (7.9) must produce, for a given sequence of devaluation probabilities $\Pi=[\pi_0,\ldots,\pi_{T-1}]$, the same sequence Π when used to compute the time path of devaluation probabilities via equation (7.7).

The last condition ensures that, in equilibrium, the devaluation probabilities reflect the fact that the policymaker's policy reaction function is consistent with the private agents' rational expectations of a currency crisis.

In this framework, the equilibrium always converges in the long run to the stationary state of a deterministic setting with a constant depreciation rate s^{δ}. The steady-state equilibrium conditions that characterise this situation, as well as the corresponding implicit connections between s^{δ} and the stance of fiscal policy, is shown in a one-good version of the model in which labour supply is inelastic:

$$A\chi\left(\frac{C/Y}{m/Y}\right)^{1+\chi}=\frac{(a+s^{\delta})(1+\rho^{*})-1}{(1+s^{\delta})(1+\rho^{*})} \tag{7.13}$$

$$\frac{C}{Y}=1+\rho^{*}\left(\frac{R}{Y}+\frac{B}{Y}\right)-\frac{G}{Y'} \tag{7.14}$$

$$\frac{G}{Y}=\left(\frac{m/Y}{C/Y}\right)\frac{C}{Y}\left(\frac{s^{\delta}}{1+s^{\delta}}\right)+\frac{C}{Y}\left[A\left(\frac{C/Y}{m/Y}\right)^{\chi}\right] \tag{7.15}$$

$$(1-\alpha)A\left(\frac{K}{L}\right)^{-\alpha}=\lambda.(\rho^{*}+\eta).[(1+s^{\delta})+(1+\rho^{*})] \tag{7.16}$$

with the exponential transactions cost technology $f=AV^{\chi}$.

The steady-state system of equations (7.13) to (7.16) shows the problem of open economies with standard preferences and trade in one-period bonds:

- the steady-state foreign asset position depends on initial conditions as discussed by Mendoza and Tesar (1998);
- given an initial prestabilisation asset position and the fact that s^{δ} is exogenous, it follows that the prestabilisation equilibrium is a block-recursive system in the variables (C/Y), (m/Y) and (G/Y) defined by equations (7.13) to (7.15);
- equation (7.16) determines the steady-state capital/output ratio and thus the level of output given by the Cobb-Douglas technology.

It also follows from equation (7.15) and the steady-state government budget constraint that, in the prestabilisation steady state, transfers are set to rebate the interest income on foreign reserves:

$$H=\rho^{*}\times R \tag{7.17}$$

By assumption at $s_0=0$, the steady-state conditions no longer hold. Introducing the peg sets the model's dynamics in motion. During every period when the peg holds, the rate of depreciation may be reset to s^{δ}: a float would then happen. But at each time period when a float may occur, the initial conditions of the corresponding deterministic postcollapse regime (that is the values of B, R and K at the date of collapse) change. Since the steady state depends on initial conditions, the deterministic long-run equilibrium to which the model converges from each possible date of collapse is then likely to differ. The assumption stating that the same s^{δ} is maintained across states of nature simplifies the analysis by ensuring that the long-run capital/output ratio and money velocity, as well as the steady-state levels of Y and K, are independent of the date of the currency collapse, following equations (7.13) and (7.16). However, the stationary equilibria of consumption, real money balances, and government purchases will still vary depending on the overall net foreign asset position (that is $R+B$) to which the economy converges from each possible devaluation date.

The same results hold in the steady-state system of the full model that includes the non-tradables sector and the endogenous labour supply. But in that case, the steady-state output and capital stock also hinge on initial conditions.

The study by Mendoza and Uribe (2000) differs from first- and second-generation models of currency crises. They consider that speculative attacks do not result from a decrease in the amount of foreign exchange reserves, a sharp appreciation of the real exchange rate, and current account and trade balance deficits. Instead Mendoza and Uribe (2000) believe that the business cycle implications of exchange-rate based stabilisation plans stem from inappropriate fiscal policies and not from abrupt variations in these policies. Besides they view crises as being triggered by market participants' loss of confidence in the policymaker's ability to keep the exchange rate fixed. In the model, this situation is represented by the policymaker's reaction function in which the probability of devaluation is a decreasing function of the level of foreign exchange reserves. Speculative attacks result from speculators' self-fulfilling expectations who launch an attack because they consider that the policymaker does not own enough foreign reserves to keep the exchange rate fixed. Hence the importance of a high stock of foreign exchange reserves to maintain a peg. There are however other means to deter attacks.

3. OPTIMAL MONETARY POLICY AND THE INTEREST RATE DEFENCE OF THE FIXED EXCHANGE RATE SYSTEM

As surprising as it may be, the policymaker can always avoid a collapse in the exchange rate. Indeed there is a nominal interest rate level that neutralises speculative attacks by increasing the demand for domestic liquid assets and, thereby, provoking a rise in foreign exchange reserves. But this is a costly strategy with respect to other economic policy objectives[3].

Theoretical studies by Garber and Spencer (1995), Bensaïd and Jeanne (1996, 1997) and Drazen (2000a) model the policymaker's arbitrages between defending the fixed exchange rate through a rise in the interest rate, and the shift to a flexible exchange rate system. Bensaïd and Jeanne (1997) represent this tradeoff by suggesting that the policymaker minimises the following intertemporal loss function:

$$L_t = \int_t^T \gamma(i_k)\exp[-\delta(k-t)]dk + \int_T^{+\infty}(C+\gamma(i_k))\exp[-\delta(k-t)]dk \qquad (7.18)$$

where i_k is the interest rate between yearly time periods k and $k+1$, $\gamma(i_k)$ the nominal interest cost with $\gamma(.)$ a cost function, d the government's discount rate, C the cost of leaving the exchange rate and T the time period where the fixed exchange rate system is abandoned.

The cost function $\gamma(.)$ reaches a minimum value normalised to 0 when the interest rate is γ^*. The interest rate γ^* is the optimal interest rate for the domestic economy that would be chosen under a flexible exchange rate regime. Function $\gamma(.)$ is defined and continuous on [0;+∞[; it is decreasing on $[0;\gamma^*[$ and increasing on $[\gamma^*;+\infty[$.

Bensaïd and Jeanne (1997) suppose that market participants do not exactly know the value of C, unlike the policymaker. To formalise this informational asymetry, speculators' beliefs are represented by a probability density function ϕ that is continuous and strictly positive on the interval $]\underline{C};\overline{C}[$, with Φ being the corresponding cumulative distribution function. By assumption speculators' initial beliefs are compatible with the truth, i.e., $C\in]\underline{C};\overline{C}[$. The policymaker is also able to resist speculative attacks indefinitely. In that case, T is infinite.

It is assumed that international capital mobility is perfect and that agents are risk-neutral. The required level of the nominal interest rate i_t is determined by rewriting the uncovered interest rate parity condition:

$$i_t = i^* + \pi_t \Delta s_t \tag{7.19}$$

where i^* is the foreign interest rate that is assumed to be constant, π_t the likelihood of exiting the fixed exchange rate system at time t, and Δs_t the variation in the exchange rate when the fixed exchange rate system is abandoned.

In the first period, the policymaker chooses the interest rate that minimises his objective function L_t in order to adjust the interest rate to its optimal level γ^* :

$$\forall\ k > T,\ i_k = \gamma^* \tag{7.20}$$

Since the analysis deals with forsaking the fixed exchange rate system, Δs_t is assumed to be positive[4]. It is also assumed that the policymaker lets the currency float indefinitely once the devaluation has occurred.

In this framework, an equilibrium is defined by the conjunction of:

- a devaluation expectations path $(\pi_t)_{t=0}^{+\infty}$;
- a date T where the fixed exchange rate is abandoned.

The path $(\pi_t)_{t=0}^{+\infty}$ stems from a rational and Bayesian updating of speculators' beliefs based on their expectations and their observations of the policymaker's past actions. T is the optimal date of the fixed exchange rate collapse that takes path $(\pi_t)_{t=0}^{+\infty}$ as given. Following these assumptions:

$$\forall\ k > \mathrm{T},\ \gamma(\gamma^*) = 0 \tag{7.21}$$

The policymaker's objective becomes:

$$\underset{T}{\text{Min}} \int_{t}^{T} \gamma(i_k)\exp[-\delta(k-t)]dk + \frac{C}{\delta}\exp[-\delta(T-t)] \tag{7.22}$$

The first derivative of this function in relation to T is:

$$\frac{\partial L}{\partial T} = \left(\gamma(i_T) - C\right)\exp[-\delta(T-t)] \tag{7.23}$$

The moment the fixed exchange rate is abandoned is therefore the unique time period T that satisfies:

$$\gamma(i_T)=C \tag{7.24}$$

If the policymaker does not devaluate at time period t, speculators infer that $C > \gamma(i_t)$ in his objective function. They update their devaluation expectations. At time t, they assess the likelihood, denoted $\pi_t dt$, that a devaluation occurs between t and $t+dt$: this is the likelihood that C is contained between $\gamma(i_t)$ and $\gamma(i_{t+dt})$. Using Bayesian updating methods:

$$\pi_t dt = \int_{\gamma(i_t)}^{\gamma(i_{t+dt})} \frac{\phi(C)}{1-\Phi(\gamma(i_t))} dC \tag{7.25}$$

which leads to:

$$\pi_t dt = \frac{\phi(\gamma(i_t))}{1-\Phi(\gamma(i_t))} \gamma'(i_t) \frac{di}{dt} \tag{7.26}$$

From equations (7.19) and (7.26), there is a differential equation in i_t that describes the dynamic of the interest rate as long the policymaker keeps the exchange rate fixed:

$$i_t = i^* + \Delta s_t \frac{\phi(\gamma(i_t))}{1-\Phi(\gamma(i_t))} \gamma'(i_t) \frac{di}{dt} \tag{7.27}$$

The solutions to equation (7.27) which may be taken into account must be compatible with a positive and non decreasing cost $\gamma(i_t)$ since this assumption is required to determine T.

Let γ^* be the level of the nominal interest rate such that relation (7.24) holds, and π^* the corresponding level of devaluation expectations such that equation (7.19) – the uncovered interest rate parity condition – is satisfied. The model has an infinity of equilibria since devaluation expectations are not predetermined. Therefore these devaluation expectations may 'jump' at any time from 0 to π^*. They follow the dynamics of equation (7.27) until date T, which is defined by condition (7.24), when the policymaker lets the currency float. He considers that there is only one optimal equilibrium such that devaluation expectations $(\pi_t)_{t=0}^{+\infty}=0$. In that case there is no devaluation. But since $(\pi_t)_{t=0}^{+\infty}$ may vary at any moment, the policymaker's optimal decision rule provides him with incentives to devaluate when the costs of defending and leaving the peg are equal. There is a currency crisis when a 'jump' from a fixed exchange rate equilibrium to a speculative attack equilibrium occurs. This 'jump' is assumed to be triggered by sunspots.

Bensaïd and Jeanne (1997) assert that a currency crisis may exclusively result from the speculators' behaviour. Their devaluation expectations increase the nominal interest rate and the costs of leaving the fixed exchange rate regime. This increase in the nominal interest rate reinforces in turn their devaluation expectations.

In this situation, the domestic economy follows a diverging equilibrium path where the continuous growth of defence costs of the fixed exchange rate system nurtures devaluation expectations. A war of attrition ensues, where speculators seek the exact value of C while the policymaker increases the nominal interest rate in order to prevent the fall of the fixed exchange rate regime.

The analysis of Bensaïd and Jeanne (1997) also allows an interpretation where the role of fundamentals is not negligible: the crisis may be viewed as resulting from the policymaker's willingness to maintain a fixed exchange rate system at any cost. But such an interpretation assumes that a high nominal interest rate systematically signals to market participants that the policymaker finds it difficult to keep the exchange rate fixed.

The authors conclude that the fixed exchange rate system is less vulnerable when the threshold of devaluation expectations π^* is high. This implies that the devaluation probability is low when $\underline{C}$ is high while i^* and Δs_t are low, i.e., when the policymaker's ability to defend the currency is important, when the interest rate policy conducted by foreign authorities is not restrictive, and when the devaluation that speculators expect is not important.

All in all, the study by Bensaïd and Jeanne (1997) asserts that:

- high nominal interest rates prevent currency crises;

- self-fulfilling speculative attacks occur if agents consider that the policymaker is not keen on increasing already high interest rates.

Their conclusions are similar to those in first-generation models, but are criticised by Drazen (2000a). He considers that Bensaïd and Jeanne (1997) do not describe in a relevant manner the speculators' behaviour. He suggests that agents face a dynamic problem of signal resolution in a framework of imperfect information. They form rational devaluation expectations in a Bayesian manner by relying on the interest rate strategies used by the policymaker during past episodes of speculative pressure. They seek to determine the point in time where the policymaker is to change his current interest rate policy and to abandon the fixed exchange rate. Speculative attacks therefore help speculators to assess the policymaker's willingness to defend the fixed exchange rate regime. In this framework, agents may interpret a rise in the interest rate as the signal that the policymaker will let the exchange rate go if the peg is once again subject to speculative pressures, even though this policy usually attracts foreign exchange reserves and prevents crises. Drazen (2000a) therefore considers that high interest rates do not systematically allow an efficient defence of a parity.

Drazen (2000a) also asserts that the relationship between increasing interest rates and keeping the exchange rate fixed is not linear.[5] This claim is supported by empirical evidence from Furman and Stiglitz (1998), Goldfajn and Gupta (1999) and Kraay (2003). The latter uses a sample of successful and unsuccessful speculative attacks in 75 developed and emerging countries between 1960 and 1997. He concludes that there is no linear relationship between rises in interest rates and the success of speculative attacks. Studies by Dekle, Hsiao and Wang (2001) and Gould and Kamin (2000) also seem to provide evidence that increases in interest rates do not always allow the policymaker to keep the exchange rate fixed, though their conclusions are not as clear-cut as those of Furman and Stiglitz (1998), Goldfajn and Gupta (1999) and Kraay (2003).

This being said, it seems possible to reconcile the traditional theory of interest rates put forward by Bensaïd and Jeanne (1997) to studies by Furman and Stiglitz (1998), Goldfajn and Gupta (1999), and Kraay (2003). If a rise in interest rate does not prevent the fall of the fixed exchange rate, this is because its size is not important enough to neutralise speculators' devaluation expectations. The latter know that the policymaker cannot maintain indefinitely high interest rates since those levels may conflict with other economic policy objectives. In such a situation, some studies ask whether the policymaker may prevent currency crises by investing in his reputation.

4. THE POLICYMAKER'S REPUTATION

Third-generation models do not only include fiscal and monetary variables in the policymaker's objective function, but also the level of unemployment, inflation or of aggregate production. These fundamentals, which are traditionally used in macroeconomic research, are called 'hard'. They are opposed to 'soft' fundamentals used in some third-generation models. 'Soft' fundamentals are the more or less cooperative rules of the game played by market participants in a fixed exchange rate regime, and above all, the policymaker's reputation. Reputation should not be confused with the costs of leaving the fixed exchange rate system. This is a fully-fledged fundamental variable, in line with the monetary policy studies of Backus and Driffil (1985a, 1985b), Horn and Persson (1988) and Andersen and Risager (1991).

Drazen and Masson (1994), Masson (1995), Bensaïd and Jeanne (1996, 2000), Velasco (1996), Agénor and Masson (1999) apply the notion of reputation to currency crises. By so doing, the policymaker's preferences for a fixed exchange rate system can be introduced: he is 'tough' if he cares about keeping the exchange rate fixed; he is 'weak' in the other case. Thus reputation provides an assessment of how the policymaker's willingness to maintain a fixed exchange rate influences the success of an attack when there is a shock on the domestic economy.[6]

In order to determine whether or not the policymaker's tough reputation neutralises speculative attacks, Masson (1995) suggests a model where the policymaker faces a tradeoff between keeping the exchange rate s_t fixed and preventing the gap ur_t between the unemployment rate and its natural output from widening:

$$L_t = (ur_t)^2 + \psi(\Delta s_t)^2 \qquad (7.28)$$

where ψ represents the policymaker's reputation, with $\psi>0$. By assumption, the 'tough' policymaker's reputation, which is denoted by the exponent ^{T}, is superior to the 'weak' policymaker's one, which is denoted by the exponent ^{W}.

Masson (1995) assumes that market participants form expectations on the policymaker's reputation, and update them on the basis of the behaviour in the preceding period.

The one-period loss function (7.28) is minimised under the following constraint:

$$ur_t = \sqrt{a[(-s_t - E_{t-1}s_t) + u_t + \lambda ur_{t-1}]} \qquad (7.29)$$

Equation (7.29) defines ur_t as a function of the exchange rate s_t, of the speculators' expectations on the evolution of the exchange rate based on lagged information available at time t, and of the shock u_t on the domestic level of employment that is uniformly distributed on the interval $[-v\,;v]$, with $v \in \mathfrak{R}^+$.

It is assumed that the policymaker devalues when the following condition holds:

$$E_t[L^{\mathrm{Fix}}(u_t)] > E_t[L^{\mathrm{Flex}}(u_t)] \tag{7.30}$$

with $E_t[L^{\mathrm{Fix}}(u_t)]$ being the anticipated value of the loss function when the policymaker keeps the exchange rate fixed, and $E_t[L^{\mathrm{Flex}}(u_t)]$ being the anticipated value of the loss function when he devalues.

The devaluation amount is assumed to be constant and equal to δ. Inequality (7.30) becomes:

$$u_t > \frac{(a+\psi)\delta}{2a} - E_{t-1}s_t + s_{t-1} - \lambda ur_{t-1} \tag{7.31}$$

Let ρ^T and ρ^W be the probabilities that the policymaker is of a 'tough' or of a 'weak' type. Let π_t be the estimate made by speculators that the policymaker is 'weak'. It follows that:

$$E_{t-1}s_t - s_{t-1} = [\pi_t \rho_t^W + (1-\pi_t \rho_t^T)] = \delta \tag{7.32}$$

with:

$$\rho_t^i = \mathrm{Prob}\left[u_t > y_t - \pi_t \rho_t^W \delta - (1-\pi_t)\rho_t^T \delta + \frac{\psi^i \delta}{2a} \middle| \text{the policymaker is of type i} \right] \tag{7.33}$$

and:

$$y_t \equiv \frac{\delta}{2} - \lambda ur_{t-1} \tag{7.34}$$

It must be reminded that u_t is uniformly distributed on the interval $[-v\,;v]$. If only corner solutions are considered, equation (7.32) leads to:

$$\mathrm{Prob}\,(u_t > u_t^*) = \frac{v - u_t^*}{2v} \tag{7.35}$$

The values of ρ^T and ρ^W may be determined:

$$\rho_t^W = \frac{(v - y_t)}{2v - \delta} - \frac{\psi^W \delta/2a}{2v - \delta} + \frac{(1 - \pi_t)(\psi^W - \psi^T)\delta^2/2a}{2v(2v - \delta)} \tag{7.36}$$

and

$$\rho_t^T = \frac{(v - y_t)}{2v - \delta} - \frac{\psi^T \delta/2a}{2v - \delta} - \frac{\pi_t(\psi^W - \psi^T)\delta^2/2a}{2v(2v - \delta)} \tag{7.37}$$

Given that:

$$\rho_t \equiv \pi_t \rho_t^W + (1 - \pi_t)\rho_t^T \tag{7.38}$$

the likelihood ρ_t of a realignment at time period t is:

$$\rho_t = \frac{v - y_t}{2v - \delta} - \frac{\psi^T \delta/2a}{2v - \delta} + \frac{\pi_t(\psi^T - \psi^W)\delta/2a}{2v - \delta} \tag{7.39}$$

At this point it is relevant to distinguish the time-dependent from the time-independent parts in the right-hand side of equation (7.39). The time-independent parts may be decomposed into stable probabilities of devaluation, respectively denoted $\overline{\rho}^W$ and $\overline{\rho}^T$, assuming speculators know whether the policymaker is 'weak' or 'tough'. If π_t=1 in (7.37), π_t=0 in (7.39), and ur_{t-1}=0 in both equations, then:

$$\overline{\rho}^W \equiv \frac{1}{2} - \frac{\psi^W \delta/2a}{2v - \delta} \tag{7.40}$$

and

$$\overline{\rho}^T \equiv \frac{1}{2} - \frac{\psi^T \delta/2a}{2v - \delta} \tag{7.41}$$

The probability of a realignment at time t is:

$$\rho_t = \overline{\rho}^T + \pi_t(\overline{\rho}^W - \overline{\rho}^T) + \frac{\lambda ur_{t-1}}{2v - \delta} \tag{7.42}$$

Equation (7.42) shows that a high unemployment rate increases agents' expectations with respect to a devaluation in the next period, since it raises the probabilities that a positive shock on the unemployment rate gives the policymaker incentives to devalue.

This devaluation is more likely to occur if the policymaker is 'weak'. If there is no devaluation in t-1, and the agents use an a priori estimate π_{t-1}, Bayesian updating methods imply that:

$$\pi_t = \frac{1-\rho_{t-1}^W}{(1-\rho_{t-1}^W)}\pi_t - 1 + (1-\rho_{t-1}^T)(1-\pi_{t-1})\pi_{t-1} \tag{7.43}$$

Replacing ρ^T and ρ^W by their values in equations (7.36), (7.37), (7.40) and (7.41) leads to:

$$\pi_t = \frac{1-\bar{\rho}^W - \dfrac{\lambda ur_{t-2}}{2v-\delta} - (1-\pi_{t-1})(\bar{\rho}^T - \bar{\rho}^W)\dfrac{\delta}{2v}}{1-\bar{\rho}^T - \lambda\dfrac{ur_{t-2}}{2v-\delta} + \pi_t - 1(\bar{\rho}^T - \bar{\rho}^W)}\pi_{t-1} \tag{7.44}$$

If equation (7.44) is linearised around ur_{t-2} and if it assumed that $\pi_{t-1}=\pi_0$, there is :

$$\pi_t = \frac{\pi_0(1-\pi_0)(\bar{\rho}^T - \bar{\rho}^W)\dfrac{\lambda}{2v}}{\left(1-\bar{\rho}^T + \pi_0(\bar{\rho}^T - \bar{\rho}^W)\right)^2} ur_{t-2}$$

$$+\pi_{t-1}\frac{1}{\left(1-\bar{\rho}^T + \pi_0(\bar{\rho}^T - \bar{\rho}^W)\right)^2}\left[(1-\bar{\rho}^T)\right.$$

$$\left.\times\left[1-\bar{\rho}^W - (1-2\pi_0)(\bar{\rho}^T - \bar{\rho}^W)\frac{\delta}{2v}\right] + \pi_0^2(\bar{\rho}^T - \bar{\rho}^W)^2\frac{\delta}{2v}\right] \tag{7.45}$$

By adding an error term η_t to equation (7.45):

$$\pi_t = \alpha\pi_{t-1} + \beta ur_{t-2} + \eta_t \tag{7.46}$$

where α and β are negative or null coefficients.

Equation (7.46) shows that speculators view a rise in the unemployment rate as a decrease in the probability that the policymaker is weak. The latter's reputation increases when he accepts a high unemployment rate. He then finds it less difficult to defend the fixed exchange rate. Investing in reputation is a relevant strategy. However this result is only valid in a one-period framework.

Consider equations (7.31) and (7.46) in a multi-period framework. Given equation (7.46), the rise in unemployment increases the policymaker's reputation. But with respect to equation (7.31), this surge in unemployment makes it more difficult to keep the exchange rate fixed; and the increase in reputation may not be of a great help.

To sum up, the more reputation grows, the more the macroeconomic situation worsens and the less important is the shock compelling the policymaker to let the exchange rate go.[7] A 'tough' reputation is therefore a hurdle that the policymaker may have to overcome if he plans to keep the exchange rate fixed. This is a paradoxical result that does not depend on the uniqueness or on the multiplicity of the macroeconomic equilibrium. Studies by Drazen and Masson (1994), Masson (1995), Velasco (1996), and Bensaïd and Jeanne (2000) all reach the same conclusion, even though the first two papers develop unique-equilibrium models while the last two use multiple equilibria.

Méon (2001) obtains similar conclusions when he introduces partisanship in this framework and distinguishes between liberal and conservative governments. Such a result even holds when the central banker is conservative *à la* Rogoff (1985). The study by Bensaïd and Jeanne (2000) indeed shows that monetary policy delegation does not prevent self-fulfilling currency crises, but is even likely to hasten them.

Reputation widens the realm of fundamentals that may be relevant during currency crises. It leads to studies dealing with the relationships between the policymaker's behaviour, macroeconomic fundamentals and speculators' expectations. It may also explain why attacks are sometimes transmitted across countries.

5. CHAPTER SUMMARY

Unlike 'early' escape clause models which assume that the policymaker is always subjected to currency crises, third-generation models of currency crises show that he may willingly abandon the fixed exchange rate system when the latter does not suit his purposes any more.

For instance the policymaker may boost public spending by devalue the currency. He then creates unanticipated inflation and thereby levies a tax on the nominal value of debts. At the same time, he may avoid a crisis. He must simply raise the level of interest rates so as to generate an increase in foreign exchange reserves. But this policy may be costly in terms of other economic objectives, as Bensaïd et Jeanne (1997) point out.

The research on optimal interest rate defence may also be related to studies linking monetary policy and currency crises, e.g., Aghion, Bacchetta and Banerjee (2000, 2001) or linking exchange-rate stabilisation plans and speculative attacks, e.g., Mendoza and Uribe (2000). The research has also sparked interest on the role of the policymaker's reputation, defined as his willingness to keep the exchange rate fixed. Studies on reputation by Drazen and Masson (1994) Masson (1995) Velasco (1996) and Bensaïd and Jeanne (2000) consider, in line with research on monetary policy, that reputation may only be improved through deteriorated fundamentals. In that case, even a policymaker with an excellent reputation may find it hard not to let the exchange rate go, since the situation has so worsened that it is impossible to maintain a fixed peg. And the deterioration of the macroeconomic situation eventually makes it hard for the policymaker to keep the exchange rate fixed, even if he has an excellent reputation.

NOTES

1. Studies on the failure of exchange-rate stabilisation plans in different countries include Helpman and Razin (1987), Mendoza and Uribe (1997) and Végh (1992).
2. Investors with Constant Relative Risk Aversion (CRRA) hold the same percentage in risky assets as their wealth increases.
3. In line with Friedman (1969) and Mankiw (1987), a high nominal exchange rate may be viewed as a tax on money. Other heuristic arguments are given by Bensaïd and Jeanne (1996, 1997). High nominal interest rates increase the service of the debt, implying a rise in future inflation. They weaken the banking sector, especially if it is indebted. They have redistributive implications between lenders and borrowers that the policymaker may want to avoid, usually for political reasons rather than economic grounds.
4. A negative Δs_t means a reevaluation.
5. This claim is also made by Flood and Jeanne (2000) and Lahiri and Végh (2003) in the framework of first-generation models. See Chapter 2, section 1.3, Sterilization and rise in interest rates.
6. The nature of the shock differs between studies: it is a variation in the unemployment rate for Drazen and Masson (1994) and Masson (1995), in inflation for Velasco (1996), in foreign exchange reserves for Agénor and Masson (1999).
7. If the policymaker's reputation ψ converges towards $+\infty$, he ignores the shocks and never lets the currency float.

8. Deteriorated Fundamentals and Currency Crisis Contagion

Research on 'pure contagion', tackled in Chapter 5, considers that currency crises are propagated across countries by speculators' self-fulfilling expectations But contagious speculative attacks may also result from fundamental interdependencies between countries.

Studies that emphasise contagion conveyed by fundamental links between countries distinguish between two types of contagious speculative attacks. Models of 'common shocks' view contagion between developing countries as the result of economic changes occurring in industrialised countries. 'Spillover' models consider that attacks are conveyed by financial, commercial or political transmission channels between countries, without any distinction between developed and emerging states.

1. MODELS OF 'COMMON SHOCKS'

Theoretical models of common shocks, also known as models with monsoonal effects, are developed by Dooley (1997) and Masson (1998, 1999). In their view, currency crises in emerging countries result from a two-step process that has its causes in major economic changes in industrialised countries.

First an external shock in developed countries triggers variations in interest rates and realignments between currencies. Capital investments in emerging markets become more attractive. These inflows increase the countries' financial dependency on the rest of the world. The likelihood of a devaluation increases since countries are vulnerable to speculators' expectations of capital outflows. Second country-specific factors determine the time of the attack, that is when the domestic macroeconomic situation has worsened too much.

Masson (1999) suggests a model of common shocks that builds upon his study of pure contagion (see Chapter 5, section 2, Pure contagion of currency crises). Emerging country A's trade balance is assumed to be a function of the logarithm of the real exchange rate, denoted RER_t^A. This variable is weighted by the exchange rates of emerging country *B*, of the United States of America, and of the rest of the world, whose respective weights are *j*, *k* and *n*, with $n \equiv 1-j-k$. Nominal exchange rates of countries *A* and *B*, and of the rest of the world, are respectively denoted s_t^A, s_t^B and $\underline{s}_t$. They are assumed to be constant and measured as the price of a dollar in local currency. Structural parameters are identical in these two countries. With $\underline{BC}$ denoting the trade balance of the rest of the world, the equations of the real exchange rate RER_t^A and the trade balance BC_t^A in country *A* are:

$$RER_t^A = s_t^A - js_t^B - n\underline{s}_t \tag{8.1}$$

and:

$$BC_t^A = \underline{BC} - \beta RER_t^A + \varepsilon_t^A \tag{8.2}$$

Both equations show the pressures of the speculators' self-fulfilling expectations on country *A*'s currency when a devaluation probability in country *B*, denoted π_t^B, exists. Similar equations exist for country *B*.

Now equation (5.39) is rewritten in order to assess the likelihood at time *t* of a crisis at *t*+1 in country *A*, in function of the likelihood π_t^B that the other emerging country *B* devalues its currency by an amount in *t*+1. Equation (5.39) is:

$$\pi_t = \text{Prob}[b_{t+1} < \alpha\pi_t] \tag{5.39}$$

Whence the likelihood at time *t*, denoted π_t^A, of a devaluation in country *A* at time *t*+1 is:

$$\begin{aligned}\pi_t^A = (1-\pi_t^B)\,.\text{Prob}[\,&\underline{BC} - \beta(s_t^A - js_t^B - n\underline{s}_t) + \varepsilon_t^A \\ &- (i^* + \pi_t^A\varphi)DE^A + r_t^A - \underline{r} < 0\,] + \\ \pi_t^B\,.\text{Prob}[\,&\underline{BC} - \beta(s_t^A - js_t^B + j\varphi - n\underline{s}_t) + \varepsilon_t^A \\ &- (i^* + \pi_t^A\varphi)DE^A + r_t^A - \underline{r} < 0]\end{aligned} \tag{8.3}$$

where i^* is the riskless interest rate in the United States and in the rest of the world, $\underline{r}$ the level of reserves where the policymaker abandons the fixed exchange rate regime, r_t^A the level of reserves in country *A* at time *t*, ε_t^A the innovation, i.e., the macroeconomic shock, in country *A* at time *t*.

Like equation (5.39), equation (8.3) shows that currency crisis transmission may result from self-fulfilling expectations when fundamentals are deteriorated. Indeed the likelihood π_t^A of an anticipated devaluation is found on both sides of this equation and is influenced by the anticipated devaluation π_t^B in country *B*.[1]

Equation (8.3) also explains that the likelihood of a devaluation in country *A* depends on common shocks. They may be related to:

- variations in the risk-free interest rate i^*;
- the evolution of emerging countries' exchange rates.

Empirical studies by Calvo and Reinhart (1996), Dooley (1997), Bacchetta and van Wincoop (1998), Chinn, Dooley and Shrestra (1999), and Moreno and Trehan (2000) seem to corroborate the existence of common shocks during currency crisis propagation. Calvo and Reinhart (1996) consider that foreign-currency-denominated private and public debts play a major role in the speculative pressure transmission in Latin America that brought about the December 1994 Mexican devaluation. In addition Dooley (1997) and Chinn, Dooley and Shrestra (1999) state that governmental guarantees given to private investors and domestic banks alike played a significant role in the increase of capital inflows and the propagation of monsoon effects. In their view, lending policies of industrialised countries and of international financial institutions are mainly responsible for these contagion phenomena. Moreover Bacchetta and van Wincoop (1998) show in a comparative study of Latin American and East Asian emerging market economies that the gradual liberalisation of economies, and the large capital inflows that followed, gave incentives to foreign speculators to rebalance their portfolio allocations. This in turn provided them with incentives to trigger speculative attacks so as to benefit from a float.

Such empirical results should not conceal the theoretical problems raised by 'common shocks'. It is unclear why they should only occur from developed countries to emerging markets. Economic changes in developing countries may also provoke currency crises in industrialised countries. Empirical studies also seem to point out that 'common shocks' mainly propagate through financial channels between developed and developing countries. But commercial and political links between these countries may also lead to currency crisis transmission.

2. 'SPILLOVER' MODELS

Unlike studies on 'common shocks', 'spillover' models do not distinguish between emerging and developed countries. They analyse macroeconomic links between countries that may convey currency crises: competitive devaluations and trade links, financial links and political links.

2.1. Competitive Devaluations and Trade Links

Using the framework of Masson (1998, 1999), the effects of a competitive devaluation may be analysed. Starting from equation (8.3) of the previous section, the effects of a competitive devaluation occurring abroad on the currency of a given country *A* may be determined:

$$\begin{aligned}\pi_t^A = (1-\pi_t^B)\,.\text{Prob}[\,\underline{BC} - \beta(s_t^A - js_t^B - n\underline{s}_t) + \varepsilon_t^A \\ -(i^* + \pi_t^A \varphi)DE^A + r_t^A - \underline{r} < 0\,]+ \\ \pi_t^B\,.\text{Prob}[\,\underline{BC} - \beta(s_t^A - js_t^B + j\varphi - n\underline{s}_t) + \varepsilon_t^A \\ -(i^* + \pi_t^A \varphi)DE^A + r_t^A - \underline{r} < 0] \qquad (8.3)\end{aligned}$$

Equation (8.3) shows that the likelihood of a speculative attack in emerging country *A* increases by an amount $\beta w\delta$ following the competitive devaluation of country *B*'s currency. Another study by Corsetti, Pesenti, Roubini and Tille (2000) shows that the collapse of the peg is more important than what is warranted by fundamentals if the devaluation game is of a non-cooperative type.

Another analysis by Gerlach and Smets (1995) focuses on crisis propagation through trade links without emphasising competitive devaluations as a source of contagion. They imply that trade links between emerging and developed countries convey speculative attacks. All major commercial partners of a country where a devaluation has just occurred are theoretically to be subjected to speculative attacks. Private agents anticipate a drop in exports towards the country whose currency has just been devalued. The current account balance of its trade partners gradually deteriorates, as a result of their trade ties and of the competition effects on third markets.

Empirical studies by Caramazza, Ricci and Salgado (2000), Eichengreen, Rose and Wyplosz (1996a), Fratzscher (1998), Glick and Rose (1998), Gelos and Sahay (2000) confirm that commercial links are potential transmission channels of speculative attacks between emerging and developed countries. Eichengreen, Rose and Wyplosz (1996a) use the methodology in Eichengreen, Rose and Wyplosz (1996b)[2] and state that the 1992–1993 EMS currency crisis propagation resulted mainly from trade links. Their methodology is used by Glick and Rose (1998) who study the transmission of attacks during various episodes of currency crises. They consider that trade links explain why currency crises are not global but always regional. Gelos and Sahay (2000) refine the analysis of Glick and Rose (1998). They distinguish bilateral trade links from indirect trade links, that is third markets where countries subjected to speculative pressures are competing. They consider that the former have less influence in promoting currency crisis contagion than the latter. Fratzscher (1998) asserts that the contagious speculative attacks in Latin America in 1994 and 1995 and in East Asia in 1997 mainly resulted from the trade and financial integration between the countries in these regions, and not from a deterioration of their fundamentals. This statement is very questionable.[3] It raises questions about financial links between countries in times of currency crisis propagation.

2.2. Financial Links

Unlike studies that explain financial contagion as a result of informational asymmetry and of the institutional constraints that speculators face (see Chapter 5, section 1, Main assumptions of pure contagion models), some research states that the propagation of speculative attacks originates in the various fundamental links of a financial nature between countries.

Pritsker (2000) analyses the role of a financial institution common to two countries, which is named the 'common creditor'. This financial institution may find it optimal to decrease the amount of loans in a given country if a currency crisis in the other nation harms its assets. Empirical studies by Caramazza, Ricci and Salgado (2000), Kaminsky and Reinhart (1998, 2000) and van Rijckeghem and Weder (2000, 2001) consider that the common lender plays a significant role in the transmission of currency crises in East Asia and in Russia.

Pritsker (2000) refines the theory of the common lender by studying the trade links between banks located in different countries. If a currency crisis makes a banking institution incur losses in a given country, it may bring back its assets held by other banks located in other countries. These banks may then be compelled to modify their investments, thereby propagating the crisis. In a perspective similar to Pritsker (2000), Allen and Gale (2000b) model the transmission of a currency crisis between lenders linked by financial arrangements, while Lagunoff and Schreft (2001) formalise contagion between institutions with similar investment projects.

Studies on the common lender are not devoid of theoretical and empirical relevance. But their perspective may seem restricted since they ignore the existence of financial markets. A shock is likely to be propagated between healthy and indebted banks through financial markets. Backus, Foresi and Wu (2002) suggest an analysis extending the banking panic model of Diamond and Dybvig (1983). They show that banks are compelled to sell their assets on financial markets when they face a 'bank run'. Huang and Xu

(2000) also use the analysis of Diamond and Dybvig (1983), and show that the interbank market and market imperfections convey speculative attacks.

However Gelos and Sahay (2000) consider that the interbank market is less responsible for contagion than is the degree of countries' integration within the international financial system. They assert that the propagation of speculative attacks is often hard to relate to trade or fundamentals factors, even though the fundamentals of the concerned countries are deteriorated. Their analysis leads to the investigation of another currency crisis transmission channel.

2.3. Political Links

Fixed exchange rate systems are often a feature of economic and political ties between nations. In that respect, political links between countries may be a possible vector of currency crises. The study by Drazen (1999) is the only empirical research dealing with the political propagation of crises. It analyses how political contagion played a significant role during the 1992–1993 European Monetary System currency crises, even though it is difficult to compare this influence to the financial and trade vectors of propagation.

Buiter, Corsetti and Pesenti (1996) analyse currency crisis propagation in a system with N+1 countries. N of these nations, called the 'Periphery', keep a fixed exchange rate system with the remaining country, the 'Centre'. The Centre is assumed to have a greater risk-aversion towards crises than the N other countries. It is less keen on conducting monetary policies meant to stabilise exchange rates.

In this framework, a negative shock leads the Centre to increase its domestic interest rate while giving incentives to the Periphery members to reconsider their exchange rate policies. Some members may decide to leave the system. The remaining Periphery countries are thus less subject to speculative pressures. The Centre currency remains overvalued, giving the Centre incentives to conduct less strict fiscal and monetary policies. As such the transmission of currency crises is incomplete. The shock hitting the Centre harms some countries but influences others positively.

Buiter, Corsetti, Pesenti (1996) show how the coordination default between countries' monetary and exchange rate policies fosters currency crisis transmission. But in the opinion of Loisel and Martin (2001), coordinated economic policies may not always prevent crisis propagation. A shock in a country may make devaluation in another unavoidable since private agents are aware of the tradeoffs faced by nations that have political links.

Loisel and Martin (2001) consider a three-country world where contagion may be propagated through trade links. There are two emerging countries which peg their currencies to the USA. Countries A and B are fully specialised in different varieties of a monopolistically competitive industrial sector. Firms of countries A and B only export to the USA. There are n_A, n_B and n_{USA} firms in each country, with $n_A+n_B+n_{USA}=N$, and each produces a different variety. The world aggregate demand Y for a composite intermediate good made of the different varieties is assumed to be exogenous and worth:

$$Y = \left[\sum_{j=1}^{j=n_A} y_{Aj}^{1-1/\sigma} + \sum_{j=1}^{j=n_B} y_{Bj}^{1-1/\sigma} + \sum_{j=1}^{j=n_{USA}} y_{USAj}^{1-1/\sigma} \right] \tag{8.4}$$

with y_{Aj} being the production of firm j in country A, and σ, with $\sigma>1$, being the elasticity of substitution between the different varieties. As the world demand for the composite good Y increases, world trade increases for a given number of firms in the world. In this framework, this type of competition may be a source of currency crisis contagion.

In countries A and B, agents, whose numbers are respectively n_A *and* n_B, share the same preferences. They derive utility from consumption of good x imported from the USA and disutility from effort in labour measured by l. The utility function of a representative agent is linear and given by:

$$U_i=x_i-\gamma(l_i+\kappa_i C_i) \qquad i=A,B \tag{8.5}$$

where γ is the relative disutility from effort, C_i, $i=A,B$, a fixed cost the agent bears when the government leaves the fixed exchange rate regime, with $\kappa=0$ if the government decides not to devalue and $\kappa=1$ if the government devalues.[4]

Equation (8.5) is maximised under the budget constraint expressed in terms of the local currency:

$$w_i l_i+hi=s_i x_i \qquad i=A,B \tag{8.6}$$

with w_i, $i=A,B$ being the agent's wage in country i, and h_i being a government transfer.

The imported good x is paid at the nominal exchange rate s_A between country A and the USA. Its price is normalised and fixed to 1 in the USA. It is assumed that there is no inflation in the USA. If the fixed exchange rate is maintained, the cost of the imported good in local currency will be:

$$s_i=1 \qquad i=A,B \tag{8.7}$$

or, if the government in country i devalues, at the exogenous rate δ:

$$s_i=\delta \qquad i=A,B \tag{8.8}$$

Next the time line of events in a period is defined as:

- wages paid in local currency are set and cannot be changed until the beginning of the next period;
- each government decides whether or not to devalue;
- monopolistic firms set their prices to maximise profits. Demands for exported and imported goods are then realised;
- work, production and consumption take place.

The price elasticity for a single producer of the export good is $-\sigma$ so that the usual profit of a monopolistic producer who maximises profits is:

$$\Pi=w\beta\sigma/(\sigma-1) \tag{8.9}$$

where β is the labour requirement which is common to all three countries in the export sector.

In order to determine the representative agent's wage, it is assumed that there is only a single union per firm. It knows the profit rule in equation (8.9) and the labour demand function. It therefore takes into consideration that the wage elasticity of production and labour is $-\sigma$. Its objective is to maximise the expected utility of the representative worker in the union subject to the budget constraint. This means that the union has to form expectations on the exchange rate policy. It is assumed that each union is small, so that it does not take into the account the fact that it influences neither the exchange rate policy nor the governmental transfer when it chooses nominal wages. This stems from the assumption that there are as many unions as firms. Loisel and Martin (2001) show that the wage rate is the mark-up over the marginal disutility from effort in labour:

$$w_i=\frac{\sigma}{\sigma-1}\gamma E_{t-1}s_i \qquad i=A,B \tag{8.10}$$

The real wage in all situations, even out of equilibrium, is to be higher than the marginal disutility of work. This imposes a parameter restriction such that the elasticity of substitution is small enough:

$$\sigma/(\sigma-1)>\delta \tag{8.11}$$

In the USA, the wage is determined in the same manner. However, the price of x is fixed in that country to 1 so that the wage rate is simply:

$$\gamma\sigma/(\sigma\text{-}1) \tag{8.12}$$

In this context, the nominal wage may be high or low,, depending on whether or not a devaluation is expected in countries A and B. Expectations on the exchange rate influence the marginal cost of monopolistic firms, and therefore their price decision. The profit expressed in local currency is:

$$\Pi_i = \beta\gamma\left(\frac{\sigma}{\sigma-1}\right)^2 E_{t-1}s_i \qquad i=A,B \tag{8.13}$$

and in dollars:

$$\Pi_i = \beta\gamma\left(\frac{\sigma}{\sigma-1}\right)^2 \frac{E_{t-1}s_i}{s_i} \qquad i=A,B \tag{8.14}$$

An unexpected devaluation decreases the price of the local good. Using the monopolistic profit rule, equation (8.9), and the fact that all firms in a specific country are symmetric and face the same exchange rate, the demand and production levels of representative monopolistic firms in countries A and B that peg their currency to the dollar may be shown to be respectively equal to:

$$y_A = Y\left[n_A + n_B\left(\frac{E_{t-1}s_A}{s_A}\frac{s_B}{E_{t-1}s_B}\right)^{\sigma-1} + n_{USA}\left(\frac{E_{t-1}s_A}{s_A}\right)^{\sigma-1}\right] \tag{8.15}$$

and

$$y_B = Y\left[n_B + n_A\left(\frac{E_{t-1}s_B}{s_B}\frac{s_A}{E_{t-1}s_A}\right)^{\sigma-1} + n_{USA}\left(\frac{E_{t-1}s_B}{s_B}\right)^{\sigma-1}\right] \tag{8.16}$$

The situation hinges on speculators expecting or not expecting a devaluation:

- Under perfect foresight, $E_{t-1}s_i = s_i$, with $i=A,B$. Fully expected devaluations do not have any real impact because a collapse of the fixed peg is exactly compensated by a higher wage and a higher marginal cost.

- If agents in countries A and B do not expect a devaluation, $E_{t-1}s_i=1$, with $i=A,B$. Nominal wages are low and a surprise devaluation in country A ($s_A=\delta>1$) increases production of firms in A while decreasing production of firms in country B.

If agents in country A expect a devaluation ($E_{t-1}s_A=\delta>1$), keeping the exchange rate fixed ($s_A=1$) is costly as national production decreases. In such a case, there may be self-fulfilling expectations leading to a currency crisis.

Monopolistic firms' profits are taxed and fully redistributed to private agents in the form of a lump-sum transfer. Given that the number of firms and the number of agents are identical, the transfer to the representative agent is the representative firm's profit:

$$h_i = \beta\gamma E_{t-1}s_i y_i \frac{\sigma}{(\sigma-1)^2} \qquad i=A,B \qquad (8.17)$$

where y_i, with $i=A,B$, is either given by equation (8.15) or equation (8.16).

In country i, the firms' profits and thus the per-capita transfer:

- decrease with exchange rate expectations;
- increase with the exchange rate of country i.

When the per-capita transfer is incorporated into the representative agent's consumer budget constraint, his equilibrium utility is:

$$U_i = \beta\gamma\left[\frac{E_{t-1}s_i}{s_i}\left(\frac{\sigma}{\sigma-1}\right)^2-1\right]y_i - \kappa_i\gamma C_i \qquad i=A,B \quad (8.18)$$

where y_i, with $i=A,B$, is either given by equation (8.15) or equation (8.16). Due to the parameter restriction ($\sigma/(\sigma-1)>\delta$), the term in brackets is always positive. Assuming the cost of leaving the fixed exchange rate regime is C_i, equation (8.18) shows that an unexpected devaluation has two welfare consequences:

- it reduces consumers' purchasing power by increasing the price of imported goods such that the term $E_{t-1}s_i/s_i$ in the brackets takes the value $1/\delta$ in the case of an unexpected situation.

- it increases domestic production profits and income as shown by equations (8.15), (8.16) and (8.17).

In this framework, the problem of each government that takes exchange rate expectations and the exchange rate policy of the other country as given is to set the exchange rate to 1 (no devaluation) or δ (devaluation) in order to maximise the utility of the representative consumer.

Assuming that the USA does not play strategically vis-à-vis countries A and B, only unions and the governments of countries A and B are relevant players. The equilibrium in this game depends on the institutional setting that governs the relations between governments of A and B, which are assumed to be known by the private sector when it forms its expectations. Three situations may be distinguished, depending on the game played by governments:

- if there is no coordination, there is a Nash equilibrium such that no government has a unilateral incentive to deviate. If there are multiple equilibria in the policy game, the government chooses the equilibrium that agents expect.
- if there is coordination among governments, policymakers settle on one solution out of several in a non-cooperative game. They do not need to trust each other, they just need to consult with each other to move simultaneously to a specific Nash equilibrium. Once they coordinate on an outcome, none of them has any incentive either to deviate unilaterally from it or to deviate in a coordinated manner from it. This stability makes coordination credible to private agents.
- if there is cooperation among governments, they choose the outcome that maximises the sum of the utility levels of representative consumers. Cooperation imposes solidarity between both governments. Since it may lead to outcomes which prove not unilaterally stable, because the equilibria are not Nash equilibria, cooperation may not appear credible to private agents. Their credibility may however be assumed to hold through a commitment technology, e.g., some institutional structure.

This framework illustrates the ambiguous effect that coordination has on the issue of regional contagion. Compared to a situation with no contagion, it reduces the possibility of simultaneous speculative crises in a region with important trade spillovers, and in this sense is welfare improving. But because the credibility of coordination itself is dependent on parameters of both countries, it introduces a new channel of contagion.

Even though a devaluation has no real impact in the equilibrium, cooperation between A and B cannot eliminate the possibility of self-fulfilling currency crises. The reason is that, even though governments can commit to each other, they still cannot commit to private agents. Out of equilibrium, they can cooperate and surprise private agents through a devaluation, and gain competitiveness relative to American firms.

Several caveats in the analysis of Loisel and Martin (2001) must be made. They are related to their assumptions:

- Wages are paid in local currency at the beginning of the period and cannot be modified until the beginning of the next period; this is a source of rigidity in the model. It justifies why devaluations may be optimally chosen.
- There are two sources of inefficiency in this set-up. The good market is monopolistic, so that production will be too low. The labor market is also monopolistic because there is a single union per firm, and thus, the wage rate will be pushed too high.
- The absence of a non-traded local good implies that the consumption price index is the exchange rate; this simplifies the analysis greatly. If such a good were introduced, the wage rate would depend on the expected price index that would comprise both local and imported goods. An expected devaluation would lead to an increase in nominal wages of lower magnitude. But because the purchasing power cost of a devaluation is lower in the presence of local goods, this should lead to a stronger incentive to devalue.

3. CHAPTER SUMMARY

Many studies attempt to demonstrate that there are links between deteriorating fundamentals and currency crisis contagion. Propagation results from macroeconomic interdependencies between countries. Research by Dooley (1997), Bacchetta and van Wincoop (1998), Masson (1998), Chinn, Dooley and Shrestra (1999) considers that speculative attacks in emerging market economies are triggered by changes in economic conditions in developed countries. Yet such 'common shocks' that are supposed to hit various states at the same time, may just be the conjunction of regional shocks transmitted through trade, financial and political links between countries.

Trade links may convey currency crises as Gerlach and Smets (1995) and Corsetti, Pesenti, Roubini and Tille (2000) show. Any important trade partner of a country where a devaluation takes place may suffer from a speculative attack. Such crises may not only result from competitive devaluations. They may also stem from private agents foreseeing a drop in export to the country whose currency has just been devalued. Glick and Rose (1998) also consider that trade links may explain why currency crises are almost always limited to a single economic zone. Likewise financial links may help transmit crises across countries, especially in regions where national financial systems are closely integrated. It is also possible to distinguish between various kinds of financial contagion. As van Rijckeghem and Weder (2000, 2001) and Pritsker (2000) show, financial contagion may result from financial institutions or from market participants reallocating their assets after a speculative attack.

All these analyses ignore the potential influence of political bonds between nations when a currency crisis occurs. Buiter, Corsetti and Pesenti (1996) demonstrate how the lack of coordination between monetary and exchange rate policies between states fosters currency crisis propagation. Yet Loisel and Martin (2001) consider that coordinating economic policies cannot always prevent contagion. Shocks in a given country may often make devaluation in another country unavoidable, insofar as market participants are aware of the tradeoff between various objectives.

NOTES

1. The equation similar to (8.3) for country *B* would be such that π_t^A has a similar effect on the devaluation in country *B*.
2. See Chapter 6, section 2.2, Early warning systems of currency crises.
3. On the 1994 and 1995 Latin American crises, see amongst others Dornbusch, Goldfajn and Valdés (1995) and Sachs, Tornell and Velasco (1996a, 1996b). See Kaminsky and Schmukler (1999), Radelet and Sachs (1998a, 1998b) and Corsetti, Pesenti and Roubini (1999a, 1999b) for differing analyses of the 1997 East Asian crisis.
4. In this study, and unlike in escape-clause models, the fixed cost C of leaving the exchange rate is borne by agents and not by the policymaker. It is modelled as a specific disruption cost, because a currency crisis implies changes in the price of imported goods in local currency. As shown by the utility function in equation (8.5), individuals are thus bound to spend a fixed effort in changing menus.

9. Deteriorated Fundamentals and Speculators' Expectations

Recent currency crisis research emphasises the influence of speculators' expectations in explaining speculative attacks when fundamentals are deteriorated. These studies focus on two aspects of crises: the links between financial crises and speculative attacks, and the coordination of speculators' self-fulfilling expectations in the context of a macroeconomic situation prone to speculative attacks.

There are three types of studies linking financial crises to speculative attacks. Some deal with the joint occurrence of banking and currency crises. Others tackle how high levels of private or public debt may entail the collapse of a peg.

Another strand of research focuses on self-fulfilling currency crises resulting from speculators' behaviour. Some consider that the agents' mimetic behaviour triggers self-fulfilling attacks. Others view their investment behaviour as reducing their incentives to launch attacks that are not warranted by deteriorated fundamentals.

1. CURRENCY CRISES AND FINANCIAL CRISES

There are three types of financial crises: debt, banking and currency crises. Some research deals with the joint outbreak of two of these three kinds of crises.

1.1. Bank Runs and Currency Crises

Following the numerous bankruptcies of financial institutions in the 1997 East Asian crisis, there has been a number of studies focusing on the similarities and common occurrences of banking and currency crises, the so-called 'twin crises'.[1] Empirical studies on this topic, such as Eichengreen and Rose (2000), Glick and Hutchinson (1999) and Kaminsky and Reinhart (1999), point out that bank runs and speculative attacks often occur.

Theoretical studies on 'twin crises' either use a first- or third-generation framework. First-generation models usually analyse the joint collapse of the banks and of the peg. Most third-generation models have the foreign exchange market unspecified.

For instance Chang and Velasco (1999) develop an open-economy version of the Diamond and Dybvig (1983) bank run model.[2] Dooley (1997) analyses the effects of an increase in financial institutions foreign-currency liabilities. When they rise to the point where they match the foreign-currency assets backing them, there is a predictable bank run and a currency crisis.[3]

Allen and Gale (2000b) also study banking and currency crises. They draw on their previous research on financial contagion and so-called 'optimal financial crises' (see Allen and Gale, 1998, 2000a). Following a shock to bank and assets returns, an optimal portfolio allocation requires the adoption of a flexible exchange rate regime. Banks go bankrupt while the policymaker abandons the fixed exchange rate system. Still investors may manage to receive profits while not incurring losses. Such a situation explains why Allen and Gale (2000b) speak of an 'optimal currency crisis'.

Chang and Velasco (1999) describe a small open economy with three periods indexed by $t=0,1,2$. There is only one good which is freely traded in the world market. It may be consumed and invested. For simplicity the price of consumption in the world market is fixed and normalised at one US dollar.

The domestic economy is populated by a large number of identical agents. Each of these domestic residents is born with an endowment of e units, with $e>0$, of this good, which are worth e dollars.

Each domestic agent has access to a constant return long-term technology. Its yield per dollar invested at $t=0$ is:

- r dollar, with $r<1$, in period 1 and
- R dollar, with $R>1$, in period 2.

The long-term technology is illiquid. It is very productive if the investment is held for two periods, but early liquidation causes a net loss of $(1-r)$ per dollar invested, with $(1-r)>0$. Only domestic residents have access to this technology.

There is a world capital market where one dollar invested at $t=0$ yields one dollar in either period 1 or period 2. Domestic agents can invest as much as they want in the market, but can borrow a maximum of f, with $f>0$, dollars.[4]

In this framework, domestic consumption is increasing:

- in e;

- in f, because the domestic technology has a higher return than the world interest rate.

In line with Diamond and Dybvig (1983), domestic agents face a non-trivial decision because they may be forced to consume early. At t =1, each domestic agent discovers his type:

- with probability λ, he is 'impatient' and derives utility from period 1 consumption.
- with probability (1-λ) he turns out to be 'patient' and derives utility only from period 2 consumption.

Type realisations are i.i.d. across agents, and there is no aggregate uncertainty. The realisation of each agent's type is private information to that agent, as in Diamond and Dybvig (1983).

Let x and y respectively denote the typical agent's consumption in period 1 if he turns out to be impatient, and in period 2 if he turns out to be patient. The expected utility of the representative agent is worth:

$$\lambda u(x)+(1-\lambda)u(y) \tag{9.1}$$

where $u(.)$ is a Constant Relative Risk Aversion (CRRA) utility function[5], with a coefficient of relative risk aversion σ >0 such that:

$$u(x)=\frac{x^{1-\sigma}}{1-\sigma} \tag{9.2}$$

This specific form of $u(.)$facilitates the ensuing analysis and is assumed to obtain closed-form solutions.

In this framework, the objective of the bank is to pool the resources of the economy in order to maximise the welfare of its depositors. The bank chooses a contingent allocation under its limited resource constraints, while not knowing the type realisations which are private information to each agent. The bank must find some way of eliciting this information.

It is assumed that the bank maximises equation (9.1) subject to:

$$k+d\leq+e \tag{9.3}$$

$$\lambda x\leq b+rl \tag{9.4}$$

$$(1-\lambda)y+d+b\leq R(k-1) \tag{9.5}$$

$$d+b\leq f \tag{9.6}$$

$$y\geq x \tag{9.7}$$

with x, y, b, k, $l\geq 0$, where d and b respectively represent net foreign borrowing in periods 0 and 1, k the amount invested in the domestic illiquid asset, l the liquidation of the domestic asset in period 1.

The above problem is called the basic social planning problem, and its solution, called the social optimum, is denoted by a bar above the variable.

Equation (9.3) restricts investment to be no larger than the sum of the endowment and of the initial borrowing from abroad.[6] Equation (9.4) is the feasibility constraint in period 1. The social optimum assigns $\bar{x}$ units of consumption to each impatient agent; this is financed by borrowing abroad $\bar{b}$ in period 1, and possibly by liquidating some portion of the long-term asset. Equation (9.5) is the feasibility constraint for period 2. Equation (9.6) is the foreign credit ceiling. Equation (9.7) is the 'truth-telling' constraint for patient agents, under the assumption that the commercial bank can monitor each agent's transactions with the domestic banking system but not his consumption or his world transactions. If a patient agent lies about his type, he will be given $\bar{x}$ units of consumption in period 1. Then the best he can do in period 2 is to exchange them at the world market for $\bar{x}$ units in period 2, instead of $\bar{y}$. Equation (9.7) may then be viewed as an 'incentive compatibility' constraint that ensures that patient depositors will not lie.

Some additional features of this social planning problem exist:

- It can be shown that $\bar{l}=0$, i.e., there is no liquidation in period 1 of the long-term investment. This should be obvious, since the bank faces no aggregate uncertainty, and liquidating the long-term asset in period 1 is costly. This is in line with the bank's objective, i.e., pooling resources to prevent the inefficient liquidation of the long-term asset. In contrast, the long-term asset must be liquidated with positive probability in autarky.
- From marginal optimality conditions, it appears that the credit ceiling in equation (9.6) is binding at the optimum. Given this, the choices of x and y must satisfy the following equation, which may be seen as the 'social transformation curve':

$$R\lambda\bar{x}+(1-\lambda)\bar{y}=eR+(R-1)f\equiv Rw \tag{9.8}$$

where $w=e+[(R-1)/R].f$ may be seen as the economy's wealth.

The final optimality condition is that the above transformation curve should be tangent to the following 'social indifference curve':

$$\left(\frac{\overline{x}}{\overline{y}}\right)^{-\sigma} = R \tag{9.9}$$

Note that since $R>1$ and $\sigma>0$,10 equation (9.9) guarantees that the incentive constraint (9.7) does not bind. It follows from equations (9.8) and (9.9) that:

$$(1-\lambda)\,\overline{y}=(1-\theta)Rw \tag{9.10}$$

$$\lambda\,\overline{x}=\theta w \tag{9.11}$$

with:

$$\theta \equiv \frac{\lambda R^{\frac{\sigma-1}{\sigma}}}{\lambda R^{\frac{\sigma-1}{\omega}}+(1+\lambda)} \tag{9.12}$$

with θ being a coefficient such that $\theta \in [0;1]$ in the unit interval.

If the coefficient of relative risk aversion σ equals 1 (the case of log utility), then $\theta=\lambda$. In that case per capita consumption is $\overline{y}=Rw$ and $\overline{x}=w$. Consumers receive the technological return corresponding to their period of consumption. Patient consumers consume more because investments kept until period 2 are more productive than period-1 investments.

If $\sigma>1$, then $\theta>\lambda$. In that case, patient consumers who consume in the 'high productivity' period cross-subsidise impatient consumers who consume in the 'low productivity' period.

Since conditions (9.4) and (9.5) hold with equality, the optimal investment strategy is given by:

$$\overline{b}=\theta w \tag{9.13}$$

$$\overline{k}=f/R+(1-\theta)w \tag{9.14}$$

$$\overline{d}=\overline{k}-e \tag{9.15}$$

The social optimum has been defined as the best allocation that the bank may achieve, given the environment. It may now be discussed how the bank may implement this allocation in a decentralised fashion via demand deposits.

Demand deposits are contracts that stipulate that:

- At t=0, each agent must surrender his endowment and his capacity to borrow abroad to the bank in period 0.
- The bank invests $\bar{k}$ in the long-term technology and borrows $\bar{d}$ in period 0 and $\bar{b}$ in period 1.
- The agent is promised the option to withdraw at his discretion, either $\bar{x}$ units of consumption in period 1 or $\bar{y}$ in period 2.

To simplify the analysis, it is assumed that the bank respects a 'sequential service constraint': it attends to the requests of depositors on a 'first come first served' basis.

As a benchmark it is assumed that the bank is committed to repay any foreign debt under all circumstances. There is therefore no foreign creditor panic and foreign debt is always repaid. The bank is committed to limit any possible liquidation of the long-term investment in period 1 to:

$$\bar{l}^{+} = (\bar{k}\,R - f)/R \tag{9.16}$$

The time line of events is as follows:

- In period 1, depositors arrive at the bank in random order. Upon arrival, each agent may withdraw $\bar{x}$ if the bank is still open.
- The commercial bank services withdrawal requests sequentially, first by borrowing abroad, up to f- $\bar{d}$, then by liquidating the long term investment up to the maximum $\bar{l}^{+}$;
- If withdrawal requests exceed the maximum liquidation value of the bank, given by to $\bar{l}^{+}.r+f-\bar{d}$, the bank closes and disappears.
- If the bank did not close in period 1, it liquidates in period 2 all of its remaining investments, repays its external debt, and pays $\bar{y}$ dollars plus any profits to agents that did not withdraw in period 1.

In this framework, depositors face a strategic decision on the withdrawal of their funds. They are players engaged in an anonymous game. The outcomes of the demand deposit system are given by the equilibria of the game:

- an equilibrium describes the strategies of each depositor and aggregate outcomes;
- the aggregate outcomes are implied by the depositors' strategies, and each depositor's strategy is individually optimal given the aggregate outcomes.

The outcomes where demand deposits exist may now be dealt with. The social optimum may be achieved because this game has an 'honest equilibrium' in which each agent withdrawal decision corresponds to his true type, i.e, equation (9.7) is satisfied. In period 1 only impatient depositors withdraw $\bar{x}$. Hence the bank does not fail and pays $\bar{y}$ to patient depositors in period 2.

The purpose of a demand deposit system in an open economy is then obvious: the bank implements an optimal allocation which improves upon what agents can achieve in autarky.

The bank may attain such an improvement only by holding fewer internationally liquid assets than its implicit liabilities. Consequently it may be subjected to a run. All domestic agents decide to attempt to withdraw their deposits in period 1 if they expect all others to do the same. In that case, the bank goes bankrupt if:

$$\bar{z}^{+} \equiv \bar{x} - (\bar{b} + \bar{l}^{+}.r) > 0 \tag{9.17}$$

Equation (9.17) states that the short-term obligations of the bank, which are given by $\bar{x}$, exceed its liquidation value: $\bar{z}^{+}$ is thus a measure of the bank's illiquidity.

A run may emerge in equilibrium if the bank is illiquid. If equation (9.17) holds, there is an equilibrium in which all agents claim to be impatient and the bank goes bankrupt in period 1. The opposite situation may also occur. If equation (9.17) is not satisfied, there cannot be equilibrium bank runs. Following equation (9.17), a bank run equilibrium occurs if and only if the bank is illiquid.

Equation (9.17) is a condition for the solution of the social planning problem. Building on equations (9.11) and (9.14) with the definition of θ in equality (9.12), it may be shown that equation (9.17) is equivalent to conditions on the agents' CRRA utility function $u(.)$:

$$R^{\frac{\sigma-1}{\sigma}} > r \tag{9.18}$$

Equation (9.18) is always satisfied if $\sigma > 1$, because $R>1$ and $r<1$ by assumption. If $\sigma < 1$, runs may be ruled out. While runs may or may not occur, the run condition is satisfied for many plausible parameter values of the utility function and of the production technologies.

So far it has been assumed that only domestic depositors may cause runs. But foreign creditors may also panic. Chang and Velasco (1999) consider that foreign lenders increase the fragility of domestic banks when new loans are not repaid in the event of a run. When there is no ongoing lending, the bank only owes $\bar{d}$ in period 2. The maximum liquidation level consistent with not defaulting on the external debt is denoted $\bar{l}^{++}$ and is worth:

$$\bar{l}^{++} = \bar{k} - \frac{\bar{d}}{R} \tag{9.19}$$

From equations (9.16) and (9.19), it appears that $\bar{l}^{++}$ is larger than $\bar{l}^{+}$.

The bank would not be able to borrow $\bar{b}$ if a run occurs in period 1. It is unable to service all of its depositors if:

$$\bar{z}^{++} \equiv \bar{x} - \bar{l}^{++}.r \tag{9.20}$$

Rewriting equality (9.20) leads to:

$$\bar{z}^{++} = \bar{x} - [\bar{k}\ r - \bar{d}\ (r/R)] > 0 \tag{9.21}$$

Comparison between equations (9.17) and (9.21) reveals that:

$$\bar{z}^{++} - \bar{z}^{+} = \bar{b}\ [(R-r)/R] > 0 \tag{9.22}$$

The run condition in equation (9.21) is more stringent than (9.17). The bank is more vulnerable to runs if foreign creditors do not engage, should a run occur. The liquid resources that the bank may have access to during a run are therefore limited since it cannot borrow $\bar{b}$ as it had planned in the event of a run.

So far the maturity of the debt incurred by the bank in period 0 has not been dealt with. It has been overlooked whether it was a one-period bond that was rolled over in period 1 or a two-period bond that matured in period 2. It has been implicitly assumed that a one-period bond was automatically rolled over, and in the same conditions, in the middle period.

Consider the implications of being explicit about the maturity structure. It is assumed that the initial debt consists of one-period loans. What happens if international creditors refuse to roll over the debt in period 1?

With no roll-over, the bank has no external debt to repay in period 2. It can liquidate the full long-term investment in case of need:

$$\bar{l}^{+++} = \bar{k} \tag{9.23}$$

The bank may go bankrupt if its short-term obligations, which now include the sum of its demand deposits and its short-term external debt, exceed the liquidation value of long-term investment. This will be the case if:

$$z^{\overline{+}++} \equiv \overline{x} + \overline{d} - r\ l^{\overline{+}++} \tag{9.24}$$

Equation (9.24) may be rewritten as:

$$z^{\overline{+}++} = \overline{x} + \overline{d} - r.\ \overline{k} > 0 \tag{9.25}$$

Subtracting (9.25) from (9.21) leads to:

$$z^{\overline{+}++} - z^{\overline{+}+} = [(R\text{-}r)/R]\ \overline{d} \tag{9.26}$$

If $\overline{d}$ is positive, equation (9.25) is more stringent than equations (9.15) and (9.21). Thus financial fragility is greater if lenders refuse to roll over existing debt in the event of a run.

In this framework, it is worth investigating what leads creditors to refuse to roll over short-term debts. This may happen because they may expect that the bank will not be able to repay its debt. Such a behaviour may entail a self-fulfilling bank run as in the case of ongoing lending. If run condition (9.25) is indeed satisfied, there would not be enough resources in period 2 to repay a loan of size $\overline{d}$ should a run occur. In that case, lenders are justified in not having been willing to roll over existing debts.

Chang and Velasco (1999) show that financial vulnerability is a function of the size of the credit limit *f*, and therefore of the size of the total inflows.

Other things being equal, a higher credit ceiling and larger capital inflows make the bank more vulnerable to runs. This raises questions about the amount and maturity of foreign-currency denominated debts that financial institutions have. Such problems are also faced by corporations, as the 1997 East Asian crisis showed.

1.2. Private Debt and Currency Crises

A major source of financial fragility in East Asia, and ultimately of currency crises, originated in foreign-currency denominated liabilities of domestic institutions. Governments were reluctant to increase interest rates, fearing that this would make many banks and companies go bankrupt.

The influence of unhealthy corporations in the joint outbreak of banking and currency crises is analysed by Krugman (2000) and Schneider and Tornell (2001). These studies focus on what has since been called the 'balance-sheet effect'. They intend to assess the influence of companies' balance sheets in determining their ability to invest. They aim at analysing the effects of capital flows on the real exchange rate. When firms and banks bear too many foreign-denominated liabilities, their investment potential decreases and capital inflows plummet. Both companies and financial institutions go bankrupt. There are capital outflows and a currency crisis occurs. Drawing on Krugman (2000), it is possible to analyse how banks' losses may lead to a currency crisis. In an open economy, a single good is produced each period, using capital and labour following a Cobb-Douglas function:

$$y_t = K_t^{\alpha} + L_t^{1-\alpha} \tag{9.27}$$

Capital is created through investment and only lasts one period. Hence capital at time t equates investment at time t-1. It is assumed that there is no maturity mismatch as in Diamond and Dybvig (1983).

The domestic good is not a perfect substitute for foreign goods. It is also assumed that there is a unitary elasticity of substitution, with a share μ on domestic goods. The rest of the world is assumed to be much larger than the domestic economy, and spends a negligible fraction of its income on domestic goods. There is a disparity between the domestic and foreign marginal propensities to spend on domestic goods: 1-μ in the case of domestic spending, 0 for foreign spending. If the foreign elasticity of substitution is 1, the value of domestic exports in terms of foreign goods may be fixed at 1. The value in terms of domestic goods is therefore $1 \times RER_t$, where RER_t is the real exchange rate at time t.

If I_t and C_t are defined as investment and consumption expenditures in terms of domestic goods, the real exchange rate may be determined. Market clearing for domestic goods requires that:

$$y_t = (1-\mu) I_t + (1-\mu) C_t + RER_t \tag{9.28}$$

Equation (9.28) may be rewritten as:

$$y_t = (1-\mu) I_t + (1-\alpha)(1-\mu) y_t + RER_t \tag{9.29}$$

The real exchange rate thus equals:

$$RER_t = y_t \left[1-(1-\alpha)(1-\mu)-(1-\mu)I_t\right] \tag{9.30}$$

From equation (9.30), it is obvious that the higher the investment, the lower the real exchange rate.

In this framework, investment is determined by entrepreneurs' limited wealth and by lenders' willingness to lend. Entrepreneurs can borrow at most λ times their initial wealth, with λ taken as given.

$$I_t \leq (1+\lambda)W_t \tag{9.31}$$

Although entrepreneurs are assumed to save all their income, they may choose not to borrow up to the limit. Above all, they will not borrow beyond the point where the real returns on domestic and foreign investments are equal. Krugman (2000) suggests determining this limit by comparing the foreign real interest rate, denoted i_t^*, with the return achieved by converting foreign goods into domestic goods, then converting the next-period return back into foreign goods. Because a share μ of investment falls on foreign goods, the price index for investment relative to that of domestic output is $RER_t^{-\mu}$. The return on investment in terms of domestic goods becomes:

$$1+i_t = \left(I_{t-1} RER^{-\mu}\right)^{\alpha} . L_t^{1-\alpha} \tag{9.32}$$

But a unit of foreign goods can be converted into RER_t units of domestic goods this period, and provide a return that is converted into $(RER_{t+1})^{-1}$ units of foreign goods next period. In that case, the return on domestic investment must be at least as large as the return on foreign goods:

$$(1+i_t)\frac{RER_t}{RER_{t+1}} \geq 1+i_t^* \tag{9.33}$$

Moreover it is assumed that investment cannot be negative:

$$I_t \geq 0 \tag{9.34}$$

Depending on circumstances, (9.31), (9.33) or (9.34) may be the binding constraint.

In this model, domestic entrepreneurs are assumed to own all domestic capital. They also have debts and/or have claims on foreigners that are denominated in terms of domestic and/or foreign goods. Since capital lasts only one period, the value of domestic capital is the income accruing to capital within the current period. Let D and F be the debts of domestic entrepreneurs that are respectively indexed to domestic and foreign goods. To simplify the analysis, D and F are referred to as 'domestic currency'- and 'foreign currency'-denominated debts.

The wealth W_t of entrepreneurs in period t is

$$W_t = \alpha y_t - D - RER_t \tag{9.35}$$

The level that domestic entrepreneurs may borrow abroad hinges on their wealth. However, the wealth of each individual entrepreneur hinges on the amount of such borrowing in the economy because the volume of capital inflow affects the terms of trade and therefore the valuation of foreign-currency denominated debts.

Krugman (2000) suggests a game in which lenders decide, in random order, how much credit to offer to successive domestic entrepreneurs. The supply of credit depends on what the lenders think will be the value of the borrower's collateral. But because some debt is denominated in foreign goods, this value depends on the real exchange rate, and therefore on the actual level of borrowing that takes place. A rational-expectations equilibrium of this game will be a path of self-fulfilling expectations, i.e., the expected level of investment implicit in the supply of credit must match the actual level of investment that takes place given this supply.

Next the relationship between investment and the wealth of entrepreneurs is derived. From equation (9.35) wealth is known to depend, other things being equal, on the real exchange rate RER_t; from equation (9.30), the real exchange rate RER_t depends on I_t. It follows that:

$$\frac{dW_t}{dI_t} = (1-\mu)\,F \tag{9.36}$$

Let I_f be defined as the 'financeable' level of investment, that is the level of investment that would occur if the leverage constraint in equation (9.31) was binding. Since the ability of entrepreneurs to borrow depends on their wealth, it follows that:

$$\frac{\partial I_f}{\partial I_t} = (1+\lambda)\,(1-\mu)\,F \tag{9.37}$$

The behaviour of the model depends on the value of $\partial I_f/\partial I_t$:

- If $\partial I_f/\partial I_t<1$, the economy has a high rate of return. Adjustment in its capital stock is delayed by financing constraints.
- If $\partial I_f/\partial I_t>1$, there are multiple equilibria. A self-fulfilling loss of confidence is warranted by debt and currency crises jointly occurring.

By assumption a currency crisis does not occur in this model as a result of short-term debt and long-term investments, unlike in the study of Chang and Velasco (1999) that was previously discussed. It does not originate in a lack of foreign exchange reserves either. In line with equation (9.37), the collapse of a peg is triggered by:

- High leverage;
- Low marginal propensity to import;
- Large foreign-currency debt relative to exports.

These factors reinforce the vicious circle – investment→real exchange rate→balance sheets→investment – that brings about crises.

The East Asian currency crisis was preceded by a rise in the foreign-currency denominated liabilities of financial institutions. Thus Burnside, Eichenbaum and Rebelo (2001b) argue, among other interpretations of the East Asian crisis, that it resulted from large prospective deficits associated with implicit bailout guarantees to unhealthy domestic banks. The expectation that these future deficits would at least be partially financed by seigniorage revenues or by an inflation tax on outstanding nominal debt, led to a collapse of the fixed exchange rate regimes. It must also be noted that a high level of sovereign debt may also entail currency crises.

1.3. Sovereign Debt and Currency Crises

Studies by Aizenmann, Kletzer and Pinto (2002), Benigno and Missale (2001), Corsetti and Mackowiak (2001), and Daniel (2001) analyse the relationship between sovereign debt and currency crises. These authors introduce debt in currency crisis models to account for some features of the Russian and Brazilian crises. In these countries, increasing fiscal deficits were a major source of financial fragility. They led to the joint outbreak of debt and currency crises.

Drawing on Fielding and Mizen (2001), a model of sovereign debt is presented in this section. An open economy is assumed to be described by the following equations:

$$(1-\beta)m_t + \beta(s_t + f_t) - p_t = -\alpha i_t \tag{9.38}$$

$$p_t = s_t p_t^* \tag{9.39}$$

$$i_t = i_t^* + E_{t-1}\Delta s_t \tag{9.40}$$

$$i_t = i_t^* + \pi_t \delta_t \tag{9.41}$$

$$m_t = s_t + f_t - \eta E_{t-1} \Delta s_t \tag{9.42}$$

$$m_t = s_t + f_t - \eta \pi_t \delta_t \tag{9.43}$$

where m_t is the domestic currency stock, f_t the foreign currency stock, i_t the domestic interest rate, i_t^* the foreign exchange rate, s_t the exchange rate, p_t the domestic price level p_t^*, π_t the probability at time t that the exchange rate collapses at the next period, δ_t the magnitude of the collapse, α the semi-elasticity with respect to the interest rate, β (respectively 1-β) the amount of foreign (domestic) currency held by domestic residents. For simplicity it is assumed that foreign residents do not hold domestic currency, and that $p_t^*=1$.

Equation (9.38) describes the equilibrium condition on the money market. Equation (9.39) is the purchasing power parity condition. Equation (9.40) and equation (9.41) respectively represent the uncovered interest parity condition under a float and under a peg. Equation (9.42) and equation (9.43) describe currency substitution by relating the demand for domestic and foreign currencies to expected depreciation of the exchange rate, respectively under a float and under a peg.

The policymaker derives a constant marginal benefit from keeping the exchange rate fixed, that amounts to κ. It is known to the policymaker but remains unknown to speculators. The loss function depends on the seigniorage revenue earned when he lets the exchange rate go, as a result of the inflationary devaluation of magnitude δ, and on the seigniorage revenue after the currency crisis. It is represented by the following equation:[7]

$$L_t = \max(SR_t) - \max(SR_{t+dt}) \tag{9.44}$$

with max(SR_t) being the maximum possible seigniorage revenue that could be earned instantly from letting the exchange rate go at time t. If the peg is forsaken at time t, SR_t is worth:

$$SR_t = (\partial p/\partial t)\exp(m_t - p_t) \tag{9.45}$$

Substituting equations (9.38) to (9.43) into equation (9.45) leads to:

$$SR_t = \delta_t \exp[-i_t^* - (\alpha + \beta\eta)\pi_t \delta_t] \tag{9.46}$$

Deriving equation (9.46) provides the maximum seigniorage revenue:

$$\delta_t = [(\alpha + \beta\eta)\pi_t]^{-1} \tag{9.47}$$

Substituting equations (9.46) and (9.47) into equation (9.44) leads to:

$$L_t = \frac{\exp\left(-\alpha i_t^* - 1\right)}{\alpha + \beta\eta\pi_t} - \frac{\exp\left(-\alpha i_t^* - 1\right)}{\alpha + \beta\eta\pi_{t-1}} \tag{9.48}$$

Deriving equation (9.49) gives the marginal cost $\partial L_t/\partial t$, that is denoted l_t: it measures the seigniorage revenue lost by delaying the float from period t to period t+1:

$$l_t = \frac{\exp\left(-\alpha i_t^* - 1\right)}{\alpha + \beta\eta\pi_t} \times \frac{\partial\pi/\partial t}{\pi^2} \tag{9.49}$$

From equation (9.49) a differential equation of π_t, which represents the probability at time t that the exchange rate collapses at the next period, is obtained:

$$\partial\pi_t/\partial t = hl\pi^2 \tag{9.50}$$

with:

$$h = \frac{\alpha + \beta\eta\pi_t}{\exp(-\alpha i_t^* - 1)} \tag{9.51}$$

Next the dynamics of π_t and l_t may be determined by assuming that speculators are Bayesian learners *à la* Bensaïd and Jeanne (1997) (see Chapter 7, section 4, The policymaker's reputation). At each time period, market participants assess the probability that the marginal cost of delaying the float equals the marginal benefit of keeping the exchange rate fixed. When the cost reaches the threshold value $\underline{\kappa}$, the policymaker lets the exchange rate go. If the peg collapses at time t+1, then $\underline{\kappa} \in]l_t; l_{t+1}[$ with $\underline{\kappa} > l_t$.

Speculators' beliefs are represented by a density function ϕ that is continuous and strictly positive on the interval $]\underline{\kappa}\,;\,\overline{\kappa}[$, with Φ being the corresponding cumulative distribution function. By assumption, speculators' initial beliefs are compatible with the 'truth', i.e., $\kappa \in]\underline{\kappa}\,;\,\overline{\kappa}[$. Using Bayesian updating methods:

$$\pi_t d_t = \int_{l_t}^{l_{t+1}} \frac{\varphi(\kappa)}{1 - \Phi(c_t)} d\kappa \tag{9.52}$$

so that:

$$\pi_t d_t = \frac{\varphi(l_t)}{1-\Phi(l_t)} dl \tag{9.53}$$

whence:

$$\pi_t = \left(\frac{\varphi(l_t)}{1-\Phi(l_t)}\right)\frac{\partial l}{\partial t} \tag{9.54}$$

In line with Bensaid and Jeanne (1997), the distribution for κ is assumed to follow a linear differential equation so as to make the model tractable. Assuming that λ is a fixed parameter, then:

$$\varphi = \lambda \exp\left[-\lambda(\kappa - \underline{\kappa})\right] \tag{9.55}$$

Equation (9.55) leads to:

$$\pi_t = \lambda \frac{\partial l}{\partial t} \tag{9.56}$$

From equations (9.50), (9.51) and (9.56), the evolution of π_t and l_t through time may be determined by:

$$\pi_t = \left[\pi_0 - hl_t t\right]^{-1} \tag{9.57}$$

and:

$$l_t = l_0 - \pi_t(t/\lambda) \tag{9.58}$$

with π_t and l_0 being the values of π_t and l_t at time $t = 0$.

In the model of Fielding and Mizen (2001), the policymaker faces a tradeoff between increasing seigniorage revenues and maintaining a fixed peg. The collapse of the peg is triggered by market participants' self-fulfilling expectations. The time period of the collapse mainly hinges on macroeconomic fundamentals. In this respect the initial fiscal situation and potential increases in seigniorage revenues play an equal role in the outbreak of the crisis. A recent study by Aizenman, Kletzer and Pinto (2002) extends the type of fiscal fundamentals that trigger currency crises. They consider that sovereign debt swaps are not neutral, in the spirit of the Modigliani–

Miller theorem. In a situation where the public debt level is unsustainable in the long run, they consider that sovereign debt swaps may worsen the macroeconomic situation and lead to a crisis. Their analysis is meant to account for some features of the Russian and Argentinean currency crises that occurred in 1998 and 2001.

All the studies that appeared in the wake of the East Asian, Russian, Brazilian and Argentinean crises do not focus on the joint outbreak of speculative attacks and banking or debt crises. Some research focuses on the role of the speculators in the outbreak of speculative attacks.

2. INVESTORS' BEHAVIOUR AND SELF-FULFILLING CURRENCY CRISES

Some recent studies investigate whether speculators may jointly launch an attack on a fixed peg that compels the policymaker to let the exchange rate go when the macroeconomic situation does not really warrant such an attack. In the unique-equilibrium model of Tarashev (2001), speculators' demand for home assets and for the domestic currency hinges on the domestic interest rate. In a framework where a stochastic disturbance on home asset supply exists, there is an equilibrium interest rate whose level may lead speculators to launch a self-fulfilling attack on the currency.

Femminis (2002) provides another analysis relieving the assumption in Tarashev (2001) that speculators' demand includes the information given by the equilibrium interest rate. He develops a framework with multiple equilibria and imperfect information about the fundamentals on the part of agents. Their devaluation expectations do not only affect the likelihood of future currency crises, but also the level of inflation. This in turn influences wage levels and the level of unemployment, which is a major component of fundamentals. Speculators thus assess the likelihood of a currency crisis based on the next period wage after observing the degree of success of speculative attacks during the previous period. As such, agents' first-period expectations influence fundamentals in the second period as well as the policymaker's ability to withstand attacks. Femminis (2002) considers that the public information provided by wage levels allows coordinated self-fulfilling attacks to be launched by agents.

In this section, two types of situation are dealt with. Market participants may either engage in mimetic behaviour that triggers currency crises, or have portfolio allocations that provide them incentives to defend a peg.

2.1. Mimetic Behaviour and the Outbreak of Self-fulfilling Currency Crises

Drawing on Tornell (1999), this section deals with the possibility of multiple equilibria stemming from contagion mechanisms of investors' behaviour.

Let $E_{t-1}\Delta s_t$ be the expected change in the exchange rate. Using the uncovered interest parity condition, it is assumed that agents keep the domestic country's assets if:

$$E_{t-1}\Delta s_t \leq i_t - i_t^* \quad (9.59)$$

Assume that each agent may hold m or 0 of these assets. Initially each agent holds m. If equation (9.59) is satisfied, he keeps his domestic assets:

$$\Delta m = 0 \quad (9.60)$$

If not, he sells them:

$$\Delta m = -m \quad (9.61)$$

There are N identical investors. At the aggregate level, if agents keep their assets, capital flows equal:

$$N\Delta m = 0 \quad (9.62)$$

If they sell them:

$$N\Delta m = -Nm \quad (9.63)$$

It is assumed that the policymaker's loss function is:

$$L_t = \Delta s_t - \alpha y_t \quad (9.64)$$

Equation (9.64) describes the policymaker's welfare as negatively related to the currency depreciation and positively to a fall in output.

It is assumed that the policymaker's foreign exchange reserves r_t can never be negative. At time $t = 0$, the reserves are worth r. The trade balance TB_t is defined as:

$$TB_t = f(\Delta s_t, y_t) - \underline{TB} \quad (9.65)$$

with the function f depending positively on Δs_t and negatively on y_t, with $f(0,0)=0$, and where $\underline{TB}$ is a strictly positive constant such that there is a structural trade deficit.

The balance-of-payments equilibrium condition is:

$$N\Delta m=\Delta r-TB_t \tag{9.66}$$

Equation (9.66) may be rewritten as:

$$N\Delta m=\Delta r-f(\Delta s_t,y_t)+\underline{TB} \tag{9.67}$$

In this framework, the policymaker faces capital outflows of size $N\Delta m$. He faces three options and may either:

- modify its foreign exchange reserves by Δr;
- let the exchange rate go such that $\Delta s_t>0$;
- modify the production level y_t.

The policymaker's behaviour depends on the evolution of the balance-of-payments:

1. If:

$$r_t\geq N\Delta m+\underline{TB} \tag{9.68}$$

the policymaker uses his reserves to defend the currency such that:

$$\Delta r=\Delta nm-\underline{TB} \tag{9.69}$$

with:

$y_t=0$
$L_t=0$
$\Delta s_t=0$

2. If:

$$\underline{TB}\leq r_t\leq -N\Delta m+\underline{TB} \tag{9.70}$$

two situations may be distinguished.

a. If equation (9.59) is satisfied, there are no capital outflows and reserves must be used. Hence:

$$\Delta r = -\underline{TB} \tag{9.71}$$

b. If equation (9.59) is not satisfied, there are capital outflows. Moreover if:

$$r_t < Nm + \underline{TB} \tag{9.72}$$

the policymaker must solve the following problem:

$$\text{Min } L_t = \Delta s_t - \alpha y_t \tag{9.73}$$

under the constraint:

$$-Nm = -r_t - f(\Delta s_t, y_t) - \underline{TB} \tag{9.74}$$

In that case, foreign exchange reserves are completely emptied so that:

$$\Delta r = -r_t \tag{9.75}$$

whence:

$$f(\Delta s_t, y_t) = Nm + \underline{TB} - \Delta r \tag{9.76}$$

Hence there is a trade surplus that exceeds capital outflows and the structural trade deficit minus the foreign exchange reserves that have been used. It is thus possible to determine an optimal rate of depreciation which is denoted δ:

$$\delta = -\frac{f'(TB_t)}{f'(\delta_t)} \tag{9.77}$$

3. The situation where reserves cannot compensate for the trade deficit may be rewritten as:

$$r_t \leq \underline{TB} \tag{9.78}$$

The policymaker is compelled to follow equation (9.77). He lets the exchange rate depreciate by the optimal rate of depreciation δ.

Here there are three macroeconomic possible situations and four equilibria, in line with 'early' escape-clause models:

1. the policymaker does not let the exchange rate go. The currency is not depreciated and there is no crisis.
2. there are two possible equilibria.

a. if $E_{t-1}\Delta s_t=0$, agents do not anticipate a depreciation. Then $N\Delta m=0$, i.e. agents keep their assets. They prevent the collapse of the exchange rate.
b. if $E_{t-1}\Delta s_t = \delta$, agents expect that the optimal depreciation will take place. There is a collapse in the exchange rate and a fall in output.

3. $E_{t-1}\Delta s_t=\delta$. Agents expect an optimal devaluation with capital outflows.

This framework bears some similarities with bank runs. If investors believe that other investors will withdraw their assets, and if reserves cannot compensate for these outflows, there is an 'asset run' bringing about a depreciation.

The only solution to avoid such a crisis is for countries to hold a sufficient amount of foreign exchange reserves, that is to satisfy the condition:

$$r_t > -N\Delta m+\underline{TB} \tag{9.79}$$

But in an era of high capital mobility, even holding an important amount of reserves may not prevent fixed exchange rate systems from collapsing.

2.2. Investment Behaviour and the Lack of Self-fulfilling Currency Crises

Some studies, e.g., Obstfeld (1996), Corsetti, Dasgupta, Morris, and Shin (2000), Corsetti, Pesenti, and Roubini (2002), deal with the strategic foundations of speculative attacks and the role of large traders in times of speculative pressure. These studies assume that speculators always benefit from the policymaker's decision to let the currency float. As pointed out by Ventura (2002), this assumption seems over-simplifying. Market participants may sometimes defend the currency, as shown by the behaviour of hedge funds that tried to prop up the Malaysian ringgit in the beginning of the East Asian crisis.[8] Such behaviours do not systematically result from errors in expectations concerning the viability of a peg, but may stem from rational assessments of potential losses that would result from a float.

Fourçans and Franck (2002) suggest that speculators may launch a self-fulfilling attack or defence of a peg, given their portfolio allocations, when the macroeconomic conditions allow it. They first determine the domestic policymaker's arbitrages as he is likely to be the largest trader on the foreign exchange market, and may not leave much leeway to private agents for speculation against the currency. They reinterpret the currency crisis model of Obstfeld (1996) in a unique equilibrium environment.[9] The domestic policymaker's tradeoff is first analysed, then the evolution of exchange rate is formalised and the policy schedule is described.

In this two-country open economy model, the domestic policymaker maintains a fixed exchange rate regime, and foreign currency prices equal domestic prices.

The policymaker's objective is to solve the problem

$$\min L_t=(y_t-y^*)^2+\psi(\Delta s_t)^2+C \tag{9.80}$$

under the constraint:

$$y_t=\bar{y}-\alpha i_t+\beta\Delta s_t-u_t \tag{9.81}$$

with:

$$i_t=i_t^*+E_{t-1}\Delta s_t \tag{9.82}$$

where y_t is output at time t, y^* the policymaker's output target, $\bar{y}$ the country's natural output level, $\Delta s_t \equiv s_t-s_{t-1}$, the change in the exchange rate s_t between t-1 and t, $E_{t-1}\Delta s_t$ the speculator's expectation of Δs_t based on lagged information deemed exogenous, i_t the domestic interest rate, i_t^* the foreign interest rate, u_t an i.i.d. shock that hits the domestic economy at each time period t such that $u_t \in \Re$, ψ the policymaker's preference for a fixed exchange rate regime, with $\psi>0$,[10] C the cost of leaving the fixed exchange rate system.

Equation (9.80) describes the policymaker's tradeoff between increasing output and keeping the exchange rate fixed. In equation (9.81), output is positively affected by devaluation expectations and negatively affected by an increase in the foreign interest rate. Assuming the Marshall–Lerner conditions verified, output is fostered by a depreciation of the exchange rate via a positive effect on net exports. Equation (9.82) represents the uncovered interest parity rate condition.

Following Obstfeld (1996), C is first omitted to simplify the presentation. In that case, the change in the exchange rate under a flexible exchange rate system is:

$$\Delta s_t^{\text{Flex}} = \frac{\beta\left(y^* - \bar{y} + u_t\right) + \alpha\beta\, i_t}{\beta^2 + \psi} \tag{9.83}$$

Output equals:

$$y_t^{\text{Flex}} = \bar{y} + \frac{\beta^2\left(y^* - \bar{y}\right) - \psi u_t - \alpha\psi\, i_t}{\beta^2 + \psi} \tag{9.84}$$

The policy loss is:

$$L_t^{\text{Flex}} = \frac{\psi}{\beta^2 + \psi}\left(y^* - \bar{y} + u_t + \alpha i_t\right)^2 \tag{9.85}$$

In a fixed exchange rate system, the change in the exchange rate is:

$$\Delta s_t^{\text{Fix}} = 0 \tag{9.86}$$

Output is:

$$y_t^{\text{Fix}} = \bar{y} - \alpha i_t - u_t \tag{9.87}$$

The policy loss is worth:

$$L_t^{\text{Fix}} = \left(y^* - \bar{y} + u_t + \alpha\, i_t\right)^2 \tag{9.88}$$

Reintroducing the costs of leaving the fixed exchange rate system C, the policymaker keeps the exchange rate fixed if:

$$L_t^{\text{Flex}} + C < L_t^{\text{Fix}} \tag{9.89}$$

In this framework, the domestic policymaker finds it optimal to let the exchange rate go if equation (9.89) is satisfied, i.e., if $u_t \in\,]-\infty;u_L[$ or if $u_t \in\,]u_H;+\infty[$, but to keep the fixed rate working if $u_t \in [u_L;u_H]$, with:

$$u_H = \left[(\beta^2 + \psi)C/\beta^2\right]^{\frac{1}{2}} - (y^* - \bar{y} + \alpha i_t) \tag{9.90}$$

and

$$u_L = -\left[(\beta^2 + \psi)C/\beta^2\right]^{\frac{1}{2}} - (y^* - \overline{y} + \alpha i_t) \qquad (9.91)$$

Building on Morris and Shin (1998a, 1998b) (see Chapter 6, section 3.3, Common knowledge between speculators and currency crisis with multiple equilibria), there are three possible unique-equilibrium macroeconomic situations:

- If $u_t \in]-\infty;u_L[$, there is a unique equilibrium such that the policymaker finds it optimal to leave the fixed exchange rate system, whatever private agents may expect or do. Following Obstfeld (1996), the exchange rate may be assumed to appreciate.
- If $u_t \in [u_L;u_H]$, the economy is 'ripe for an attack' (Morris and Shin, 1998a, 1998b). Macroeconomic conditions are such that a currency crisis only happens if many market participants expect other speculators to attack the currency. Following Obstfeld (1996), it may be assumed that the policymaker is only compelled to let the exchange rate go if the size of the self-fulfilling speculative attack is equal or superior to $E_{t-1}\Delta s_t$.
- If $u_t \in]u_H;+\infty[$, there is a unique equilibrium such that the policymaker finds it optimal to leave the fixed exchange rate system, whatever private agents may expect or do. Following Obstfeld (1996), the currency is devalued.

Next focus on the case where $u_t \in [u_L;u_H] \cup]u_H;+\infty[$, and rule out the case in which speculators may trigger self-fulfilling appreciations of the currency. The following results may be easily adapted to the case in which $u_t \in]-\infty;u_L[$.

If the domestic policymaker keeps the exchange rate fixed at time t-1 so that $s_{t-1}=s_{t-1}^{Fix}$, then the exchange rate at time t is $s_t = s_t^{Fix}$ if the exchange rate remains fixed; or $s_t = s_t^{Flex}$ if there is a float, with $s_t^{Flex} > s_t^{Fix}$.

It is possible to determine s_t^{Flex} the exchange rate under a flexible exchange rate system at time t as a function of s_{t-1}^{Fix}, the fixed exchange rate at time t-1. Given equation (9.83), it is found that:

$$s_t^{Flex} = \frac{\beta\left(y^* - \overline{y} + u_t\right) + \alpha\beta\, i_t}{\beta^2 + \psi} + s_{t-1}^{Fix} \qquad (9.92)$$

Here a self-fulfilling attack is theoretically possible, but it is unclear whether speculators may have incentives to launch it. The speculators' tradeoff must therefore be dealt with. It is assumed that there is a foreign exchange market between the foreign state and the domestic country. There are no derivative markets and no domestic speculators.

Let U_k and W_k be respectively the kth speculator's utility function and wealth. It is assumed that no speculator is wealthy enough to launch a successful attack on his own.

Let Z_{jt}^F and Z_{jt}^D be respectively the prices of the jth foreign and domestic stocks at time period t that follow a random walk; M^D the amount of foreign-denominated currency held for speculation or hoarding that the speculator buys and sells when he expects a currency crisis; ρ_{jk}, τ_{jk}, and ω_{jk} respectively the weights associated with Z_{jt}^F, Z_{jt}^D and M^D in the kth speculator's portfolio.

To simplify the analysis, it is assumed that foreign exchange markets are such that:

- There is the same m-number of stocks on the domestic and foreign markets;
- $\forall\, j=1,\ldots m$, $\rho_{jk}\geq 0$, $\tau_{jk}\geq 0$, and $\omega_{jk}\geq 0$, that is short sales are not allowed;
- $\forall\, j=1,\ldots m$, $\text{Cov}(Z_{jt};s_t)=0$ and $\text{Cov}(Z_{jt}^D;s_t)=0$, that is a currency crisis does not have any impact on stock prices;
- $\sum_{i=1}^{m} E(Z_{it}^F) < \sum_{i=1}^{m} E(Z_{it}^D)$ and $\sum_{i=1}^{m} E\left[Z_{jt}^F - E(Z_{jt}^F)\right]^2 = \sum_{i=1}^{m} E\left[Z_{jt}^D - E(Z_{jt}^D)\right]^2$.

This last feature suggests that the sum of stocks' expected returns is higher on the domestic market than on the foreign market, while the sum of variances of stocks are equal on the domestic and foreign markets, that is risk on both markets is the same. Without this assumption, foreign speculators would not have any incentives to invest in the domestic country.

The kth foreign speculator's objective is to solve the following problem:

$$\text{Max } E[U_k(W_k|u_{t-1})] \tag{9.93}$$

with:

$$W_k = \sum_{j=1}^{m}\left(\rho_{jk} Z_{jt}^F + \tau_{jk}\frac{Z_{jt}^D}{s_t}\right) + \omega_k \frac{M^D}{s_t} \tag{9.94}$$

Each speculator maximises his expected wealth given the shock which occurred at the previous period.

If speculators cannot modify their portfolio allocations during a time period, their actions take the following line of events:

- Beginning of period: depending on the shock of the previous period and their preferences, foreign speculators allocate their wealth between domestic and foreign stocks, or hold liquidity in order to speculate against the domestic currency.
- The policymaker and the speculators observe the shock u_t.
- End of period: exchange rate stability depends on the shock u_t, the policymaker's arbitrages and the speculators' behaviour.

The speculators' payoffs may now be determined. Let *cs* be the lump sum that speculators pay for entering the foreign exchange market. Let *A* be equal to:

$$A=\left(\frac{-\dfrac{\beta\left(y^{*}-\bar{y}+u_{t}\right)+\alpha\beta\, i_{t}}{\beta^{2}+\psi}}{s_{t-1}^{Fix}\left(s_{t-1}^{Fix}+\dfrac{\beta\left(y^{*}-\bar{y}+u_{t}\right)+\alpha\beta\, i_{t}}{\beta^{2}+\psi}\right)}\right)\left[\sum_{j=1}^{m}\rho_{jk}Z_{jt}^{D}+\omega_{k}M^{D}\right] \quad (9.95)$$

Table 9.1 gives each speculator's wealth variation between time *t*-1 and time *t*, depending on the success or the failure of the speculative attack at time *t*.

Table 9.1 The change in the speculator's wealth following an attack on the currency

The speculator's action when the attack is launched	The speculator's payoff when the attack fails	The speculator's payoff when the attack succeeds
The speculator attacks the currency	-*cs*	*A*-*cs*
The speculator takes no action	0	*A*
The speculator defends the currency	-*cs*	*A*-*cs*

Table 9.1 suggests that two kinds of speculators may be distinguished. There are those who would benefit from a currency crisis, either resulting from unsound fundamentals or self-fulfilling expectations, and those who would lose from a collapse in the fixed exchange rate system.

Each speculator may benefit or lose from a successful attack on the currency, depending on the macroeconomic fundamentals and his portfolio allocations, as shown in Table 9.2.

Table 9.2 The macroeconomic shock and the speculators' behaviour

The macroeconomic shock	The behaviour of speculators who gain from a float	The behaviour of speculators who lose from a float
$u_t \in]-\infty; u_L[$	No action taken	No action taken
$u_t \in [u_L; u_H]$	Currency attack	Currency defence
$u_t \in]u_H; +\infty[$	Currency attack	No action taken

Fourçans and Franck (2002) provide an explanation as to why some foreign speculators may defend a fixed exchange rate system in order to prevent a devaluation. The most risk-taking market participants among foreign speculators invest in the domestic country despite the exchange rate risk, whereas the most risk-averse ones do not. When the domestic macroeconomic situation worsens, the risk-taking speculators defend the currency because they will incur losses if a float happens. The risk-averse foreign speculators launch an attack because they do not have any vested interests in the domestic economy. This situation happened in Malaysia just before the float of the ringgit in July 1997. Hedge funds, which are traditionally the most risk-taking foreign speculators, defended the currency. Institutional investors, which are usually the most risk-averse foreign speculators, attacked the peg.

This model also implies that speculators attack or defend the fixed peg on rational grounds. Sunspots or problems in information transmission are not required to justify the occurrence of 'self-fulfilling' currency crises. There are portfolio allocations such that the speculators are given incentives to launch self-fulfilling attacks or defences of a fixed peg.

Fourçans and Franck (2002) also show that self-fulfilling speculative attacks are unlikely to happen. As there may be substantial changes in stock prices that may affect market participants' wealth, they consider that speculators cannot find the portfolio allocations that provide them with incentives to launch self-fulfilling attacks before the policymaker lets the currency float. Thus the authors do not rule out self-fulfilling currency crises a priori, but believe that they are unlikely to occur since they require additional conditions which may not be met on the foreign exchange market.

3. CHAPTER SUMMARY

Recent studies, e.g., Dooley (1997), Irwin and Vines (1999), try to formalise the relationships between deteriorated fundamentals and speculators' self-fulfilling expectations in times of currency crises. Often these deteriorated fundamentals are unhealthy financial institutions, as seen from the role they appear to have played in the 1997 East Asian crisis. Studies on these 'twin crises', focusing on the similarities and common occurrences between banking crises and currency crises, include Chang and Velasco (1998, 1999, 2000a, 2000b, 2001), Glick and Hutchinson (1999), Kaminsky and Reinhart (1999) and follow different paths as shown by the survey of Marion (2000). For instance Chang and Velasco (1999) extend the bank run framework of Diamond and Dybvib (1983) to account for self-fulfilling features of banking and currency crises. Some third-generation models, such as Krugman (2000) and Schneider and Tornell (2001), also study the 'balance-sheet effect'. They attempt an assessment of the influence of companies' balance sheets in determining their ability to invest, and the effects of capital flows in affecting the real exchange rate.

Another characteristic of third-generation models deals with the influence of speculators' expectations on the launching of speculative attacks. A theory of what triggers speculators' expectations when the economy is 'ripe for an attack' is lacking. Following Morris and Shin (1998a, 1998b), several studies, e.g., Tornell (1999), Femminis (2002), Fourçans and Franck (2002), try to account for this. Different approaches have been suggested, which focus on the behaviour of large traders and their influence on speculators, on wage-setters in the domestic economy, or on market participants' portfolio allocations.

NOTES

1. Marion (2000) analyses the similarities and differences between currency and banking crises.
2. See also Chang and Velasco (1998, 2000a, 2000b, 2001).
3. Dooley (1997) may also be viewed as a study on contagion through 'common shocks'. See Chapter 8, section 1, Models of 'common shocks'.
4. Chang and Velasco (1999) treat the credit ceiling as exogenous but consider that it could be justified by recourse to the many theories of international borrowing under sovereign risk. It can also be thought of as the result of domestic restrictions (a regulated capital account) that prevent domestic residents from borrowing more than f dollars).
5. Under Constant Relative Risk Aversion, the percentage of wealth invested in risky assets is always the same.
6. Notice that d can be positive or negative. It is positive if f is sufficiently large relative to e so that investment in the illiquid asset takes up the whole of the initial endowment, the difference being made up by period 0 borrowing.

7. After the currency crisis, seigniorage revenue depends on the current interest rate and on a set of fixed parameters, notably a time-invariant interest rate. It is assumed that the government is myopic and only takes into account the seigniorage from the inflationary devaluation. In any case, equation (9.44) is an approximation of the policymaker's real loss function.
8. On the role of hedge funds during the East Asian crisis, see Eichengreen and Mathieson (1998), Brown, Goetzmann and Park (2000) and Brown (2001).
9. By assumption multiple equilibria are ruled out in this framework.
10. In this framework, the parameter ψ measures the policymaker's preference for a fixed exchange rate. The higher ψ is, the stricter the monetary and fiscal policies.

PART FOUR

Currency Crises and the International Financial System

This part aims at providing a double assessment of the relevance of the currency crisis literature. On the one hand it aims at determining whether currency crisis studies provide appropriate explanations of actual currency crises. On the other hand it discusses the pertinence of reform proposals of the international financial system that are based on the results of these studies.

Hence this part contains a case study of the propagation of the East Asian crisis to Russia and Brazil. It discusses its causes and consequences, and whether or not theoretical and empirical studies in currency crises give an accurate account of this currency crisis contagion which lasted 18 months, from July 1997 to January 1999.

These recent currency crises in emerging countries moreover provide incentives to analyse international financial arrangements and reforms that may prevent similar speculative attacks in the future. Two bearings may be distinguished: the choice of the exchange rate regime, and the role of international financial institutions.

In the current debate about the choice of the exchange rate regime, some argue that fixed and super-fixed exchange regimes, that is currency boards and dollarisation, may be harmful to emerging economies, and that flexible exchange rates may be too risky for these countries.

Discussions on the international financial system also focus on the role of international financial institutions. Their policies or even their existence are called into question because they are said to be unable to prevent currency crises or to mitigate the real effects of speculative attacks. Some of their proponents believe that they should act as international lenders of last resort.

Reform proposals obviously hinge on one's analyses of the causes of currency crises. They are the normative implications of positive statements on the origins of speculative attacks, and are shaped by one's views on the self-fulfilling or fundamental sources of crises. Readers should also look to studies by Fischer (2002), Meltzer (2000), Summers (2000) or Tirole (2002) for other analyses that bear similarities and dissimilarities with ours.

10. The Spread of Currency Crises in Emerging Countries from 1997 to 1999: A Case Study

When researchers at the World Bank published in 1993 a report on the development of East Asian countries (World Bank, 1993), they did not realise the controversy they would raise from their conclusions. They did not know that, on 2 July 1997, a financial crisis would occur and refute the bulk of their analyses. The report asserted that several Asian countries, i.e., Hong Kong, Indonesia, Japan, Malaysia, South Korea, Taiwan and Thailand, had been benefiting for the past decades from high levels of growth thanks to interventionist public policies and private endeavours: this was the 'Asian Miracle'.

At first glance, it may seem surprising that the report included Japan and excluded China. Japan did not start its economic development after 1945, but during the second half of the nineteenth century. It was not an emerging market, but a developed economy. An explanation for the inclusion of Japan is that Japanese high-level civil servants had in fact 'influenced' economists of the World Bank into writing a text praising interventionist policies in Japan and in the Far East.[1] Yet the exclusion of China from this report appears to be justified, despite the assertions of Naisbitt (1995) or Rohwer (1995). China had benefited from high levels of growth for the previous 15 years. But state interferences with the economy, as well as the unequal repartition of growth benefits which has so far only benefited the state bourgeoisie, excluded China from the Asian miracle.

If there was an Asian miracle, it only happened in South East Asian countries. Their development characteristics differ from those in China and Japan. The development of the 'Dragons' (Hong Kong, Singapore, South Korea and Taiwan) and of the 'Tigers' (Indonesia, Malaysia, the Philippines and Thailand) respectively started at the end of the 1950s and at the end of the 1970s. While formerly praised, these countries have since been accused of being at the origin of the currency crises that hit Russia in August 1998 and Brazil in January 1999.

Radelet and Sachs (1998a, 1998b) consider that a sudden change in market participants' trust in South East Asian economies was the main reason for the crisis contagion. In line with the 'pure contagion' models of Masson (1998, 1999) dealt with in section 2 of Chapter 5, they consider that the crisis did not result from the deterioration of fundamentals – although the macroeconomic performances of some countries had deteriorated during the 1990s. The crisis stemmed from a panic that gradually spread to local and foreign investors in Asia, and that was reinforced by the inopportune interventions of international financial institutions, especially the IMF. Yet Corsetti, Pesenti and Roubini (1999b) suggest that the 1997 financial panic simply revealed the structural problems of the region. In line with third-generation models of currency crises, macroeconomic disequilibria triggered the crisis, which in turn intensified the problems of the financial and real sectors of the economy.

In our opinion, these explanations focusing on market participants and macroeconomic disequilibria miss the peculiar situation of the industrial and financial sectors of South East Asian countries. They were heavily indebted shortly before the outbreak of the crisis, following an accumulation of investment failures. This situation may seem paradoxical for firms that had been praised for their capacity to adapt to the evolution of demand on international markets. It stemmed from the suppression of domestic financial markets sought by politicians and high-level civil servants. Both were then able to influence investment decisions without taking into account the lack of transparency and profitability, or so they believed. The Russian and Brazilian private sectors also suffered from such deficiencies, as well as from the politicians' inability to implement state reforms.

This chapter analyses the cause of currency crises that successively hit South East Asian countries, Russia and Brazil between 1997 and 1999. First it examines the heralding signs of speculative attacks, that is, the slowdown of trade throughout East Asia, the rise in the emerging economies' debt and the deficiencies in domestic private sectors. Second it investigates the economic problems of South East Asian countries in the months prior to the crisis, then analyses the reaction of these countries following its outbreak. It also deals with the propagation of speculative attacks in Russia and Brazil that forced both countries to let their exchange rate go.

1. HERALDING SIGNS OF CURRENCY CRISES

The analysis of heralding signs of the currency crises in South East Asia, Russia and Brazil cannot only rely on financial indicators. The problems created by the reduction of trade in South East Asia, and by the rise in the debt level of the countries of that region – as well as in Russia and Brazil – must also be dealt with.

1.1. The Reduction of Trade

For over 30 years, exports were a major of source of growth for East Asian countries. The decrease in exports that occurred in 1996 could not do anything but slow down their economic growth: it was a first signal of their future problems.

1.1.1. Cyclical and structural reasons for the slow decrease in exports

Among the various causes of the export decrease, cyclical and structural factors must be distinguished. The former reflect regional and global trends. World growth in exports underwent a sharp decline between 1995 and 1996, from 20% to 4%.[2] It decreased by the same proportion in the Far East. Table 10.1 shows that some countries were more affected than others. Thailand was clearly the most affected nation, even experiencing a fall in exports.

Table 10.1. Share of exports in the GNP (US dollar)

	1994	1995	1996	1997
Hong Kong	11	13	4	4
Indonesia	8	12	9	7
Malaysia	20	21	6	1
Philippines	17	24	14	21
Singapore	24	18	5	-1
South Korea	14	23	4	5
Taiwan	9	17	4	4
Thailand	19	20	-1	3
China	25	19	2	21
USA	9	12	7	10
Japan	9	10	-8	2
World	14	20	4	4

Source: International Monetary Fund (1998a), World Bank (1998)

This drop hurt East Asian countries all the more insofar as the electronic sector was the most affected, especially the chip and semi-conductor sectors in which they were specialized. The demand for manufactured industrial products, such as textile, was relatively more stable.

If the strong decline of exports in 1996 may be partially attributed to various cyclical factors, it also resulted from structural factors. In 1990, East Asian countries' exports were mainly in raw materials and low-technology products.[3] Only 30% of Malaysian and Singaporean exports were high-tech products. But in 1996, only raw materials constituted Indonesia's exports, even though the share of high-tech products in Indonesian exports also gradually rose.

Several interpretations may be given to the rapid development of high-tech industries in South East Asia. The quick accumulation of human and technological capital is said to have fostered the growth of high-tech productsin Asian economies. The growing competition from China, where labour costs are comparatively low, is supposed to have caused the competitiveness of South East Asian countries to deteriorate.[4] Finally direct investments from industrialised countries and the delocalisation of manufactured products from the 'Dragons' to the 'Tigers' would also have played their role. These explanations may be relevant but omit a decisive factor of Asian economies: the mercantilist convictions of politicians and high-level civil servants. They influenced investments in domestic industries, which are eventually not driven by market demand. In spite of their capacity for adaptation,[5] Asian countries could not withstand the 1997 crisis: they were the victims of a production structure commanded by political imperatives.

1.1.2. Regional trade as a crisis factor in South East Asia

The South East Asia countries' openness is probably one of the factors explaining their spectacular growth over the past two or three decades. First exports were mainly towards Western countries, but intra-regional trade was gradually developed. Table 10.2 shows that, in 1996, 53% of Singaporean and Malyasian exports were to neighbouring countries; yet only 40% of the Philippines were to East Asian countries.

If regional trade may foster growth, its drop may amplify crises, as documented by Glick and Rose (1998) and other studies on crisis propagation through trade links that were discussed in section 2.1 of Chapter 8. Moreover Asian countries did not benefit from the advantages of a genuine economic integration. They could not fully specialise following their comparative advantages as their governments implemented selective industrial policies in areas more or less disconnected from real comparative advantage, ranging from cars to high-tech. Yet Asian economies were not very protectionist, as Table 10.3 demonstrates.

Table 10.3 shows that Indonesia's degree of openness is the lowest. It went from about 26% to 28% between 1990 and 1997, while the ratios for South Korea, Philippines and Thailand were higher during the period. Taiwan's ratio almost reached 50% in 1997 while Malaysia's was over 90% and Hong Kong's was above 100%.

Table 10.2. Intra-regional exports in East Asia as a percentage of total exports in 1996

	Hong Kong	Indonesia	Malaysia	Philippines	Singapore	South Korea	Taiwan	Thailand	China	Japan	East Asia
Hong Kong	0	1	1	1	5	1	3	1	27	5	47
Indonesia	4	0	2	1	8	6	4	2	4	27	58
Malaysia	5	1	0	1	20	5	3	4	3	13	53
Philippines	5	1	2	0	5	5	3	5	1	16	40
Singapore	9	1	19	2	0	9	4	6	2	8	53
South Korea	8	2	2	1	5	0	3	2	7	14	45
Taiwan	23	2	3	1	4	3	0	3	13	12	63
Thailand	5	1	3	1	14	5	2	0	3	17	48
China	24	1	1	1	2	4	2	1	0	19	56
Japan	6	2	4	2	5	6	7	4	5	0	42
East Asia	10	2	4	1	6	0	4	3	5	4	49

Source: World Bank (1998)

Table 10.3. Degree of openness of East Asian countries (measured by the mean of exports and imports divided by GNP, 1990-1997)

	1990	1991	1992	1993	1994	1995	1996	1997
Hong Kong	129.93	135.28	140.37	137.18	138.92	151.67	142.28	132.68
Indonesia	26.30	27.18	28.23	25.26	25.94	26.98	26.13	28.22
Malaysia	75.23	86.52	76.64	87.72	92.15	97.42	91.50	93.55
Philippines	30.40	31.09	31.58	35.58	36.98	40.26	44.90	54.20
South Korea	30.04	29.38	29.38	29.04	30.47	33.59	34.36	38.48
Taiwan	44.27	45.14	42.34	43.29	43.16	47.80	46.63	48.07
Thailand	37.76	39.24	38.98	39.69	40.99	44.88	44.19	46.69

Source: Corsetti, Pesenti and Roubini (1999b).

All the above-mentioned factors provide an explanation for the fall in trade in East Asia. They also cast light on the structural difficulties of these countries, especially the explanation of their high level of debt. However, the economic problems of Russia and Brazil did not have the same causes. Their weaknesses were mainly due to the high level of sovereign debt that is commonplace in emerging markets and countries in transition.

1.2. The Debt Level of Countries in Crisis

South East Asian countries' debt did not result from high-spending public policies and budgetary deficits, but from disequilibria in their current account stemming from the private sector's indebtness. The Russian and Brazilian crises also resulted from the unhealthy situation of their domestic financial and industrial sectors, though in both countries sovereign debt played a major role in the outbreak of speculative attacks. As such, some characteristics of the East Asian crisis may be related to elements of first- and third-generation models, while the main features of the Russian and Brazilian crises are more easily related to third-generation models.

To explain the fragility of the crisis countries, it is necessary to analyse, on the one hand, their public deficits and their current account disequilibria, and, on the other hand, the nature of their short-term debt and capital inflows.

1.2.1. Public deficits and current account disequilibria

As noted by Krugman (2000), the East Asian currency crisis did not result from wide public deficits, unlike the 1970s and 1980s emerging market crises.

In the months prior to the devaluation of the Thai baht, the macroeconomic indicators traditionally associated with a crisis triggered by a public deficit did not provide any heralding signs of future financial problems in the region. Table 10.4 shows that, in the 1990s, only three countries have significant inflation rates for one or two years. The rate in the Philippines almost reached 20% in 1991, but went back to 5% in 1997. Hong Kong had an inflation rate of 11% in 1991 but of 6% in 1997. Inflation in China reached 24% in 1994, but it went down to 8% in 1996 and to 3% in 1997. As can be seen, the inflation rate in Asian countries was not very high just before the outbreak of the crisis, especially when compared to what happened in some Latin American countries during the 1980s.

While the Asian financial crisis did not seem to result from high public deficits and high inflation rates, things were different for Russia and Brazil. The Russian economic situation was more worrying than in most South East Asian countries, as shown in Table 10.5. Table 10.6 also shows that the deficit of the Russian federal government remained significant, in spite of the subsidies granted by the IMF since 1992 and the surveillance programme established in 1995. Unlike Asian countries, a large share of the Russian government budget is devoted to monthly interest payments. To meet its obligation, the Russian government was compelled to use extra-budgetary funds, especially social security funds.

Table 10.4 Inflation rates (1990–1997) (in %)

	1991	1992	1993	1994	1995	1996	1997
China	2.50	6.30	14.60	24.20	16.90	8.30	2.80
Hong Kong	11.60	9.32	8.52	8.16	8.59	6.30	5.83
Indonesia	9.40	7.59	9.60	12.56	8.95	6.64	11.64
Malaysia	4.40	4.69	3.57	3.71	5.28	3.56	2.66
Philippines	18.70	8.93	7.58	9.06	8.11	8.41	5.01
Singapore	3.40	2.32	2.27	3.05	1.79	1.32	2.00
South Korea	9.30	6.22	4.82	6.24	4.41	4.96	4.45
Taiwan	3.63	4.50	2.87	4.09	3.75	3.01	0.90
Thailand	5.70	4.07	3.36	5.19	5.69	5.85	5.61

Source: International Monetary Fund (1998a, 1998b)

Table 10.5 Russian economic indicators

	1992	1993	1994	1995	1996	1997	1998
Variation of the GNP (in %)	-14.5	-8.7	-12.7	-4.2	-6	0.9	-4.9
Industrial production (in %)	-18	-14.1	-20.9	-3.3	-5	2	-5.2
Agricultural production (in %)	-9	-4	-12	-8	-5.1	1.5	-13.2
Consumption price index (yearly mean)	1528.7	875	309	197.4	47.8	14.7	27.8
Official unemployment rate (in % of the labour force)	4.7	5.5	7.5	8.9	10	11.2	13.3

Source: Rucker and Crosnier (2000)

Table 10.6 General Budget of the Federal Russian Government (in % of GNP)

	1992	1993	1994	1995	1996	1997	1998 Jan-Jun	1998 Jul-Dec	1998 Jan-Dec
Receipts	15.6	13.70	11.8	12.2	13.0	10.0	10.5	7.80	9.0
Spending	26.0	20.2	23.2	17.3	22.1	16.8	15.6	12.60	13.9
Debt service	0.7	1.90	2.0	3.3	5.7	4.7	5.4	2.90	4.0
Difference	-10.4	-6.5	-11.4	-5.4	-9.1	-6.8	- 5.1	-4.80	-4.9

Source: International Monetary Fund (1998b), Organisation of Economic and Commerce Development (2000)

At the beginning of the 1990s, Brazilian public finances were not in a good shape, and inflation reached 50% per month. To deal with this situation, the government launched a stabilisation programme in July 1994, the so-called *real* plan. It established a new currency unit the *real*, which was to follow a crawling peg to the US dollar. It also implied a freer trade policy that helped to maintain GNP growth, as can be seen from Table 10.7.

Table 10.7 Brazilian economic indicators

	1994	1995	1996	1997	1998
GNP variation (in %)	5.9	4.2	2.8	3.7	0.2
Export growth (in %)	12.9	6.8	2.7	11.0	-3.5
Import growth (in %)	31.0	51.1	6.7	15.4	-6.2
Penetration ratio of imports[a]	10.9	15.6	16.4	19.2	20.5
Export propensity[b]	13.7	14.0	14.5	N.a.	17.0

Notes: [a] The penetration ratio of imports is the ratio of imports to the supply of manufactured goods, with supply= production – exports + imports.
[b] The export propensity is obtained by dividing exports by the sales of manufactured goods.
Source: Franco (2000)

As shown by Milesi-Feretti and Razin (1998), a high current account deficit is usually a good leading sign of future currency crises. This is all the more true as Brazil had a high level of foreign-currency denominated short-term debt.

Table 10.8 shows a persistent disequilibrium of the current account in Indonesia, Malaysia, South Korea, Thailand and the Philippines over the 1990s. Other East Asian countries usually have surpluses in their current accounts. The surplus in the Singaporean current account was on average worth more than 10% of GNP between 1990 and 1993 and more than 16% in 1996. Taiwanese current accounts are also in surplus over the period.

Russia had a surplus in its current account from the fall of the Soviet regime to the outbreak of the crisis as Table 10.9 shows. The evolution of the current account cannot therefore be taken as an indicator of the Russian crisis. Yet it is relevant for Brazil.

In spite of the *real* plan, the deficit of the current account kept on growing, as shown in Table 10.10. Brazilian authorities did not however try to curb these deficits. They considered that these disequilibria could not harm the stabilisation programme as they were the result of the increase in foreign direct investments following the privatisation programme. They also believed that the Brazilian Central Bank had sufficient foreign exchange reserves to defend the *real*. Furthermore Brazilian interest rates were quite high, providing incentives to foreign investors for holding assets in *real* and hence dissuading them from launching speculative attacks. Future events showed that the views of the Brazilian authorities were erroneous.

Table 10.8 East Asian countries' current account disequilibria as a percentage of GNP (1990–1997)

	1990	1991	1992	1993	1994	1995	1996	1997
China	3.02	3.07	1.09	-2.19	1.16	0.03	0.52	3.61
Hong Kong	8.40	6.58	5.26	8.14	1.98	-2.97	-2.43	-3.75
Indonesia	-4.40	-4.40	-2.46	-0.82	-1.54	-4.27	-3.30	-3.62
Malaysia	-2.27	-14.01	-3.39	-10.11	-6.60	-8.85	-3.73	-3.50
Philippines	-6.30	-2.46	-3.17	-6.69	-3.74	-5.06	-4.67	-6.07
Singapore	9.45	12.36	12.98	8.48	18.12	17.93	16.26	13.90
South Korea	-1.24	-3.16	-1.70	-0.16	-1.45	-1.91	-4.82	-1.90
Taiwan	7.42	6.97	4.03	3.52	3.12	3.05	4.67	3.23
Thailand	-8.74	-8.01	-6.23	-5.68	-6.38	-8.35	-8.51	-2.35

Source: International Monetary Fund (1998b).

Table 10.9 Russian balance-of-payments (1992–1998)

	1992	1993	1994	1995	1996	1997	1998
Current account (in percentage of the GNP)	N.a	N.a	4.1	2.6	2.9	0.9	0.7
Foreign direct investments (in billions US$)	1454	1211	640	2016	2479	6639	2761
Trade balance (in billions US$)	N.a.	N.a.	28201	33160	39516	33059	28570

Source: Rucker and Crosnier (2000).

Table 10.10 Brazilian balance-of-payments (1994–1998, in billions US dollars)

	1994	1995	1996	1997	1998
Current account	-1.7	-18.0	-23.1	-33.4	-35
In percentage of GNP	-0.3	-2.6	-3.0	-4.2	-4.5
Foreign direct investments	2.6	5.5	10.5	18.7	26.1
Net portfolio investments	7.3	2.3	6.0	5.3	-1.8
Exchange reserves variation	7.2	12.9	8.7	-7.9	-7.6

Source: Franco (2000).

From these stylised facts it would appear that the current account might have been a leading signal of the Asian and Brazilian crises. But this was not the case for Russia.

1.2.2. Short-term international debt and capital inflows

If there is a specificity of the Asian crisis as opposed to the 1970s and 1980s emerging market crises, it has to do with the nature of the debt. It was mainly composed of short-term loans in foreign currency. When a large part of a country's external debts is short-term, a financial crisis may lead to a shortage of liquidity: reserves may not be sufficient to cope with the service of the debt. This may appear when foreign creditors refuse to renew loans because of their expectation of a forthcoming speculative attack, or because a devaluation has just happened. This was the case in East Asia, following the debts contracted by the domestic private sector from foreign financial institutions.

Table 10.11 shows that in 1996, the share of loans whose maturity is less than a year amounted to about 50% or more in China, Malaysia, the Philippines, Indonesia, Thailand and South Korea. In Hong Kong, Taiwan and Singapore, this share was higher, reaching 82%, 84% and 92%. In the last three countries, the high level of short-term debts did not merely result from mismatches in the maturity structure of liabilities, as in other East Asian countries: it also reflected their significance in the financial exchanges in the region.

Table 10.11. East Asian countries' short-term debt from foreign financial institutions (in % of total debts) in 1996

China	49	Hong Kong	82	Indonesia	61
Malaysia	50	Philippines	58	Singapore	92
South Korea	67	Taiwan	84	Thailand	65

Source: Bank of International Settlements (1998a, 1998b)

As shown by these data, the foreign liabilities of East Asian financial institutions were mostly in the short term. But most of the loans they granted to domestic firms were in the mid and long run. Hence financial institutions not only faced maturity mismatches between assets and liabilities, but also a high exchange risk as a result of the modalities of financial intermediation: local banks borrowed from foreign financial institutions in foreign currency, then lent in domestic currency to domestic investors. These characteristics belong to the 'balance-sheet' approach to currency crisis developed by some third-generation models, as documented in Chapter 9, section 1.2, Private debt and currency crises.

The situation in Russia and Brazil is similar to that of South East Asia in at least one respect: both countries faced a liquidity crisis. The Russian government had to borrow from foreign creditors to cope with public spending. It could not reform its tax system in order to raise taxes efficiently. Moreover from 1995 onwards, the IMF forbade the government to borrow from the Central Bank. To find a new source of financing the Russian government issued that same year short-term (GKOs) and long-term (OFZs) bonds.

Although the economic situation in Brazil might not have been as problematic as in Russia, the government also had budgetary problems. As shown by La Chapelle Bizot (2000), its debt did not decrease, unlike in other Latin American countries such as Venezuela or Chile, despite the implementation of the so-called Brady plan. The benefits of the *real* plan were also mixed. Brazil is the only South American country whose financial situation deteriorated as inflation diminished. This deterioration resulted from various factors, notably the removal of the indexation of tax resources and of public spending. More important was the lack of political willingness to reform the Brazilian state. During his first term (1994–1998), President F.H. Cardoso never found the required two-thirds majority in both houses of Parliament to implement the constitutional reforms needed to carry on the *real* plan.

Table 10.12 Share of FDIs to current account financing (in % of current account deficit)

	1990	1991	1992	1993	1994	1995	1996	1997	1998
Brazil	N.a.	N.a.	-19.37	-18.75	-46.56	-37.47	-133.4	238.15	195.76
Indonesia	36.58	34.79	63.92	95.16	75.54	67.58	80.83	97.11	21.03
Malaysia	268.05	95.58	239.1	180.1	98.27	90.10	110.84	139.28	N.a.
Philippines	19.67	52.61	22.8	41.05	53.93	74.65	38.38	29.12	N.a.
Russia[a]	N.a.	N.a.	N.a.	N.a.	3.36	24.30	14.42	95.25	13.52
South Korea	45.16	14.19	18.43	-59.39	20.92	20.88	10.11	34.82	N.a.
Thailand	33.57	26.60	33.52	28.35	16.90	15.26	15.90	103.84	N.a.

Note: [a] Russian data for the early 1990s are not available because this country became an IMF-member only on 1 June 1992.

Source: International Monetary Fund (1998a), OECD (2000), World Bank (1998).

This lack of reform explains why foreign direct investments (FDIs), which are non-debt creating long-term capital inflows, did not foster the growth of the Brazilian economy in the 1990s. This is surprising as Brazil was able to attract FDIs to finance its current account imbalances, as Table 10.12 shows. Table 10.12 shows that the FDIs in Russia did not contribute greatly to the financing of the current account. Such a fact may be explained by the reluctance of foreigners to make long-term investments in a country where too many political, juridical and economic uncertainties were thought to exist.

Table 10.12 also shows the paradoxical situation of some East Asian countries whose investments were mainly in the short rather than in the long term. South Korea and Thailand obviously favoured short-term inflows in the years preceding the crisis, due to the willingness of politicians and high-level civil servants to prevent too great an involvement of foreign investors in the domestic economy. Still East Asian countries like Indonesia and Malaysia encouraged FDI inflows.

All in all there was a lack of long-term investments in most South East Asian countries, which instead received large amounts of short-term capital inflows. Hence the growing debt of South East Asian firms and financial institutions and their loss of competitiveness.

1.3. Private Sector's Weaknesses

Brazilian and Russian firms and banks were never models for European and American competitors. Yet the industrial and financial private sector in South East Asia was seen as very competitive until the outbreak of the speculative attacks. It is therefore surprising that these countries were so much affected by the crisis. To understand this apparent paradox, one must go deeper into the study of the private sector.

There are similarities between the industrial and trade sectors in East Asia, Russia and Brazil, besides the bad working conditions in these countries.[6] Corruption was a common factor, and influenced firms' profitability.

1.3.1. The industrial and commercial sectors

Over the 1990s, the South East Asian private sector's debt kept on growing. This growth resulted from the strong acquisition of assets fostered by the real estate and financial speculation that existed throughout the decade, and was aggravated by the decline in investment profitability.

The decrease in profitability can be measured by the return on shareholders' investments. Table 10.13 presents the 'Return on Equity' (ROE), i.e., 'Net Profit' (after tax) over 'Capital'. A comparison between the means of the ROEs between the countries of the region gives an assessment of the profitability of domestic firms. Some ROEs are relatively high throughout the period, especially in Hong Kong, Indonesia and Malaysia. Other countries, e.g., South Korea, have lower ROEs, sometimes with values like those of France and Germany, two industrialised countries in crisis. The 'Asian Miracle' does not therefore seem to have benefited industrial and commercial firms in every country. It clearly benefited Hong Kong, where corruption was low and where government officials did not interfere with the choice of private investments.

Table 10.13. Estimation of the return on investment after tax (in %)

	1992	1993	1994	1995	1996	Mean
Hong Kong	29	24	27	24	21	25.0
Indonesia	14	12	12	15	13	13.2
Malaysia	12	14	14	14	13	13.4
Philippines	4	7	16	12	9	9.6
Singapore	10	10	9	8	8	9.0
South Korea	5	4	8	11	N.a.	7.0
Taiwan	12	10	14	12	8	11.2
Thailand	13	10	11	9	5	9.6
Latin America	3	6	10	12	14	9.0
France	7	3	6	3	6	5.0
Germany	7	3	8	6	11	7.0
Japan	5	3	2	2	4	3.2
USA	4	8	16	16	18	12.4

Source: Pomerleano (1998)

Russia and Brazil were also among the most corrupt countries in the world. The establishment of Russian conglomerates, studied by Sapir (1996, 1998), is an example of the barriers to economic development resulting from corruption. These conglomerates, via the financial and banking institutions they owned, played an instrumental role in the August 1998 Russian crisis.

The Russian industry also faced numerous barriers. It was hindered by the government's trade policy and the weaknesses of the banking system. Hence most firms were highly indebted before the earliest speculative pressures on the rouble. Many were not profitable and incurred heavy losses, as shown by Table 10.14.

The Russian industry mainly consisted of large low-capital plants. It did not use its production capacities in an optimal manner and products were usually not competitive. This accounts for the decline in industrialisation that has occurred from 1996 onwards in all regions, except those where natural resources were exploited. Tables 10.15 and 10.16 show that oil and gas constitute a large share of national exports and receipts. The decrease in the price of these two commodities in the midst of 1997 worsened the budgetary difficulties of the Russian state: it was undoubtedly one of the cyclical factors of the August 1998 crisis.

Table 10.14 Russian firms' lack of profitability and losses

	January – October 1996		January – October 1997	
	Percentage of non profitable Russian firms	Total losses (billions of ruble)	Percentage of non profitable Russian firms	Total losses (billions of ruble)
Industry	42.0	34025	47.5	43212
including:				
- electricity	23.9	1490	28.4	1296
- combustibles	44.8	6028	49.7	6210
oil extraction	25.3	1009	28.3	967
petrol refining	11.9	117	25.5	674
gas	34.8	1578	43.5	122
coal	58.0	3307	64.3	4037
- iron and steel industry	30.6	1964	42.5	4765
- non-ferrous metallurgy	66.1	2742	63.9	2849
- petrochemistry	39.0	4804	44.4	5353
- metal transformation	40.2	7035	44.6	9394
- wood industry	61.3	4199	70.4	5494
- construction materials	46.5	1308	54.4	1808
- glass, earthenware and porcelain	53.2	180	55.8	245
- textile and clothing industry	55.6	1508	60.3	2134
- food industry	34.2	2196	41.3	3018
- cereal industry	27.7	123	35.2	217
- microbiological industry	50.0	86	56.4	103
- medical industry	20.8	69	16.5	87
- printing	13.3	13	17.6	19
- other branches	38.8	280	42.2	220

Source: Gicquiau (1998)

Table 10.15 Russian exports and production in 1996

	Exports outside CIS[a]	Exports towards CIS	Production	Share of exports in the domestic production (in %)
Crude oil (thousands of tons)	105031.6	20612.7	301000	41.7
Petroleum products (thousands of tons)	54875.8	1605.8	n.a.	n.a.
Natural gas (thousands of cubic metres)	127996.0	68457	601000.0	32.7
Coal (thousands of tons)	20703.9	4846.2	257000.0	9.9
Coke (thousands of tons)	521.5	892.1	n.a.	n.a.
Iron ore (thousands of tons)	7946.0	3376.0	72100.0	15.7
Cast iron (thousands of tons)	2040.4	66.0	37200.0	5.7
Copper (thousands of tons)	527.4	2.2	n.a.	n.a.
Crude aluminium (thousands of tons)	2616.9	2.2	n.a.	n.a.
Crude nickel (thousands of tons)	166.9	0.3	196.6	84.9
Mineral fertilisers (thousands of tons)	3565.8	40.8	9076.0	39.7
Wood (thousands of cubic metres)	5636.0	281.4	n.a.	n.a.
Paper pulp (thousands of tons)	1044.1	48.3	3076.0	35.5
Newspaper (thousands of tons)	777.9	121.2	1245.0	72.3
Cars (per thousand units)	137.0	11.9	868.0	17.2
Lorries (per thousand units)	6.6	7.3	136.0	10.1
Frozen fish (thousands of tons)	1154.1	5.4	n.a.	n.a.

Note: [a] Community of Independent States
Source: Gicquiau (1998)

Table 10.16 Volume and amount of main industrial Russian exports in 1996

	Volume in thousands of tons	Amount in millions US$	Share in total exports
Total exports	----	88400.0	----
Natural gas (thousands of cubic metres)	196453.0	15772.2	17.80
Crude oil	125644.3	15668.0	17.70
Machines and transport equipment	n.a.	8180.2	9.30
Oil products	56481.6	7409.3	8.40
Ferrous metals	n.a.	6676.4	7.60
Crude aluminium	2619.1	3929.8	4.40
Crude nickel	167.2	1217.2	1.40
Frozen fish	1159.5	1138.3	1.30
Cooper	529.6	1135.2	1.30
Nitrate fertiliser	8430.3	1073.3	1.20
Coal	25550.1	1011.1	1.10
Wood (thousands of cubic metres)	15850.4	939.7	1.10
Synthetic rubber	373.7	525.3	0.60
Paper pulp	1092.4	452.3	0.50
Newspaper	899.1	440.9	0.50
Ammonium	3263.9	408.5	0.50
Ferrous metals	278.8	319	0.40
Cast iron	2106.4	294.9	0.30
Iron alloy	11256.8	282.1	0.30
Potassium fertiliser	3606.6	278.9	0.30
Calcium phosphate	3777.2	193.1	0.20
Coke	1412.6	95.5	0.10
Méthanol	466.2	54.4	0.06

Source: Gicquiau (1998)

If the Brazilian government was compelled to let down the crawling peg of the *real* five months after the Russian crisis, the Brazilian industry encountered difficulties before this time period. Following the 1994 establishment of the *real* plan, the gradual decrease in inflation alongside the development of consumption credit led to a rise in demand. Yet demand decreased again after the Mexican crisis which triggered numerous bankruptcies and layoffs in Brazil. The Brazilian industrial sector then went through a series of changes that brought about the creation of small-sized firms, as shown in Table 10.17.

As the less competitive Brazilian firms went bankrupt, the government gradually called into question its free-trade policy set up at the beginning of the *real* plan – in spite of the rules of the World Trade Organization (WTO). This change influenced the amount of capital inflow towards Brazil from 1995 onwards, investors being more reluctant to invest in Latin America in the wake of the Mexican crisis. They preferred to invest in South East Asian countries.

As can be seen, the Mexican crisis also explains market participants' subsequent reluctance to invest in Latin America, as ever-increasing capital inflows to East Asia. These inflows helped local banks to finance domestic projects without concern for their profitability.

Table 10.17 Number and mean size of industrial Brazilian firms per region

Region	Number of firms per region			Mean size of firms per region [a]		
	1989	1997	Variation	1989	1997	Variation
North	3584	5591	56.00%	48	25	-48.10%
North-East	14664	23711	61.70%	46	23	-48.90%
South-East	114496	128929	12.60%	35	22	-38.50%
South	44800	60324	34.70%	28	19	-33.20%
Centre-West	7911	12096	52.90%	15	14	-4.10%
Total	185455	230651	24.40%	34	21	-38.40%

Note: [a] The mean size of firms is obtained by assessing the number of employees.
Source: Saboia (2000).

1.3.2. Financial institutions

If the 1997 crisis revealed the weaknesses of the financial sector in South East Asia, Frankel (1998) notes that numerous observers had noticed them before the outbreak of speculative attacks.

Before July 1997, Asian financial systems were characterised by the low capitalisation of onshore markets. Banks were the main providers of financial intermediation.[7] They borrowed from foreign banking institutions on the offshore markets of the region, then lent to domestic firms. When the latter began to have difficulties, South East Asian banks could not reimburse their foreign-currency denominated debts with national-currency denominated credits on insolvent firms. The banking system was therefore at the origin of a generally high growth of loans to industrial and commercial firms. Table 10.18 assesses the 'lending boom', i.e., the rise in loans granted by financial institutions from 1990 to 1996, by estimating the growth rate from 1990 to 1996 of the commercial banks' credits to the private sector divided by nominal GNP. The volume of loans granted to industrial and commercial firms kept on rising from 1990 to 1996. It recorded a rise of 151%, 58% and 31% in the Philippines, Thailand and Malaysia. These three countries were among the first to be hit by speculative pressures in 1997.

The loans mainly financed investments whose profitability was low, or even null. This is reflected in Table 10.19 where the proportion of non-reimbursed loans to the total granted in 1996 is listed. Domestic banks were also weakened by the real estate crisis in South East Asian countries. Indeed an important share of banks' foreign-currency denominated loans was used to buy real estate assets. Depending on countries, these investments were directly made by financial institutions or, indirectly, by industrial and commercial firms, leading to the speculative bubble of the mid-1990s. Table 10.20 shows that at the end of 1997, the exposure of financial institutions to real estate risk was especially high in Hong Kong, Malaysia, Singapore and Thailand.

Table 10.18 The lending boom in East Asia (1990–1996)[a]

China	7%	Indonesia	10%	Philippines	151%	South Korea	11%
Hong Kong	26%	Malaysia	31%	Singapore	17%	Thailand	58%

Note: [a] Growth rate from 1990 to 1996 of the commercial banks' credits to the private sector divided by nominal GNP.
Source: International Monetary Fund (1998a).

Table 10.19 Percentage of non-reimbursed loans out of the total banking loans in 1996

China	14	Hong Kong	3	Indonesia	13
Malaysia	10	Philippines	14	Singapore	4
South Korea	8	Taiwan	4	Thailand	13

Source: International Monetary Fund (1998a).

Table 10.20 The banking system exposure to real estate risk (in % of assets, on 31 December 1997)

	Exposure to real estate risk	Share of real estate non-reimbursed loans out of the total loans
Hong Kong	40–55	1.50
Indonesia	25–30	11.00
Malaysia	30–40	7.50
Philippines	15–20	5.50
Singapore	30–40	2.00
South Korea	15–25	16.00
Thailand	30–40	15.00

Source: International Monetary Fund (1998a).

Like South East Asian banks, Russian financial institutions were indebted and were not able to deal with a crisis, even though Russian banks had not had special difficulties after the fall of the Soviet Union. Until the 1995 IMF-stabilisation plan, they benefited from a lax legislation and made high profits, although barter began to develop throughout the country as documented by Woodruff (1999). They also benefited from inflation, from the continuous depreciation of the exchange rate, and from the financing of import–export activities.

The liquidity crisis which occurred in August 1995 heralded the end of this 'good period'. It compelled the Russian government to seek the IMF's help and to apply its economic directives, mainly aimed at reducing inflation. Numerous banks went bankrupt and the Russian banking system was consolidated. The small number of small regional deposit banks went from more than 2600 at the beginning of 1995 to only 1800 at the end of 1997. There was also one state-run bank known as the 'Sberbank', which dominated the national banking sector: it held three quarters of households' deposits.

Yet banks' profits generally remained high between 1995 and mid-1997. A new source of gain had indeed appeared: operations on the GKOs, the short-term public bond market. The mean real return on this market reached 75% in 1996. But from 1997 onwards, the decrease of inflation diminished banks' profitability. Banks compensated this loss by undertaking speculative operations on the foreign exchange markets using forward contracts and currency options. But the rise in the number of these operations happened at the same time as the outbreak of the Asian crisis and the opening of the asset market to non-resident investors by a government that anticipated to pay back its foreign creditors. The latter started purchasing forward contracts on the rouble from November 1997 onwards, in the expectation of a possible contagion of the Asian financial crisis to Russia. Russian banks also borrowed in foreign currency from foreign financial institutions. The share of their foreign-currency denominated debts on their assets rose from 7% in 1994 to 17% in 1997. Russian banks were all the more weakened as their assets were mainly made of public bonds. In such a context, a sharp decline of the rouble was bound to lead Russian banks to bankruptcy.

The problems of the Brazilian banking sector were close to Russia's. Before the *real* plan, Brazilian banks' profits mainly stemmed from the financing of international activities that relied on the continuous depreciation of the exchange rate that resulted from inflation, just like Russian banks before the 1995 IMF plan. Afterwards Brazilian financial institutions had to focus on traditional banking activities. They seem to have been unable to adapt quickly to economic reforms, and many fell into trouble.

To prevent a banking crisis, the government created an insurance system, the so-called Guarantee Credit Fund. It was meant to help the Brazilian state to disengage gradually from the banking sector and develop an alternative programme to reform the financial system. The role of the Brazilian Central Bank in the supervision of the domestic financial system was also increased.

Table 10.21 Assets and deposits of Brazilian commercial banks (in millions of real*)*

Assets	Dec-94	Dec-95	Dec-96	Dec-97	Dec-98
Subsidiaries of foreign institutions	14.764	17.294	36.884	66.208	84.079
Offshore loans	35.348	54.429	60.370	65.683	64.516
State banks	141.316	154.754	170.262	161.093	162.031
Domestic private banks	94.086	120.292	159.598	186.739	179.835

Deposits	Dec-94	Dec-95	Dec-96	Dec-97	Dec-98
Subsidiaries of foreign institutions	11.722	14.137	30.097	53.109	62.288
State banks	121.996	141.661	155.836	173.404	138.599
Domestic private banks	78.989	104.925	140.770	166.562	159.267

Source: Peek and Rosengren (2000)

This privatisation programme led a great number of foreign financial institutions to invest in the Brazilian banking sector, as shown in Table 10.21 by the growing number of Brazilian assets and deposits held by subsidiaries of foreign institutions. There was not however any mass entry of foreign banks into the capital of Brazilian banks. Each entry was handled differently under the control of monetary authorities and under the condition that foreign financial institutions would recapitalise banks in trouble or develop specific financial activities.

Table 10.21 also shows the importance of offshore banking in the financing of the Brazilian economy. Yet the Brazilian financial sector withstood the crisis, unlike Asian banks. This resulted from the gradual establishment of foreign banks in Brazil. They diversified the risks and chose investments on financial criteria, not on the 'opinions' of politicians or civil servants, as was the case in most South East Asian countries.

1.3.3. Corruption and the unfinished economic liberalization

Financial institutions of countries in crisis were in a difficult situation before the first speculative attacks appeared. Several explanations are given to explain the reasons for this situation characterised by a high debt level and repeated choices of financing unprofitable projects.

The World Bank (1999, pp. 63–67) suggests that banks in these countries, especially in South East Asia, are not to blame. They borrowed to finance the development of national industries, but were later hurt by a cyclical drop in the profitability of investments. Furthermore the liberalisation of financial systems, which had begun at the end of the 1980s, was largely responsible for their fragility, consequently for the difficulties of the domestic private sectors. Moreover the deregulation of banking activities was not accompanied by an appropriate reinforcement of prudential regulations and by an adequate supervision. The IMF (1998b) agrees with such an assessment. Krugman (1998) and Radelet and Sachs (1998a, 1998b) also consider that the financial liberalisation was responsible for the Asian crisis. But they imply that the IMF is inefficient in dealing with these problems.

These views neglect the role of government intervention in these countries. Politicians regulated the activities of financial institutions when they liberalised capital movements. The prudential ratios adopted by banks were more or less in line with the recommendations of the Basle committee. In fact some governments let financial institutions circumvent these recommendations. In countries where corruption was widespread, such as Indonesia, South Korea and Thailand, the financial system was in a weaker position than in Hong Kong or Singapore where the ruling political elite was relatively scrupulous.[8]

Public interference is therefore often the cause of the weaknesses of the South East Asian banking sector, leading to an increase in borrowing on offshore markets, as documented by Goh and Olivier (2002).[9] This explains why the repeated financing of projects with doubtful returns did not always result from a hypothetical cyclical drop in these returns. The flaws in the selection and supervision of banking loans did not come from too quick a financial liberalisation. Financial systems in South East Asia were too dependent on the state, with the lack of transparency that follows. It notably resulted from a lack of liquidity on onshore capital markets. Banks were therefore able to call on foreign banks' investments without revealing their real debt level or the doubtful nature of their investments projects.

In Russia and Brazil, where corruption was widespread, politicians did not apparently make decisions about conglomerates' investments. But they did not implement the necessary reforms, especially in terms of financial liberalization. This discouraged capital inflows and led firms to increase their long-term debt.

All in all it can be said that the responsibility for the outbreak of speculative attacks in emerging markets or countries in transition did not rest entirely on the private sector.

2. MACROECONOMIC PRESSURES AND CRISES IN EAST ASIAN COUNTRIES

From 1995 onwards South East Asian countries had to deal with macroeconomic difficulties. They increased during the first half of 1997, especially in Thailand where the government was compelled to abandon the parity between the domestic currency and the US dollar on 2 July 1997. The crisis then spread throughout South East Asia, and subsequently, to Russia and Brazil.

2.1. Macroeconomic Pressures in South East Asia before the Crisis

2.1.1. The deterioration of the economic perspectives in 1995 and 1996

The growth of South East Asian countries did not change much between 1995 and 1996, as shown in Table 10.22. Yet from Table 10.23, it can be seen that this sustained growth was mainly related to the 1990s stock market bubble, which also affected the real estate market.

Table 10.22 GNP growth between 1991 and 1997

	1991	1992	1993	1994	1995	1996	1997
China	9.19	14.24	12.09	12.66	10.55	9.54	8.80
Hong Kong	4.97	6.21	6.15	5.51	3.85	5.03	5.29
Indonesia	6.95	6.46	6.50	15.93	8.22	7.98	4.65
Malaysia	8.48	7.80	8.35	9.24	9.46	8.58	7.81
Philippines	-0.58	0.34	2.12	4.38	4.77	5.76	9.66
Singapore	7.27	6.29	10.44	10.05	8.75	7.32	7.55
South Korea	9.13	5.06	5.75	8.58	8.94	7.10	5.47
Taiwan	7.55	6.76	6.32	6.54	6.03	5.67	6.81
Thailand	8.18	8.08	8.38	8.94	8.84	5.52	-0.43

Source: International Monetary Fund (1998a, 1998b).

Table 10.23 Evolution of stock market indexes between 1990 and 1997

	1990	1991	1992	1993	1994	1995	1996	1997
Hong Kong	3024	4297	5512	11888	8191	10073	13451	10722
Indonesia	417	247	274	588	469	513	637	401
Malaysia	505	556	643	1275	971	995	1237	594
Philippines	651	1151	1256	3196	2785	2594	3170	1869
Singapore	1154	1490	1524	2425	2239	2266	2216	1529
South Korea	696	610	678	866	1027	882	651	376
Taiwan	4350	4600	3377	6070	7111	5158	6933	8187
Thailand	612	711	893	1682	1360	1280	831	372

Source: International Monetary Fund (1998a, 1998b).

In 1995 the Indonesian currency was hit by speculative attacks. The Indonesian government was reluctant to change its policies. It only followed a slightly deflationary budgetary policy and implemented a minor change in monetary policy.[10] The Indonesian Central Bank only increased the required reserve ratio of commercial banks from 2% to 3% in January 1996, even though it used moral suasion to slow down the expansion of bank credit. The Indonesian Central Bank had to deal with a dilemma common to most Asian countries, and whose features have been studied by third-generation models: to defend the fixed exchange rate without increasing interest rates. High interest rates increase capital inflows but make it more difficult for firms and banks to pay back their debts. And a devaluation of the currency is also likely to create problems since financial institutions and firms would find it difficult to reimburse their foreign-currency denominated debts. The Indonesian Central Bank therefore widened the band of fluctuation of the rupee to limit speculation.[11] Yet market participants triggered a new fall of the rupee each time its bands were widened.

Unlike Indonesia, Malaysia was not subjected to speculative attacks before the outbreak of the crisis. It was however in a difficult situation. Its current account deficit worsened in 1995 and reached 8.8% of GNP. The trade balance went from equilibrium to a deficit of 3.75% of GNP. The Malaysian Central Bank increased the required reserve ratio on domestic commercial banks. It implemented administrative controls on consumption loans. It also increased its interest rate each time the Malaysian currency, the ringgit, had a tendency to depreciate. These increases in the interest rate fostered important capital inflows, from 2400 billion US$ in 1995 to 11300 billions US$ in 1996. These inflows led to a 30% increase in bank credits, essentially for investments on the stock and real estate markets.

There was also a deterioration of the South Korean macroeconomic environment before the outbreak of crises. Short-term foreign debts kept on growing. Between 1995 and 1997, the growth rate of industrial production was cut by half. The stock market lost 34% between 1995 and 1996. In the middle of 1996, the economic crisis was patent. It remains to say that the Asian crisis started in Thailand after speculative attacks against its currency during the first half of 1997.

2.1.2. First semester of 1997: the South East Asian countries' financial distress

Macroeconomic conditions in East Asia once again deteriorated in the first months of 1997. Most financial institutions and conglomerates which officially went bankrupt after the crisis were already insolvent. Governments were not completely inactive against the looming financial disaster. In Thailand several financial institutions received public subsidies in January 1997. Their amount was approximately worth 8 billion US$, 17.5% of which was for 'Finance One', the most important Thai financial company.[12] On 10 March 1997, the Thai government announced its intention to buy back financial institutions' real estate debts for an amount of 3.9 billion US$. On 15 May, it established capital controls.[13] On 23 May, it tried to save 'Finance One', by attempting to merge it with two other financial companies. The failure of this project compelled the government to promise a buy back of the equity of this institution. It however reneged on this promise: it will neither save 'Finance One', nor any other financial companies in trouble. On that same day, the Thai financial ministry revealed that foreign exchange reserves were only a fraction of previous official estimates. During the spring of 1997 28 billion US$ were used to defend the bath.[14] The Thai government, which could not bail out the domestic private sector, attempted a defence of the currency: the Thai Prime Minister Chavalit Yongchaiyudh solemnly announced on television on 30 June that the baht would not be devalued. Two days later, the devaluation occurred. The financial disaster that had threatened Thailand for the past months was triggered. It quickly spread to the other countries of the region, notably Malaysia.

Before the devaluation of the baht, Malaysia's macroeconomic difficulties had worsened, especially during the first half of 1997. They resulted from the accumulation of debts stemming from unsuccessful real estate and financial investments, as well as from the speculative bubble on the stock market. But the Malaysian Central Bank was slow to react. It only started imposing limits on the amounts of real estate loans and purchased assets in March 1997. Kuala Lumpur's stock index dropped by 6.6% in one week.[15] On 15 May, Kuala Lumpur's stock index reached a sixteen-month low. The policy of the Malaysian Central Bank did not however stabilise the domestic economic situation. It seems to have been as inefficient as the Indonesian Central Bank's policy.

The latter tried to stop the growth of domestic firms' debt, but without any real success. It lowered the interest rate by 0.5% in March 1997, thereby hoping to promote exports and diminish the amount of interest reimbursements.[16] Such a policy led to an increase in loans on international capital markets: the private and public debt of Indonesia was said to exceed 200 billion US$ on 24 December 1997.[17]

South Korea was in no better shape, with many conglomerate bankruptcies in 1997 that resulted from their inability to repay the loans granted by domestic financial institutions, especially banks. The latter suffered from this situation, given the high level of bad loans, and found it hard to pay back their foreign creditors.

Financial institutions in the Philippines faced similar difficulties during the first half of 1997, following unsuccessful domestic real estate investments. But their debts represented a mere fraction of South Korean banks' liabilities.

Finally countries such as Hong Kong and Singapore were relatively spared and had better macroeconomic fundamentals than neighbouring countries. The spread of the Thai currency crisis nevertheless showed that no country in the region was safe from speculative pressures.

2.2. Financial Market Crises

South East Asian countries were most heavily affected by the July 1997 financial panic and its spread in the following months.

2.2.1. The financial panic in July 1997

Wednesday 2 July 1997 was the day when the financial panic in South East Asian markets started. That day, the Thai Central Bank stopped defending the domestic peg: the baht lost 14% on the onshore market and 19% on the offshore market. Paradoxically enough, foreign investors' first reactions to the float of the baht were positive. On 3 July, the Thai stock market index increased by 8%. But forecasts quickly became pessimistic as the severe situation of Thai financial companies became blatant. The volatility of the baht increased at the beginning of the second week of July 1997. At the same time, the differentials in the interest rate and in the exchange rate between the offshore and onshore markets rose, due to the capital controls established in May 1997.

The first consequence of the float of the baht was the intensification of speculative pressures on the Philippine peso and on the Malaysian ringgit. In the Philippines, the Central Bank intervened on the spot market and increased its interest rate by 32% in a single month. It even prevented domestic banks from trading forwards contracts on the peso. This policy was inefficient: between 2 and 10 July, the Philippine Central Bank lost more than 1.5 billion US$ of foreign exchange reserves. It stopped its interventions on 11 July, thus letting the peso depreciate by 11.5% in one day. The amount of pesos traded fell sharply.[18]

As in the Philippines, the Malaysian Central Bank defended its currency until Friday 11 July. Then it stopped intervening on the foreign exchange market. The ringgit lost 2.4% of its value. Afterwards the Central Bank intervened again, provoking an appreciation of the ringgit, and made speculators incur losses. Yet the value of the ringgit decreased again until the end of July. In all likelihood the Malaysian Central Bank did not have sufficient reserves to defend the currency.

The Indonesian Central Bank relentlessly defended the value of the rupee. It widened the floating band from 8% to 12% on 11 July. Again an inefficient policy: on 21 July, the rupee depreciated from 8%. In reaction, the Indonesian Central Bank increased the domestic interest rate from 12% to 13% on 23 July and intervened on the foreign exchange market. It was only on 14 August 1997 that it stopped intervening.

On the whole the currency crises and the financial crises in South East Asia only reflected the bad economic situation of the countries involved. Their fundamentals were quite similar, and during the first months of the crisis, they led comparable monetary policies. They tried to prevent a contraction in their money supply by sterilising their interventions on the spot and forward markets. But in line with the IMF-led policies discussed in Chapter 12, they had to follow more restrictive monetary policies and increase interest rates. They also weakened foreign investors' confidence in the capacity of these countries to overcome their difficulties. In this situation the policies penalised the highly indebted private sector.[19]

2.2.2. The transmission of the crisis in South East Asia

In the summer of 1997, the currencies of the countries in crisis continued to fall. On 31 August 1997, the fall of the Thai, Indonesian, Malaysian and Philippine currencies were respectively 34%, 37%, 17% and 14% compared to their levels on 1 January 1997. On 31 September, the baht had lost 42% of its value, the rupee 37%, the ringgit 26% and the peso 29%. As most trade and finance transactions were within the Asian region, it was unavoidable that the zone as a whole was affected. Singapore decided at the beginning of August not to defend its currency and to let it fall. At the end of September, the Singaporean dollar had lost 8%. This depreciation resulted from the difficulties faced by Singapore's trading partners, especially Malaysia, and not from the domestic economic situation, which was rather sound. A similar observation may be made for Taiwan, whose economic situation was sound.

The speculation against the Taiwanese currency is surprising. It fell regularly from 1992 to July 1997, and made it an unlikely target of speculative attacks. The fundamentals of Taiwan also differed from those of other South East Asian nations, except Hong Kong and Singapore. Taiwanese exports were mainly of high added-value goods. The budget was in surplus and the Central Bank had significant foreign exchange reserves. However the exchange rate had greatly appreciated in real terms between July and September 1997 due to the devaluations in neighbouring countries. Thus on 20 October 1997, the Taiwanese authorities decided to let the currency depreciate.

The fall of the Taiwanese and Singaporean currencies ultimately triggered speculative attacks against the Hong Kong dollar. Even if it was on a par with the US dollar, this policy had been for some time called into question, as documented by Lingle (1998). The Hong Kong dollar had appreciated by 30% in real terms since 1990, while the trade balance had a large structural deficit in 1995. The reunification with China introduced an additional political risk. Tung Chee-hwa, the new governor appointed by Beijing, took his new job on 1 July 1997, i.e., the day before the devaluation of the baht, and announced that he would lead interventionist economic policies. These policies were not implemented, as speculative pressures began to appear on Hong Kong financial markets.

These observations suggest that speculative attacks on the Hong Kong dollar at the end of October did not stem from speculators' expectations, but from the deterioration of macroeconomic fundamentals. Yet the situation in Hong Kong was not as severe as in Thailand. The domestic monetary authorities were successful in maintaining the parity between the US and Hong Kong currencies.[20] Thanks to its restrictive monetary policy, Hong Kong was able to convince market participants of its willingness to defend the peg with the US dollar and to prevent capital outflows.

South Korea's situation differed from Hong Kong's insofar as the country had been through a crisis since the second half of 1996. But speculative attacks against the won only started at the end of October 1997. These belated attacks may be explained by the continuous depreciation of the won during the decade: between 1 January 1990 and 1 January 1997, it lost 15% of its value. This decrease lasted throughout the first half of 1997 where it lost 14%.

But from July 1997 onwards, the successive devaluations of South East Asian currencies triggered the appreciation of the Korean currency. On 30 October 1997, the won had appreciated by 37%, 36%, 20% and 15% with respect to the Thai, Malaysian, Indonesian and Philippine currencies, compared to their levels on 1 January 1997. As a result, the won lost 25% of its value during the sole month of November.[21] The first consequence of this rapid depreciation was the intensification of the domestic financial crisis. It compelled the Korean government to implement a 60-billion US$ bailout plan of the financial system.[22] The won remained stable from then onwards, just like the other currencies that had been devalued in those last six months.

All in all in December 1997, the appreciation of the dollar compared to Malaysian, Philippine, Thai, South Korean and Indonesian currencies respectively reached 52%, 52%, 78%, 107% and 151%. The devaluations in the countries the least affected by the crisis, i.e. Singapore and Taiwan, were of lesser magnitude, around 18%. Eventually the South East Asian currency crisis ended in December 1997. Its effects on the real sector of the economy however lasted throughout 1998 when many industrial and commercial firms, as well as financial institutions, went bankrupt. In Indonesia these bankruptcies provoked the panic of depositors and bank runs in March 1998. Unemployment rose throughout South East Asia.

Such crises were bound to have political consequences. Among the elected officials in July 1997, only the Malaysian Prime Minister Muhatir Muhammad was still in power two years afterwards.[23] Even the Japanese Prime Minister Ruytaryo Hashimoto had to resign in July 1998, after his party lost many seats in the upper house of parliament.[24]

3. THE SPREAD OF THE EAST ASIAN CRISIS TO RUSSIA AND BRAZIL

In August 1998, i.e., thirteen months after the devaluation of the Thai baht, the Russian government abandoned the crawling peg of the rouble. Five months later, in January 1999, the Brazilian government abandoned the crawling peg of the domestic currency. This section investigates the determinants of the currency crises in both countries. It analyses whether they resulted from speculators' self-fulfilling expectations or from domestic macroeconomic disequilibria.

3.1. The Spread of the Crisis to Russia

From the beginning of 1998 onwards, the economic situation in Russia deteriorated. Weakened by a lack of fiscal receipts and a high level of debt, the Russian economy had to face an increase of the real exchange rate and a drop in oil prices. This situation compelled the government to let the exchange rate go on 14 August 1998.

3.1.1. The first semester of 1998: increased financial difficulties

There was little international trade and capital movement between South East Asia and Russia. The increase of the real exchange rate did not therefore result directly from the 1997 crisis in Asia. Rather speculators expected that the rouble could not be maintained at its current rate. These pressures increased as the price of Russia's two main exports, i.e., oil and non-ferrous metals, dropped. As shown in Table 10.24, the price of the Russia barrel diminished by 31% over the first half of 1998. The 6.4% rise in the volume of oil exports did not prevent a 25.5% drop in receipts.

Table 10.24. Oil price and Russian export receipts in 1997 and 1998

	Jan – July 1997	Jan – July 1998	Variation (in %)
Oil export price, US$ per ton	118.1	81.2	-31.2
Russian oil exports, millions of ton	72.9	79.1	8.4
Export receipts, in billion US$	8.6	6.4	-25.5
Total	24.1	27.2	12.6
Total in cash[a]	22.2	23.6	6.0

Note: [a] A part of the receipts is traded against food.
Source: Illiaronov (2000)

The Russian crisis stemmed from the conjunction of bad macroeconomic fundamentals, the Asian crisis, the drop in oil prices and, also, a restrictive monetary policy. As documented by Aglietta (2000) and Chapman and Mulino (2000), the authorities aimed at maintaining the nominal exchange rate within its fluctuation band while inviting non-resident speculators to trade on the short-term public bond market (GKOs), the main source of governmental income.

In the last days of May, the Central Bank increased the interest rate by 150%. Half of the fiscal receipts were then devoted to the debt service and the government was compelled to find 20 billions US$ before the end of the year. It appealed to the IMF that was already supportive of the Russian crawling peg policy.

3.1.2. The Russian currency crisis

On 13 July 1998, the IMF granted 22.6 billion US$ to prevent the bankruptcy of the Russian state and the devaluation of the rouble. These funds were to be used until the end of 1999. The first grant, worth 4.8 billion US$, disappeared within two weeks through intervention in the foreign exchange market. It might then have been appropriate to let the rouble float and to lower the interest rate. The IMF opposed such a move: it considered that the measure would only worsen the economic situation. Its programme quickly appeared to be at odds with Russian economic conditions.

The IMF wanted to raise fiscal receipts, whereas Parliament had for a long time opposed the necessary reform of the fiscal system. The IMF bailout plan aimed at exchanging the GKOs, i.e., short-term government bonds, against dollar-denominated long-term bonds. That implied that Russian banks, which made up the bulk of GKO resident owners, rolled them over at maturity. But Russian banking institutions were unable to repay foreign creditors who held crossed claims on their debts. In other words, banks were compelled to repay the loans of banks that could meet their obligations.

At the beginning of August, Russian commercial banks' foreign debt amounted to 16 billion US$, including 6 billion US$ of 'dollar–rouble' swaps with non-resident investors. The latter believed they hedged their GKO purchases. But when they started anticipating the crisis, they closed their positions on the Russian markets, i.e. the GKOs, the long-term bonds (OFZs) and the swaps. Russian banks then faced foreign financial institutions' refusal to roll over their debts: they were compelled to sell government bonds at a loss, and to buy foreign currencies to repay their debts. In the process, they were deprived of their liquidities and unable to reimburse interbank loans.

All in all, the Russian banking system went through a lack of liquidity that ultimately led to the collapse of the financial system. The Central Bank could not fulfil its role as a lender of last resort as the IMF had forbidden to monetise the public debt. Market participants became convinced that the Russian authorities were unable to solve the problems of the domestic financial institutions, and on 11 August 1998, financial markets became bearish. Two days later, the Central Bank restrained the convertibility of the rouble. This measured intensified speculative pressures on the exchange rate and on the GKOs.

On 17 August 1998, the Russian government postponed the reimbursement of the short-term debt and let the rouble float. This decision, which the IMF agreed upon, allowed Russian banks not to have to repay their debts on the GKO and OFZ markets to foreign creditors during 90 days.[25] Like in Asian countries, the Russian crisis had political consequences. Prime Minister Sergey Kirienko was dismissed on 26 July 1998.

On the whole, both the devaluation of the rouble and the reorganisation of the Russian debt seemed unavoidable. The establishment of temporary capital controls suggested by Desai (2000) would probably not have prevented the crisis either, just as the IMF bailout plan did not. It is also probable that the spread of the crisis to Brazil was also barely avoidable.

3.2. The Fall of the Brazilian Currency

The Asian and Russian crises had had an impact on Latin American countries. During the second half of 1997, as well as in August 1998, international investors pulled their funds out of South America. Each time, Brazil was the most affected. Speculators expected that the stabilisation programme would lead to an overvaluation of the Brazilian currency. No surprise then that attacks hit Brazil after East Asia and Russia. They compelled the government to abandon the crawling peg of the *real* on 13 January 1999.

3.2.1. Brazil after the Asian and Russian crises

At the end of October 1997, South American stock markets began to fall, especially in Brazil. This is one channel of transmission of the Asian financial crisis to Latin American countries as investigated by Miotti, Quenan and Ricoeur-Nicolaï (1999).

In Brazil, capital outflows increased while inflows diminished. By the end of October 1997, more than 8 billion US$ left Brazil. Consequently the Brazilian Central Bank increased its interest rate from 21.6% to 43.4%. Such a hike made the situation of domestic firms worse, and increased the public debt. But it stopped the fall of the stock market, at least temporarily. The government could resume its sales of bonds in February 1998.

Brazilian financial markets went through a relatively calm period during the first half of 1998. No significant capital inflows or outflows occurred. This situation could not last as the government's budget deficit kept on increasing, in spite of reform proposals to limit civil servants' wages and to diminish retirees' pensions.

The outbreak of the Russian crisis in August 1998 ended Brazilian hopes of avoiding speculative pressures that already existed on other emerging markets. Capital outflows amounted in the month of September to more than 17 billion US$. Added to that was the uncertainty created by the election of October (F.H.Cardoso was re-elected). The following month he called upon the international financial institutions to bail out the Brazilian economy.

3.2.2. The fall of the *real*

The *real* plan, the objective of which was to re-establish financial orthodoxy, started in 1994 without the supervision of international financial institutions. Brazilian politicians made electors accept unpopular reforms by using nationalistic arguments. The government changed its rhetoric when it asked international financial institutions to intervene.

The IMF, the World Bank, the Interamerican Bank of Development, and the Bank of International Settlements, devised a 41.5-billion-US$ programme to support the Brazilian economy, most of it, i.e., 37 billions US$, for the following twelve months. This programme was conditional on the Brazilian government implementing measures aimed at curbing the budget deficit.

In spite of this programme, the crawling peg of the *real* vis-à-vis the dollar could not be maintained. On 11 January 1999, the band of the crawling peg of the *real* was widened. Two days later the currency floated. Around mid-March, the *real* had lost 40% from its 1-January-1999 value with respect to the dollar.

The failure of the crawling peg of the *real* bears similarities with what happened in Russia in July 1998. Neither called into question the existence of the crawling peg nor accepted the establishment of a moratorium on short-term debt held by foreign creditors. The IMF indeed dreaded that the float of the *real* might trigger an economic and financial crisis in Brazil that would spread throughout Latin America.

Leaving the crawling peg did not trigger the recession that the Brazilian authorities and the international financial community feared. It stimulated exports and did not stop the policy of public debt reduction. However, more than four years after the fall of the *real*, the Brazilian economy had not recovered from the crisis.[26]

4. CONCLUSION

Emerging markets and countries in transition were hit by currency crises between 1997 and 1999. These crises resulted from the countries' economic and financial difficulties. The first nations to be affected were those with the worst economic situation. Indonesia, Malaysia, the Philippines and Thailand had already been experiencing a growth slowdown since 1996. South Korea had been in crisis since the second half of that year. Countries like Singapore or Taiwan had lesser economic problems, but were still compelled to let their exchange rate go. Their currencies had become overvalued following the devaluations in the neighbouring countries, their main trading partners.

On the whole the currency crises seemed unavoidable in South East Asia, but also in Russia, and in Brazil. Governments did not have much leeway, if any, to defend the currencies. They underestimated the magnitude of the financial crisis. So did international financial institutions.

To conclude on that matter, there was an important side effect to the crises: a renewal of the debate on the appropriate exchange rate system in crisis countries. And more generally, on the implications of the Asian, Russian and Brazilian crises for the international financial architecture.

NOTES

1. Lingle (1998) provides an interesting perspective on this subject.
2. The growth in exports is measured in US dollars. Source: World Bank (1998).
3. In 1990, the share of raw materials in exports was 40% for China, Thailand and Singapore; they represented 54% for Malaysia and 72% for Indonesia. Furthermore Hong Kong, South Korea and Taiwan depended for 60% of their exports on low-tech products. Source: World Bank (1998).
4. The consequences on the competitiveness of the East Asian countries of the 50% devaluation of the Chinese currency in January 1994 have been debated. The World Bank (1998) considers that it led to a rise in Chinese exports. Corsetti, Pesenti and Roubini (1999b) believe that the majority of Chinese trade transactions were paid at the exchange rate on the swap market, not at the official exchange rate.
5. In Hong Kong and in the Philippines, firms were in a much better financial situation than in Thailand and in South Korea.
6. See Lingle (1998) on this.
7. Non-banking financial institutions also participated in financial intermediation in South East Asia. It is however difficult to assess their importance since no reliable statistical data are available. See Corsetti, Pesenti and Roubini (1999a, 1999b).
8. The situation of Hong Kong has been more uncertain since its reattachment to China in July 1997.
9. The two most important offshore markets in Asia are the 'Japan Offshore Market', established by the Japanese government in 1986 (433 billion US$ in 1994), and the 'Bangkok International Facility', created in Thailand in 1993 (managing 31 billion US$ in 1996). The 'Labuan International Offshore Financial Centre', set up in 1990, seems to hold a major position in financial exchanges both in Malaysia and in South East Asia. No reliable information were however available on the right amount of transactions in this market.

10. The apathy of the Indonesian government is partly explained by its willingness not to damage the interests of people close to power, especially the relatives of President Suharto.
11. In January 1996 the Indonesian Central Bank widened the floating band of the currency from 2% to 3%. It was broadened to 5% in June 1996, and to 8% in September 1996.
12. Subsidies to financial institutions were distributed by the 'Financial Institutions Development Fund', an agency of the Thai Central Bank.
13. The high level of foreign-currency debt of the Thai financial sector made it vulnerable to a rise in the interest rate traditionally used in the defence of the exchange rate. This is why the Thai government chose to establish control over capital transactions. It aimed at protecting the private sector from a hike in the interest rate and to increase the cost of speculation for foreign financial institutions. Thus on 15 May 1997, it decided to prevent banks from granting domestic-currency denominated loans. The day after, they were also precluded from selling swaps on the domestic currency and from selling baht against dollar to offshore market participants. These regulations were however inefficient as far as Thai banks circumvented them.
14. Before the speculative attacks in the spring of 1997, Thai foreign exchange reserves officially amounted to 30 billion US$.
15. Kuala Lumpur's stock index, known as the 'Kuala Lumpur Commercial Index', is mainly composed of shares of financial institutions and construction companies.
16. The Indonesian Central Bank had already lowered the domestic interest rate by 0.5% in December 1996.
17. This estimation has been made by Corsetti, Pesenti and Roubini (1999b). Officially, Indonesia's debt amounted to 117 billion US$.
18. The daily amounts traded on the spot market decreased from 220 million US$ (daily mean from 1 January 1997 to 30 June 1997) to 75 million US$ (daily mean from 14 July 1997 to 24 July 1997).
19. Alba, Bhattacharya, Claessens, Ghosh and Hernandez (1999) and Agénor, Aizenman and Hoffmaister (2000) talk of a 'credit crunch' phenomenon.
20. This success led to debates on the relevance of currency boards, as seen in Section 1 of Chapter 11. Concerning Hong Kong it seems that the existence of a currency board was less significant as a defence mechanism of the peg than the sharp increase in short-term interest rates that occurred.
21. This depreciation corresponds to a 39% drop since the beginning of 1997.
22. This bailout plan received the approval of the IMF.
23. In South Korea and the Philippines, candidates from the incumbent party lost. In Thailand, Chavalit Yongchaiyud resigned from the office of the Prime Minister after the devaluation of the baht. A long period of governmental instability followed. In Indonesia political protests compelled President Suharto to resign in May 1998. He was replaced by one its protégés, Bucharuddin Jusuf Habibie. In June 1999 B.J. Habibie lost the first free elections in Indonesia for the past 40 years. He however managed to remain in power for some time before being replaced by Abdurahman Wahid, a long-time opposition leader. Finally it needs to be remembered that there are no democratic elections in China and even in Hong Kong.
24. A member of the ruling Liberal-Democrat party became Prime Minister: Obuchi Keizo managed to build around him a majority coalition in the lower house of parliament.
25. On the rescheduling of GKOs and OFZs, see Organisation of Economic and Commerce Development (2000). On Russian banks in the wake of the crisis, see Buch and Heinrich (1999).
26. On the Brazilian situation after the crisis, see International Monetary Fund (2001).

11. Currency Crises and Exchange Rate Regimes

Frankel (1999) considers that no exchange rate regime fits every country through time. Such a position is debatable. Sticking to a given exchange rate, which may not always be optimal for economic development, may still be preferable to repeated changes in exchange rate regimes.

Following the 1990s currency crises, some studies have argued that 'corner solution' regimes, that is exchange rate regimes that are fully fixed or fully flexible, should be favoured over 'intermediary' regimes. As such this chapter focuses on the pros and cons of several exchange rate systems.

The chapter also deals with the relationship between the choice of an exchange rate regime and the outbreak of speculative attacks. The policymaker faces a tradeoff between the advantages of choosing an exchange rate regime which he finds optimal, and the risks of undergoing speculative pressures that jeopardise his exchange rate policy.

1. FEATURES OF EXCHANGE RATE REGIMES

The expression 'super fixed exchange rate regime' designates a fixed exchange rate system that is perfectly credible and that provides few incentives to market participants to launch self-fulfilling attacks. Two super-fixed exchange are distinguished: currency boards and dollarisation. The pros and cons of establishing one of these two regimes in relation to fixed and flexible exchange rate systems must be discussed.

1.1. Fixed and Flexible Exchange Rate Systems

When it comes to discussing the advantages and disadvantages of fixed and flexible exchange rate systems, it must be said that the 1990s currency crises introduced new arguments into the debate. This section distinguishes new and old rationales for the establishment of fixed or flexible exchange rate systems. It must however be acknowledged that the 'new' arguments bear similarities with the 'old' ones.

It must be noted that fixed exchange rates have often been a major influence in currency crises. Indeed throughout the currency crisis literature, speculative attacks are seldom, if ever, seen as taking place under flexible exchange rates. It is indeed worth investigating whether currency crises may occur under a floating exchange rate system. It is also worth wondering if fixed exchange rates are indeed crisis prone. It is indeed obvious that speculators get a one-way bet under a peg.

Traditional arguments in favour of the fixed exchange rate system come in many ways. It is said to:

- offset the impact of monetary shocks;
- prevent monetary financing of the fiscal deficit;
- ease disinflation;
- diminish domestic interest rates by reducing the spread with the world market interest rate;
- diminish the cost of access to international financial markets by lowering the risk premium;
- limit the exchange risk for international transactions and foreign investments.

The fixed exchange rate is criticised on several grounds. It is said to:

- make the pegging country depend on the monetary policy of the peg country;
- transmit external shocks to the domestic economy;
- amplify the effects of real domestic shocks;
- increase the risk of real exchange appreciation and strong current account deterioration;
- provide the illusion of financial and economic stability that leads to a costly adjustment in case of a crisis.

Flexible exchange rates provide the traditional alternative to fixed exchange rate systems. It is considered that they:

- offset the effects of external shocks;
- offset the effects of real shocks;
- offset the effects of inflation on export competitiveness.

There are also criticisms against flexible exchange rates. They are said to:

- allow for strong volatility that has a negative impact on trade and financial transactions;
- allow the import of inflation;

- increase regional instability in case of competitive devaluation;
- lead policymakers to delay required structural adjustments.

Recent approaches on the choice of exchange rate regimes focus on other considerations. Some rely on political factors to favour the choice of an exchange rate system. For instance Collins (1996) argues that countries lacking political stability are given incentives to adopt a flexible exchange rate regime. This they do because they cannot find the support for unpopular measures that is required to keep the exchange rate fixed. Besides, the collapse of a fixed exchange rate entails costly political consequences. In that case a floating exchange rate may be appropriate since rate adjustments are less obvious to the public. A different approach is taken by Edwards (1996). Building on the policymaker's dynamic inconsistency, he considers that governments may seek to increase inflation in order to reduce unemployment, even if it is only in the short run. Establishing a fixed exchange rate system may prevent such an inflation-prone policy from being implemented. The empirical investigation by Méon and Rizzo (2002) supports the idea that such political considerations account for the choice of the exchange rate regime in most countries.

Other research emphasises what has been called 'fear of floating', following the title of a paper by Calvo and Reinhart (2002). Proponents of this approach also include Baliño, Bennet and Borensztein (1999) and Berg and Borensztein (2000). In their view, countries adopt *de jure* a flexible exchange rate system while they establish de facto a fixed exchange rate regime.

Currency mismatches in balance sheets explain why countries want to peg their currency to a foreign currency when the bulk of corporate and banking liabilities and/or assets is denominated in that foreign currency. Usually these countries have high unhedged foreign currency denominated debt and, correspondingly, a high exchange rate risk exposure. They cannot hedge because they find it impossible to borrow abroad in their own currency. Moreover nonresidents are reluctant to take net long positions in the domestic currency.

The 'fear of floating' theory is at odds with studies by Krugman (2000) and Schneider and Tornell (2001) (see Chapter 9, section 1.2, Private debt and currency crises). They consider that corporate debt and currency mismatches may be a source of currency crises. As such a flexible exchange rate system avoids balance sheet disequilibria that ultimately lead to speculative attacks.

Debts are not however the sole focus of the 'fear of floating' approach. If foreign currency denominated assets are widely used as financial assets or for hoarding, the choice of the exchange rate is more ambiguous since this case is similar to a situation with high capital mobility. Hence the policymaker gets incentives to adopt a flexible exchange rate. Yet a fixed exchange rate regime would be more appropriate if the bulk of shocks is monetary.

The 'fear of floating' theory also emphasises dollarisation, that is currency substitution, as a means of avoiding currency crises. This is why the pros and cons of dollarisation should now be discussed.

1.2. Dollarisation

Dollarisation is a monetary arrangement in which a country abandons its domestic country currency and replaces it by the currency of a foreign country which then serves as the legal tender. The term dollarisation is used because the foreign currency that is adopted is usually the US dollar. Historically the first dollarised economies were Liberia and Panama, that is territories under American domination.[1]

Traditionally the theoretical benefits of a dollarisation consist in:

- the offsetting of exchange risk linked to strong adjustments in the exchange rate;
- the stabilisation of capital flows;
- the decrease in interest rates since the country adopts a currency that is less risky than its own;
- a means to ease the financial and economic integration of the dollarised economies vis-à-vis the rest of the world.

The 'fear of floating' approach, notably studies by Baliño, Bennet and Borensztein (1999) and Berg and Borensztein (2000), also suggests that dollarisation may be an appropriate exchange rate regime for currency crisis prone countries where political factors play a major role in the outbreak of currency crises. Dollarisation is said to prevent political interferences. If foreign currency denominated assets are widely used for transactions, there is also a case for currency substitution in the economy, and dollarisation may be a relevant choice.

But dollarisation has some disadvantages since it:

- requires the policymaker to hold a certain minimal amount of foreign exchange reserves;
- prevents the policymaker from intervening as a lender of last resort;
- prevents the policymaker from letting the exchange rate go when the country faces important real or external shocks.

The empirical studies by Edwards (2001a, 2001b) consider that dollarised economies have an inflation rate which is significantly inferior to non-dollarised economies. Their growth rate is also lower. And dollarisation does not provide a significantly better fiscal discipline. It does not seem to prevent current account deficits or speculative attacks. Even though few economies remain dollarised for a long time period, it would be hasardous to generalise such conclusions. It must be acknowledged that dollarisation does not seem to prevent the various macroeconomic disequilibria that cause banking and financial crises. The same remark also seems to hold for currency boards.

1.3. Currency Boards

A currency board is a monetary arrangement stricter than a fixed exchange rate regime: the domestic monetary aggregate must be fully backed by foreign exchange reserves.

The first currency boards were established in 1849 between Mauritius and Great Britain. Currency boards were widely used thoughout the British empire. Studies by Williamson (1995) and Schuler (1996) seem to indicate that they provided monetary stability and eased trade between Great Britain and its colonies. They disappeared during the second half of the twentieth century, not as a result of economic changes but because of political upheaval caused by the independence of British colonies. The transition from a currency board to a fixed exchange rate system occurred without any major incident. However, the financial stability in the time periods where currency boards were established contrasts with the numerous crises that hit developing countries afterwards.

It is unclear whether currency boards suit the needs of emerging or crisis-prone economies. Their proponents argue that currency boards prevent:

- the artificial creation of money, thus avoiding the financing of unessential public spending and/or a rise in inflation;
- monetary policy from being discretionary;
- the policymaker acting as a lender of last resort.

It must be noted that proponents of currency boards like Hanke, Jonung and Schuler (1993) consider that they can only foster growth if they are a part of a wider package of economic reforms. They consider that currency boards cannot promote economic recovery if other policies are inappropriate.

Critics of currency boards, such as Schwartz (1993) and Roubini (1998), consider that they cannot provide stability even if other economic policies are fine. In their view, currency boards do not prevent speculative attacks. The events in Argentina in 1995 and in Hong Kong in 1997 show that their existence does not dissuade speculators from launching attacks. In both cases the countries withstood speculative pressures, though more as the result of rises in interest rates that they were willing to make than thanks to the existence of a currency board. But such hikes in interest rates made it hard for firms to repay their loans, thus making many financial institutions and banks go bankrupt. This is to some extent the outline of the Argentinian crisis that culminated at the end of 2001.

Another criticism against currency boards lies at the heart of their existence. As has already been mentioned, they are said to suppress the dynamic inconsistency of monetary policy. Critics of currency boards consider this argument to be a fallacy. When the government creates the currency board, it prevents the Central Bank from running monetary policy but does not abolish the dynamic inconsistency problem. Instead dynamic inconsistency falls upon the government itself: it creates the currency board and may then abolish it when it sees fit. The government may decide to act as a lender of last resort under popular pressure, by bailing out banks for instance. It thereby restores a power that is supposed to disappear with the establishment of the currency board.

It is still unclear whether currency boards may provide monetary stability more efficiently than banks. In this respect the wager between K. Schuler and and W. Salater comparing the performance of several central bank and currency board-like systems regarding several criteria over the period 2001–2005 is of the utmost interest: it should help determine whether countries in transition that have adopted currency boards made the right decision.[2] As can be seen, currency boards do not seem to offer an efficient protection against speculative attacks. But it is unclear whether there is an exchange rate regime that deters currency crises more efficiently than others.

2. CURRENCY CRISES AND THE OPTIMAL EXCHANGE RATE REGIME

Drawing on Cukierman, Goldstein and Spiegel (2002), the relationship between the exchange rate regimes and the outbreak of speculative attacks is investigated. It is assumed that the policymaker dislikes nominal exchange rate uncertainty. The rationale for this hypothesis is of a public-choice type. While the policymaker seeks re-election, business lobbies that influence his electoral platform face losses resulting from exchange rate variations. They want to reduce risk uncertainty about the nominal exchange rate and give incentives to the policymaker to prevent a float.

Initially the policymaker sets an exchange rate band $[\underline{s}\,;\overline{s}\,]$ around the pre-existing nominal exchange rate s_{t-1}. The nominal exchange rate s_t is allowed to move freely within the band in accordance with market forces. If the nominal exchange rate reaches the boundaries of the band, the policymaker is committed to intervene and keep it from moving outside the band. The exchange rate band thus defines a interval of changes in the exchange rate $[\underline{e}\,;\overline{e}\,]$, such that $\underline{e}<0$ and $\overline{e}>0$ with:

$$\underline{e}=\underline{s}-s_{t-1} \tag{11.1}$$

and:

$$\overline{e}=\overline{s}-s_{t-1} \tag{11.2}$$

Denoting Δs_t the change in the exchange rate that equals $s_t- s_{t-1}$ under laissez-faire, the domestic currency:

- appreciates if $\Delta s_t \in [\underline{e};0[$, where $\underline{e}$ is the maximal rate of appreciation;
- depreciates if $\Delta s_t \in [0;\overline{e}]$, where $\overline{e}$ is the maximal rate of depreciation.

The policymaker faces a tradeoff between nominal exchange rate uncertainty and the cost of adopting a band. He has the following loss function:

$$L_t = -\psi E_t(e) - E_t[\text{Min } g(\Delta s_t, \alpha), C] \quad (11.3)$$

where ψ is the parameter that measures the policymaker's aversion to nominal exchange rate uncertainty, with $\psi \in \Re^+$, e the actual change in the exchange rate, C the costs of leaving the exchange rate band, α the fraction of speculators that attack the band, and $g(.)$ the function that assesses the policymaker's costs of intervention on the foreign exchange market with:

- if $\Delta s_t \geq \overline{e}$, then $g(\Delta s_t, \alpha) = \Delta s_t - \overline{e} + \alpha$;
- if $\underline{e} \leq \Delta s_t \leq \overline{e}$, then $g(\Delta s_t, \alpha) = 0$;
- if $\Delta s_t \leq \underline{e}$, then $g(\Delta s_t, \alpha) = \underline{e} - \Delta s_t + \alpha$.

The first component of L_t represents the policymaker's aversion to variations in the nominal exchange rate. The second component is the cost of adopting an exchange rate band. This cost either equals $g(\Delta s_t, \alpha)$ if the policymaker defends the band, or C if he does not. In the latter case, the exchange rate is realigned.

There is a continuum of speculators whose number is normalised to one. When the exchange rate reaches the upper or lower boundaries of the band, each speculator observes independently a noisy signal on the exchange rate that should prevail under laissez faire. The signal observed by speculator k is assumed to be:

$$x_k = \Delta s_t + \eta_k \quad (11.4)$$

where η_k is a white noise, independent among speculators and distributed uniformly on the interval $[-\eta;+\eta]$.

Based on x_k, each speculator k decides whether or not to attack the currency. For simplicity it is assumed that speculators will always attack the band if they believe that Δs_t is such that the policymaker will get rid of the band.

If the exchange rate s_t is at the high price of $\underline{s}$, speculators can short-sell the currency and buy the same amount on the market to clear their position. If the exchange is at the upper bound of the band, speculators can buy the foreign currency at price $\overline{s}$. Denoting cs the nominal transaction cost associated with switching between currencies, speculators' payoffs may be determined, as shown in Table 11.1.

Table 11.1 The speculators' payoffs following the policymaker's successful or failed defence of the band

	The policymaker fails to defend the band	The policymaker manages defend the band
Attack on the lower bound of the band	$\underline{s}-s_t-cs$	$-cs$
Attack on the upper bound of the band	$s_t-\overline{s}-cs$	$-cs$
No attack	0	0

In this framework, the time line of events is:

1. The policymaker determines a band around the existing nominal exchange rate s_t. He is committed to intervene on the foreign exchange market when $\Delta s_t<\underline{e}$ or $\Delta s_t>\overline{e}$.

2. The 'free float' change in the exchange rate is realised and persists over the remaining stages of the game. There are now two possible cases.
   a. If $\underline{e}\leq\Delta s_t\leq\overline{e}$, the nominal exchange rate is allowed to move freely within the boundaries of the band, and is determined by market forces. Since Δs_t persists, the exchange rate immediately adjusts to $(1+\Delta s_t)\,s_{t-1}$ and remains at this value for the remainder of the period.
   b. If $\Delta s_t<\underline{e}$ or $\Delta s_t>\overline{e}$, the policymaker intervenes in the exchange market and keeps the exchange rate from moving outside the band. As a result the exchange rate is either at the upper or at the lower bound of the band. Simultaneously each speculator gets the signal x_k on Δs_t and decides whether or not to attack the currency. Those decisions determine the fraction α of speculators who launch an attack against the band.

3. The policymaker observes Δs_t and α. He evaluates the total cost of continuing to defend the band. If he keeps on defending the band, the exchange rate stays at the boundary of the band and he incurs the cost $g(\Delta s_t, \alpha)$. If the policymaker gets rid of the band and there is realignment, the exchange rate moves to its freely floating rate: the rate of change in the exchange rate is worth Δs_t while the policymaker incurs a future credibility loss, the present value of which is C.

In this framework, Cukierman, Goldstein and Spiegel (2002) show that the exchange rate band gives rise to two 'Ranges of Effective Commitment' (RECs) such that the policymaker defends the band only if x falls inside one of these ranges.

There is a positive REC, $[\bar{e}\,;\bar{e}+\rho]$, and a negative REC, $[\underline{e}-\rho\,;\underline{e}]$, where ρ is the width of the RECs that equals:

$$\rho=\sqrt{\frac{cs}{s_{t-1}}+\frac{(C-1)^2}{4}}+\frac{C-1}{2} \tag{11.5}$$

The two RECs are such that:

- When Δs_t falls inside the positive REC, the policymaker defends the currency and ensures that the rate of depreciation is not larger than $\bar{e}$.
- When Δs_t falls inside the negative REC, the policymaker defends the currency and ensures that the rate of appreciation is not larger in absolute value than $\underline{e}$.
- When Δs_t falls below the negative REC, above the positive REC, or inside the band, the policymaker lets the exchange rate move freely in accordance with market forces.
- The width of the RECs, denoted ρ, increases with cs and with C, but is independent of $\underline{e}$ and $\bar{e}$ that define the boundaries of the band.

The policymaker's choice of the band width may now be determined. It is assumed that:

- the value of Δs_t is drawn from a distribution function $f(\Delta s_t)$ on $\Re$ with cumulative distribution function (c.d.f) $F(\Delta s_t)$;
- $f(\Delta s_t)$ is unimodal with a mode at $\Delta s_t=0$, that is $f(\Delta s_t)$ is increasing for all $\Delta s_t<0$ and decreasing for all $\Delta s_t>0$.

The policymaker's expected payoff is computed and given in the appendix to this chapter. It is possible to determine the boundaries of the band, $\underline{e}$ and $\bar{e}$, with respect to the policymaker's aversion to nominal exchange rate uncertainty.

In equilibrium, the exchange rate band has the following properties:

- If $\psi\leq 1$, then $\underline{e}=-\infty$ and $\bar{e}=+\infty$, so the optimal regime is a free float. When the policymaker is not too concerned with nominal exchange rate variability, that is $\psi\leq 1$, he sets a free float and avoids the cost of maintaining a band.
- The band is nondegenerate if:

$$1<\psi<\underline{\psi}(-\rho)\equiv 1+C\Big/\int_{-\rho}^{0}\left[\frac{f(\Delta s_t)}{f(-\rho)}-1\right]d\Delta s_t \tag{11.6}$$

then $-\infty<\underline{e}<0$. Likewise if:

$$1<\psi<\bar{\psi}(\rho)\equiv 1+C\Big/\int_0^{\rho}\left[1+\frac{f(\Delta s_t)}{f(\rho(}\right]d\Delta s_t \qquad (11.7)$$

then $0<\bar{e}<+\infty$. In intermediate cases, the policymaker balances his two objectives, i.e., limiting exchange rate uncertainty and minimising the cost of intervention by setting a nondegenerate band. Intervention occurs only when Δs_t falls inside the negative or the positive RECs.

- If V is concave in $\underline{e}$ and in $\bar{e}$, and if the policymaker is sufficiently concerned with nominal exchange rate variability:

$$\psi>\text{Max}\{\underline{\psi}(-\rho), \psi(\rho)\} \qquad (11.8)$$

then $\underline{e}=\bar{e}=0$: the optimal regime is a peg.

- If $f(x)$ is symmetric around 0, so that $f(-\Delta s_t)=f(\Delta s_t)$ for all Δs_t, the band is symmetric around 0 in the sense that $-\underline{e}=\bar{e}$. A sufficient condition for the band to be symmetric is that the distribution of shocks $f(x)$ is symmetric around 0, that is depreciations and appreciations are equally likely under laissez faire.

Let us focus on the case in which the policymaker's problem has a unique interior solution, that is $-\infty<\underline{e}<0<\bar{e}<+\infty$. In this situation ψ is above 1, but not by 'too much'. And as the policymaker becomes more concerned with exchange rate uncertainty, that is as ψ increases:

- $\underline{e}$ and $\bar{e}$ shift closer to 0 so that the band tightens;
- the probability that a speculative attack occurs increases.

These results imply that the policymaker sets a tighter band, and thereby allows the exchange rate to move freely within a narrower range around the centre rate, as he becomes more concerned with exchange rate stability. They also show that the tightening of the band raises the likelihood of a speculative attack. Hence when ψ increases, the policymaker is willing to set a tighter band despite the fact that it makes speculative attacks more likely.

All in all it seems that the choice of the exchange rate regime depends on the policymaker's aversion to nominal exchange rate uncertainty that is influenced by the sensitivities of lobbies to exchange rate risk. Policymakers and lobbies of a key currency country are less sensitive to nominal exchange rate variations than policymakers and lobbies of smaller countries. Cukierman, Goldstein and Spiegel (2002) thus explain why the USA, Japan, and the euro area have flexible exchange rates while emerging and developing countries, e.g., East Asian and Latin American countries, establish pegs, currency boards, or dollarise their economy.

3. CONCLUSION

This chapter provides an overview of the features of exchange rate regimes and discusses whether they are able to deter speculative attacks. It also analyses how the choice of the exchange rate regime may influence the outbreak of currency crises.

Many recent studies deal with exchange rate regimes, especially in the context of emerging countries where most of the 1990s currency crises took place. In these countries fixed exchange rates did not seem appropriate since they did not provide a discipline for policymakers that compelled them to conduct strict macroeconomic policies.

Super fixed exchange rate regimes appear at odds with the macroeconomic situation of a country that is subjected to speculative pressures, or that has just undergone an attack. Flexible exchange rate regimes are risky, but this risk may provide policymakers with incentives to conduct strict policies in order to prevent the outbreak of currency crises.

4. APPENDIX

This Appendix provides additional elements related to the study of Cukierman, Goldstein and Spiegel (2002) which is discussed in Section 2 of this chapter.

The expected payoff of the policymaker, given $\underline{e}$ and $\overline{e}$, is:

$$
\begin{aligned}
L_t = \psi [& \int_{-\infty}^{\underline{e}-\rho} \Delta s_t f(\Delta s_t) d(\Delta s_t) + \int_{\underline{e}-\rho}^{\underline{e}} \underline{e} f(\Delta s_t) d(\Delta s_t) + \int_{\underline{e}}^{0} \Delta s_t f(\Delta s_t) d(\Delta s_t) \\
& - \int_{0}^{\overline{e}} \Delta s_t f(\Delta s_t) d(\Delta s_t) - \int_{\overline{e}}^{\overline{e}+\rho} \overline{e} f(\Delta s_t) d(\Delta s_t) - \int_{\overline{e}+\rho}^{+\infty} \Delta s_t f(\Delta s_t) d(\Delta s_t)] \\
& - \int_{-\infty}^{\underline{e}-\rho} C f(\Delta s_t) d(\Delta s_t) - \int_{\underline{e}-\rho}^{\underline{e}} (\underline{e} - \Delta s_t) f(\Delta s_t) d(\Delta s_t) \\
& - \int_{\underline{e}-r}^{\overline{e}} (\Delta s_t - \overline{e}) f(\Delta s_t) d(\Delta s_t) - \int_{\overline{e}+r}^{+\infty} C (\Delta s_t) d(\Delta s_t)
\end{aligned}
\tag{11.9}
$$

The term in brackets represents the policymaker's loss from exchange rate uncertainty while the last line represents the expected cost of adopting a band.

The policymaker chooses the boundaries of the band, $\underline{e}$ and $\overline{e}$, so as to maximise his expected payoff. The first-order conditions for an interior solution to the policymaker's problem (that is $-\infty < \underline{e} < 0 < \overline{e} < +\infty$) are :

$$\frac{\partial L_t}{\partial \underline{e}} = -\,[\rho(\psi\text{-}1)+C]f(\underline{e}\text{-}\rho)+(\psi\text{-}1)+\int_{\underline{e}-\rho}^{\underline{e}} f(\Delta s_t)d(\Delta s_t)$$

$$=\psi\int_{\underline{e}-\rho}^{\underline{e}}[f(\Delta s_t)\text{-}f(\underline{e}\text{-}\rho)]\,d(\Delta s_t)\text{-}[\int_{\underline{e}-\rho}^{\underline{e}}[f(\Delta s_t)\text{-}f(\underline{e}\text{-}\rho)]\,d(\Delta s_t)+C.f(\underline{e}\text{-}\rho)]=0 \qquad (11.10)$$

and

$$\frac{\partial L_t}{\partial \overline{e}} = \text{-}[\rho(\psi\text{-}1)+C]f(\overline{e}+r)+(\psi\text{-}1)+\int_{\overline{e}}^{\overline{e}+\rho} f(\Delta s_t)\,d(\Delta s_t)$$

$$=\text{-}\psi\int_{\overline{e}}^{\overline{e}+\rho}[f(\Delta s_t)\text{-}f(\overline{e}+\rho)]d(\Delta s_t)\text{-}[\int_{\overline{e}}^{\overline{e}+\rho}[f(\Delta s_t)\text{-}f(\overline{e}+\rho)]d(\Delta s_t)+ C.f(\overline{e}+\rho)]=0 \qquad (11.11)$$

Equations (11.10) and (11.11) show that by altering the bounds of the band, policymakers move along a tradeoff between reduction of exchange rate uncertainty and minimisation of the costs of maintaining a band.

NOTES

1. It must also be noted that a monetary union may be seen as a form of 'dollarisation' since countries adopt a new currency instead of adopting an already existing currency of a foreign country. In the case of the single currency of the European Monetary Union, it could have been said that there was a 'euroisation'.
2. On the central banking vs. currency boards wager between K. Schuler and W. Salater, see Kurt Schuler's webpage at dollarization.org. On the currency boards that operate at present, see Sevic (2002).

12. The Role of International Financial Institutions

International financial institutions (IFIs) argue that they can restrain crises, and even prevent them. They assert that they compensate for the weaknesses of domestic monetary authorities. They provide guarantees on the stability of the international financial system. The high number of institutions is said to demonstrate their ability to solve the problems faced by countries. The International Monetary Fund (IMF) manages public funds in developed and developing countries alike. The World Bank focuses on the alleviation of poverty in developing countries by providing resources, technical assistance and policy advice to domestic policymakers.[1]

In the wake of every crisis, IFIs come under attack and are accused of mismanaging countries. For instance Meltzer (2000, p.6) considers that the IMF 'gave too little attention to improving financial structures in developing countries and too much to expensive rescue operations'. Some economists, such as Radelet and Sachs (1998a) and Schwartz (1998), went as far as demanding their termination, after the East Asian crisis. Criticisms against IFIs fall into three categories: their methods of crisis prevention are inefficient; their economic policies and their management of countries are inappropriate; the principles that govern their existence and their actions are questionable since they imply moral hazard.

1. CRISIS PREVENTION

IFIs acknowledge that they had not foreseen the magnitude of the crisis triggered by the collapse of the Thai baht, but consider that they had anticipated the financial disaster that threatened Thailand. The IMF states that it had engaged a dialogue with Thai authorities at the beginning of 1996 during which they suggested that radical reforms should be implemented.[2] Furthermore the IMF advises governments but cannot compel them to follow its recommendations as long as there is no crisis. It cannot voice its concerns over the financial and macroeconomic situation of a given country since this may trigger the very crisis it aims at avoiding.

Such a defence of IFIs, which is used by Krueger (2000), is quite shrewd. But it has weaknesses. If the IMF admits that it had not forecasted the magnitude and the spread of the crisis in East Asia before July 1997, it seems that it had not updated its forecast after the fall of the baht. The IMF 1997 Annual Report of the Executive Board (International Monetary Fund, 1997) published on 1 October of that year, states that '[IMF] Directors welcomed Korea's continued impressive macroeconomic performance' (p. 59) and 'praised the authorities for their enviable fiscal record' (p.60). Hence just two months before the fall of the won, the IMF 1997 Annual Report only suggested that some financial reforms be implemented. It does not mention that the Korean conglomerates had been facing financial difficulties since 1996 or that financial market regulations prevented an effective allocation of capitals. The IMF started dealing with these problems after the collapse of the won.

Similar criticisms are levelled against the IMF in the wake of the Russian and Brazilian crises. In both cases, the IMF is said not to have acted in the best of the countries' interests. Desai (2000) believes that the policy against inflation led in Russia by the IMF was at odds with the fiscal situation of the Russian government, which was not able to collect taxes efficiently. In addition, repeated announcements of exchange rate stabilisation made by the IMF and the Russian government quickened the fall of the Russian ruble by entailing multiple equilibria on the foreign exchange market. The IMF policies in Brazil were also extremely questionable. It initially supported the government in its maintaining the crawling peg. It then approved the governmental decision to let the exchange rate go in January 1999.

All in all it seems that the IMF and other international financial institutions alike were unable to prevent crises in the 1990s. They belatedly discovered the economic difficulties of East Asian countries, and their policies prior to the Russian and the Brazilian crises lacked consistency.

2. CONTROVERSIAL RESPONSE PROGRAMMES TO CRISES

Various criticisms are levelled against the implementation of economic policies led by IFIs in countries hit by crises. They are said to ignore the social consequences of the crises, especially in East Asia. They are also accused of leading inappropriate economic policies that do not really address the real causes of the crises, particularly the private sector's debt.

2.1. Some Facts on IFIs' Rescue Programmes

Lane, Ghosh, Hamann, Philipps, Schulze-Ghattas and Tsikata (1999) provide a rationale for IFIs' actions during the 1990s.[3] They consider that the financial and economic stabilisation of emerging countries hit by a crisis implies some austerity measures. There must be structural reforms, as well as official financial lending designed to keep countries solvent. Tables 12.1 and 12.2 provide examples of international financial institutions' programmes in three East Asian countries, Indonesia, South Korea and Thailand.

Table 12.1 IFIs' funding in Indonesia, South Korea and Thailand in the wake of the crises (in billion US dollars)

	IMF	World Bank and Asian Bank for Development	Other sources	Total
Indonesia	11.2	10.0	21.1	42.3
South Korea	20.9	14.0	23.3	58.2
Thailand	4.0	2.7	10.5	17.2
Total	36.1	26.7	54.9	117.7

Source: International Monetary Fund (1998b).

Interest rate policies are probably the most controversial aspect of IFIs' response programmes to crises. In the short run, some consider that hikes in interest rates do not prevent devaluations but increase the magnitude of crises by provoking bankruptcies. There is a credit crunch, i.e., a contraction in the supply of credit that makes firms, which would otherwise be solvent, go bankrupt.[4] The general decrease in profitability increases the number of loans that are not reimbursed. The economic situation worsens and another contraction in credit ensues.

Others believe that expansionary monetary policies and low interest rates are not an appropriate response to crises. In the case of the East Asian crisis, restrictive policies would have led to an increase in the foreign-currency denominated debt of domestic banks and corporations that would have brought about a new round of devaluation.

The optimal monetary policy in the wake of a crisis in these countries should depend on the degree of overvaluation of the currency, on the level of public and private debt which may be either domestic- or foreign-currency denominated, and on the strengths and weaknesses of the industrial and financial domestic sectors. Optimality in matters of monetary policy in the wake of the East Asian crisis is the focus of differing analyses by Furman and Stiglitz (1998), Radelet and Sachs (1998a, 1998b) and Corsetti, Pesenti and Roubini (1999a, 1999b).[5]

Table 12.2 Structural reforms impelled by IFIs in Indonesia, South Korea and Thailand

	Indonesia	South Korea	Thailand
Domestic trade	Termination of monopolies on food and wood distribution		
Foreign trade	Decrease in custom rights on goods and industrial products	Alignment of import certificates on international norms	
	Termination of quotas	Allowing foreigners to trade on financial and real instate markets	
Fiscal reforms	Termination of subsidies and hikes in prices of gas, electricity, sugar and other products	Revision and rationalisation of the subsidy programme	
	Termination of fiscal and commercial advantages granted to the domestic aeronautic and car ventures		
Privatisation	Privatisation of state firms in the mid-term	Privatisation of state firms	Privatisation of state firms in rail, energy, telecommunication and water

Source: World Bank (1998)

Monetary policy in East Asia is not the only difficulty faced by IFIs, especially by the IMF. The latter must also deal with the debt of the private sector. In that case, policies combining financial orthodoxy with strict fiscal policies may not be appropriate, though they fit countries with debt problems, e.g., Brazil and Russia.

A leading critic of IMF policies is the former World Bank Chief Economist, Joseph Stiglitz (Stiglitz, 2002). He considers that the IMF mismanaged the consequences of the 1990s currency crises in emerging countries by forbidding them to finance their needs by borrowing. But as Kenneth Rogoff, the 2001 appointed IMF Chief Economist notes (Rogoff, 2002), evidence from the 1990s crises suggests that countries which increased their sovereign debt did not improve their macroeconomic situation. In addition, Radelet and Sachs (1998a, 1998b) consider that the inconsistent economic programmes of all the IFIs are at the root of the bank runs which took place in Indonesia in September 1997 and in Japan one year later. This view goes too far. These two countries did not implement the IMF plans designed to prevent banking panics. South Korea and Thailand implemented them and did not suffer from bank runs.

As can be seen, IMF policies may not be as inefficient as its critics say.[6] This may well justify the case for official lending to currency-crisis-prone countries in times of speculative pressures.

2.2. Pros and Cons of Official Lending

Bordo and Schwartz (1997) analyse the effects of bailouts in the wake of crises. They consider that some countries fared better without bailouts than others that were granted rescue packages. Their observations indicate that rescue packages may have counterproductive liquidity effects. Official lending may lead investors to massively leave a country by financing a run. Yet Meltzer (2000) considers that the IMF should lend to countries when they experience short-term liquidity problems.

This subsection investigates the official lending strategy by drawing on Zettelmeyer (2000). The exchange rate of one country is pegged to the US dollar at rate 1 and it is assumed that there are N investors. Each investor owns a unit of a domestic currency denominated asset. Domestic fundamentals, denoted ψ, may either be good or bad, and are respectively denoted G and B. A currency crisis is defined as a shift from the peg to a flexible exchange rate system that is caused by a run on the policymaker's foreign exchange reserves.

The time line of events is as follows:

- At time 0, investors learn the state of fundamentals ψ and the level of reserves $\underline{r}$;
- At time 1, investors may choose to leave the domestic market. They liquidate early and convert their domestic asset into dollars. A currency crisis ensues if $n>\underline{r}$, where n is the number of investors leaving the market, with $n\in[0;N]$.

In this framework, the *k*th speculator's payoffs per unit of investment are given in Table 12.3.

Table 12.3 The kth *speculator's payoffs per unit of investment*

	Investor leaves the market	Investor remains in the market
No crisis	$1\text{-}cs$	$\rho^{k}_{\psi,\text{Flex}}$
Crisis	$(\underline{r}/n)+(1-\underline{r}/n)/s_{\text{Flex}}-cs$	$\rho^{k}_{\psi,\text{Fix}}$

Here cs is the early fixed liquidation cost and s_{Flex} the flexible exchange rate that prevails after the currency crisis. The variables $\rho^{k}_{\psi,\text{Flex}}$ and $\rho^{k}_{\psi,\text{Fix}}$ represent gross returns under the flexible and fixed exchange rate systems, that is in the non-crisis and crisis cases, depending on the state of fundamentals ψ.

Several assumptions are laid out:

- The investment is assumed to be a sunk cost:

$$\rho^{k}_{\psi,\text{Flex}} \geq 0 \qquad (12.1)$$

- All investors know that leaving the domestic market is the best response, depending on the state of fundamentals but also on the total number of investors exiting:

$$cs-s_{Flex}< \rho^{k}_{\psi,\text{Flex}} \qquad (12.2)$$

- There are two kinds of investors with different market strategies. There are N_1 type-1 investors who are such that:

$$\rho^{1}_{\psi,\text{Flex}} <1$$

$$\rho^{1}_{\psi,\text{Fix}} >1$$

$$cs=0$$

There are N_2 type-2 investors who are such that:

$$\rho^2_{B,j} < 1\text{-}cs$$
$$\rho^2_{G,j} > 1\text{-}cs$$
$$cs \geq 0$$

with j=Fix,Flex denoting the exchange rate system that prevails.

Here type-1 investors do not face early liquidation costs while type-2 ones do. Type-1 investors care more about potential devaluations than about the state of fundamentals. Conversely the market strategy of type-2 investors hinges more on the state of fundamentals than on the exchange rate regime.

The equilibrium outflows that depend on the state of fundamentals are now characterised. Let n_1 and n_2 be the number of type-1 and type-2 investors that leave the market such that $n \equiv n_1 + n_2$.

Table 12.4 sums up the results if the state of fundamentals is good.

Table 12.4 Investors' behaviour when fundamentals are good

	Type-1 investors	Type-2 investors
No crisis	No exit: $n_1=0$	No exit: $n_2=0$
Crisis	Exiting may be the best response: $n_1=\underline{r}\alpha_G^1$ (see below for an explanation)	No exit: $n_2=0$

If there is a crisis, type-1 investors may find it optimal to leave the domestic market, that is to obtain foreign exchange at rate $s_{Fix}=1$. Such a strategy obviously hinges on the amount $\underline{r}$ of foreign exchange reserves that the policymaker has, and on the number n_1 of type-1 investors exiting. It is optimal for speculators to leave if:

$$(\underline{r}/n_1)+(1-\underline{r}/n_1)s_{\text{Flex}} \geq \rho^1_{G,\text{Flex}} \tag{12.3}$$

Condition (12.3) may be rewritten as:

$$\underline{r} \geq n_1\, \alpha^1_G \tag{12.4}$$

with $\alpha^1_G \equiv \dfrac{s_{\text{Flex}} - \rho^1_{G,\text{Flex}}}{s_{\text{Flex}} - 1}$.

The number of type-1 investors that leave the market becomes:

$$n_1 = \underline{r}\,\alpha_G^1 \qquad (12.5)$$

From equation (12.5), it is clear that the higher the amount of reserves, the higher the number of type-1 investors exiting.

If the state of fundamentals is bad, the behaviour of type-1 investors is similar to the case with good fundamentals. The strategy of type-2 investors is different. If the fixed exchange rate system is maintained, they will want to leave the domestic market. If a float happens, they incur losses either by remaining on the domestic market though fundamentals are bad, or by liquidating their assets at the flexible exchange rate.

Hence different situations may be distinguished:

- If $\underline{r} \geq N_2$, no type-1 investor leaves the domestic market while all type-2 investors exit. The peg is maintained;
- if $\underline{r} < N_1 + N_2$, there is a shift to a flexible exchange rate system. The number of investors leaving the domestic market depends on the amount of foreign exchange reserves. If type-1 and type-2 investors have the same opportunity costs, that is if:

$$\rho_{B,\text{Flex}}^1 = \rho_{B,\text{Flex}}^2 + cs \qquad (12.6)$$

the results are similar to those with 'good fundamentals', except that they are now extended to all the investors.[7]

Now it is possible to deal with the effects of financial assistance by an IFI, that is to see whether or not an increase in the level of reserves triggers a currency crisis. It seems that official lending:

- does not trigger currency crises, but
- increases the number of investors who leave the domestic market when a crisis occurs.

Speculative attacks cannot be averted by a rise in reserves or triggered by a decrease in reserves, because movements in foreign reserves are unable to trigger a switch from a fixed exchange rate equilibrium to a crisis equilibrium, at least in the framework of Zettelmeyer (2000).[8] Such mixed results on the effects of official lending raise questions on the need for an international lender of last resort.

3. THE INTERNATIONAL LENDER OF LAST RESORT

Following the 1990s crises, many studies tried to reconsider the role of IFIs. While some called for their suppression, others suggested that there should be an international lender of last resort (ILLR). Fischer (1999) considers that this role falls on the IMF which should then aim at preventing both governments and financial institutions from being illiquid.

The doctrine of the lender of last resort was elaborated by Thornton (1802) and Bagehot (1873). They considered that the Central Bank may be allowed to lend under certain conditions to illiquid but solvent banks. Bordo (1990), Kaufman (1991) and Schwartz (1998) consider that the theory of lender of last resort of Thornton (1802) and Bagehot (1873) is irrelevant nowadays since efficient interbank markets prevent solvent banks from being illiquid. Interventions on aggregate liquidity (monetary policy) may be warranted but individual interventions (banking policy) are not any more. Rochet and Vives (2002) believe that the ideas of Thorton (1802) and Bagehot (1873) may still be valid, even with efficient interbank markets. However it is unclear whether an ILLR may be established nowadays, and what its task would be.

The existence and interventions of an ILLR raise theoretical and practical difficulties. An ILLR is said to create moral hazard. Creditors and borrowers are given incentives to undertake risky financial operations since they know they will be bailed out by the ILLR should a crisis occur. It is indeed likely that the significant capital inflows in East Asia in the second half of 1995 are related to expectations of a possible international bailout, as in the wake of the December 1994 Mexican crisis. Sachs (1995) notices that the Mexican crisis led the IMF to break its own rules. It granted Mexico a loan worth seven times its quota. There may be grounds for questioning the existence of an institution that does not abide by its own regulations if it believes it to be necessary.[9]

Chang and Velasco (1998) consider that crises occurred before any international financial institution ever existed. Moral hazard cannot therefore be a relevant argument. They consider that the existence of an ILLR would guarantee the stability of the international financial system. Chari and Kehoe (1998) hold the opposite view and believe that an ILLR is likely to be inefficient.

A model for the ILLR may be presented by drawing on Goodhart and Huang (2000). In a framework which builds on Diamond and Dybvig (1983), they consider J open economies. Each economy has two depositors whose financial capacity is normalised to 1: one is domestic, the other international. The time line of events is as follows:

- At time $t=0$, each depositor invests in the economy an amount I_0 that is normalised to 1.
- At time $t=1$, type-1 depositors have access to an unverifiable trading opportunity of gross return B_1, provided they invest an amount I_1 in this new project, with $I_1>I_0$.
- At time $t=2$, type-2 depositors have access to an unverifiable trading opportunity of gross return B_2, provided they invest an amount I_2 in this new project, with $I_2>I_0$.

Each country has one private bank and one Central Bank. Each bank invests the deposits it receives in a project that is partially illiquid. The return Z_t, $t=1,2$, is fully liquid at time $t=1$ but is not at time $t=2$. If a run does not compel the bank to liquidate all its assets at $t=1$, then the bank generates additional liquidity beyond Z_1 until date $t=2$ to obtain an amount worth γZ_2, with $\gamma<0$.

The Central Bank's objective is to maintain a fixed exchange rate that is initially pegged at rate 1. Let f_t and r_t be respectively the capital outflows and the policymaker's foreign exchange rate reserves at time t. If:

$$f_t < r_t \tag{12.7}$$

the Central Bank keeps the exchange rate fixed. If condition (12.7) is not satisfied, there is a currency crisis in the country.

Some additional assumptions on the features of each economy must be made:

- Z_1 is fully liquid but Z_2 remains illiquid until time period $t=2$.
- Any liquidation of the remaining investment at time $t=1$ only generates $\gamma<1$ for each unit of foreign currency invested.
- If there is a currency crisis, the currency is devalued by δ, with $\delta<1$; the domestic return is $\gamma\delta$, whereas the foreign currency return is γ.
- The liquidity shock is derived from depositors' outside investment opportunities, rather than from shocks on their preferences.
- A self-fulfilling rational bank run can break out at time $t=1$.
- The existence of foreign investors makes it possible that a bank run becomes a currency crisis that may be propagated across countries.

Several cases need to be distinguished, depending on the existence of liquidity shocks, interbank markets and an ILLR.

1. No liquidity shock.

In this situation, banks do not face any uncertainty on their investment. There is perfect competition between banks, that is between countries, for deposits. The optimal deposits contract is:

$\rho_1=1$
$\rho_2=Z_1+Z_2-1$

2. Potential liquidity shocks.

In this situation, bank runs are possible. It is assumed that:

$(Z_1,Z_2)=(\bar{Z}_1, \bar{Z}_2)$ with probability μ
$(Z_1,Z_2)=(\underline{Z}_1, \underline{Z}_2)$ with probability $1-\mu$

with:

$\underline{Z}_1 <1 < \bar{Z}_1$
$1 <\underline{Z}_2< \bar{Z}_2$
$\underline{Z}_1+\underline{Z}_2 > 2$

There is a probability μ that the optimal contract of case 1 holds:

$\rho_1=1$
$\rho_2=Z_1+Z_2-1$

However there is a probability $1-\mu$ that type-1 depositors will not be able to withdraw their deposits at time $t=1$. If:

$$(1-\alpha)\underline{Z}_2\leq 1 \qquad (12.8)$$

with:

$$\underline{Z}_1+\alpha\gamma\delta\underline{Z}_2=1 \qquad (12.9)$$

the bank must have to liquidate a share α of its investment at time 1 to meet the demand withdrawal for type-1 depositors. The heavy discount factor γ, with $\gamma<1$, may make the required portion for liquidation α so large that there is nothing left for type-2 depositors. Type-2 depositors thus have incentives to withdraw at date 1 as well.

This bank run only occurs because there are foreign investors. They trigger a panic because they believe that the Central Bank does not own enough foreign exchange reserves to convert their deposits into foreign currency. Had there only been domestic depositors, the Central Bank might have been able to prevent a panic by lending $1\text{-}\underline{Z}_1$ to the commercial banks, while expecting a reimbursement of $\underline{Z}_2$, with $\underline{Z}_1<1$ and $\underline{Z}_2>1$.

Hence with no international interbank market or an ILLR, there is a probability $1\text{-}\mu$ that a bank run and a currency crisis occur.

3. Potential liquidity shocks and lending through an international interbank market.

It is assumed that there is an international interbank market that links the J banks of the N countries in order to provide liquidity if need be. There are also M banks, that is M countries, that face a liquidity shock, while the remaining $J\text{-}M$ banks do not, with $M<J$.

In this situation, these M banks face liquidity shocks and are unable to meet the international depositors' withdrawals at time $t=1$. Still their returns have not been changed and they face the following liquidity shock:

$$(Z_1, Z\text{-}Z_1) \tag{12.10}$$

with:

$$\underline{Z}_1<1<Z\text{-}\underline{Z}_1$$
$$\underline{Z}_1+\underline{Z}_1>2$$

The remaining $J\text{-}M$ banks face liquidity constraints and their returns are:

$$(Z_1, Z\text{-}Z_1) \tag{12.11}$$

with:

$$\underline{Z}_1>1$$
$$Z=\underline{Z}_1+\underline{Z}_2>2$$

Here the M banks have incentives to borrow from the $J\text{-}M$ other banks in order to meet withdrawals at time $t=1$ and avoid bankruptcy. They may be able to borrow if:

$$M\underline{Z}_1+(J\text{-}M)Z_1\geq J \tag{12.12}$$

If condition (12.12) holds, there is enough liquidity in the interbank system to rescue illiquid banks. If it is not satisfied, some countries may face currency crises and bank runs.

When one bank fails to meet its withdrawals at time $t=1$ such that:

$$\underline{Z}_1+\alpha\gamma\delta(Z-\underline{Z}_1)=1$$
$$(1-\alpha)(Z-\underline{Z}_1)\leq 1$$

then depositors and banks in the J countries know that the international interbank market cannot provide liquidity at time $t=1$. Type-2 depositors launch bank runs and currency crises.

Comparing Cases 2 and 3 allows the probability of an international banking crisis to be evaluated. If there is no international interbank market as in Case 2, the crisis occurs with probability:

$$\phi\equiv(1-\rho)^J \tag{12.13}$$

If there is an international interbank market as in Case 3, the crisis occurs with probability:

$$\omega\equiv\sum_{i=1}^{M^*}\binom{J}{i}\mu^i(1-\mu)^{J-i} \tag{12.14}$$

with M^* being the largest integer satisfying:

$$M^*\underline{Z}_1+(J-M^*)Z_1<J \tag{12.15}$$

As J grows and μ decreases, $\omega>\phi$. The collapse of the whole international interbank system is more likely to happen than when each bank acts separately.

4. The role of an ILLR in a framework with potential liquidity shocks with lending by an international interbank market.

Building on Case 2, and assuming condition (12.12), the total liquidity L needed in the system is:

$$L\equiv J-[M\underline{Z}_1+(J-M)Z_1] \tag{12.16}$$

Building on Case 3, the liquidity L^+ needed is worth:

$$L^+=M(1-\underline{Z}_1) \tag{12.17}$$

It appears that $L^+>L$: the international interbank market provides an amount that is strictly positive and worth $(J-M)(Z_1-1)$. The existence of an international interbank market decreases the amount that the ILLR has to provide to guarantee the stability of the international banking system.

If it were not for the intervention of an ILLR, countries hit by speculative attacks would find it even more difficult to stabilise their financial and economic situations. But the ILLR must not be seen as omnipotent. It cannot bail out all banks and firms that suffer from crises, as far as its financial means are likely to be lower than the private sector's total losses. Political considerations may then interfere with the action of the ILLR when choosing firms and banks to be bailed out.

4. CONCLUSION

In the wake of the 1990s currency crises, many studies have investigated the role of IFIs in the ever ongoing reform process of the international financial system. Some, such as Radelet and Sachs (1998a, 1998b) and Schwartz (1998), favour abolishing IFIs. Others such as Fischer (1999) advocate that out of the current IFIs should emerge an international lender of last resort. Few, if any, consider that IFIs should not be reformed.

It must be acknowledged that the record of IFIs in limiting the economic and financial consequences of crises in emerging countries is mixed, even poor. But IFIs should not be blamed for crises that they do not cause. The root of speculative attacks is often found in domestic problems, not in international financial transactions. If governments were to lead the 'right' policies, crises would seldom occur.

Moreover corruption in many countries is a major hindrance to reforms. World Bank funds that should be channelled to the poor are too often kept by governments and ruling elites, as documented by Easterly (2001). The IMF cannot expect policymakers to implement codes and standards of transparency that would result in their losing influence and/or personal benefits. Failures of IMF-designed programmes in various countries, which ultimately failed to prevent crises, may often be attributed to corrupted governments. Russia is a case in point as Nagy (2000) shows.

All in all, such observations raise questions about the rationale for development policies and financial reforms to be implemented through public endeavour and spending.

NOTES

1. Other IFIs whose competencies are limited to a single region, like the Asian Development Bank, act jointly with the IMF and the World Bank.
2. See International Monetary Fund (1998b).

3. See also Masson and Mussa (1997), Lane and Philipps (2000), Jeanne and Zettelmeyer (2001) on this matter. Evrensel (2002) discusses the effectiveness of IMF-supported adjustment programmes in developing countries from 1971 to 1997.
4. On credit crunch, see for instance, Alba, Bhattacharya, Claessens, Ghosh and Hernandez (1999) and Agénor, Aizenman and Hoffmaister (2000).
5. See the discussion on monetary policy in third-generation models which is largely inspired by the events in East Asia in Chapter 7, section 1.1, The policymaker's optimal commitment to exchange rate stability.
6. When criticising the IMF policies, the then Malaysian Prime Minister Muhatir Muhammad showed to his electorate that he is independent-minded. In September 1998, he established capital controls against the advice of the IMF. He claimed that he thereby stopped the crisis in his country. But the financial panic per se ended in January 1998 and Malaysia had not yet overcome the consequences of the East Asian crisis. Except for Kaplan and Rodrik (2002), studies dealing with Malaysian capital controls, such as Furman and Stiglitz (1998), Radelet and Sachs (1998a), Corsetti, Pesenti and Roubini (1999b), doubt their efficiency.
7. If the two types of investors do not have the same opportunity costs, different cases may be distinguished where type-1 and type-2 investors may find it optimal to exit or stay in the market.
8. This result holds even if there are multiple equilibria.
9. Studies on the Mexican crisis and IMF policies include Dornbusch, Goldfajn and Valdés (1995) and Sachs, Tornell and Velasco (1996a, 1996b).

References

Admati, A.R. (1985), 'A noisy rational expectations equilibrium for multi-asset securities markets', *Econometrica*, **53**, 629–57.

Agénor, P.R. and J. Aizenman (1998), 'Contagion and volatility with imperfect credit markets', *International Monetary Fund Staff Papers*, **45**, 207–35.

Agénor, P.R., Aizenman, J., and A. Hoffmaister (2000), 'The credit crunch in East Asia: what can bank excess liquid assets tell us ?', *National Bureau of Economic Research Working Paper*, **7951**, Cambridge, MA: National Bureau of Economic Research.

Agénor, P.R., Bhandari, J.S., and R.P. Flood (1992), 'Speculative attacks and models of balance-of-payments crises', *International Monetary Fund Staff Papers*, **39**, 357–,94.

Agénor, P.R. and P.R. Masson (1999), 'Credibility, reputation, and the Mexican peso crisis', *Journal of Money, Credit and Banking*, **31** (1), 70–84.

Agénor, P.R. and P.J. Montiel (2000), *Development Macroeconomics*, Princeton, NJ: Princeton University Press.

Aghion, P., Bacchetta, P., and A. Banerjee (1999), 'Capital markets and the instability of open economies', *Centre for Economic Policy Research Discussion Paper*, **2083**, London, UK: Centre for Economic Policy Research.

Aghion, P., Bacchetta, P., and A. Banerjee (2000), 'A simple model of monetary policy and currency crises', *European Economic Review*, **44**, 728–38.

Aghion, P., Bacchetta, P., and A. Banerjee (2001), 'Currency crises and monetary policy in an economy with credit constraints', *European Economic Review*, **45**, 1121–1150.

Aglietta, M. (2000), 'La crise financière russe, un révélateur de la fragilité des marchés financiers', *Revue Economique*, **51** (3), 649–58.

Aizenman, J., Kletzer, K., and B. Pinto (2002), 'Sargent-Wallace meets Krugman-Flood-Garber, or: why sovereign debt swaps don't avert crises', *National Bureau of Economic Research Working Paper,* **9180**, Cambridge, MA: National Bureau of Economic Research.

Alba, P., Bhattacharya, A., Claessens, S., Ghosh, S., and L. Hernandez (1999), 'The role of macroeconomic and financial sector linkages in East Asia's financial crisis', in Pierre-Richard Agénor, Marcus Miller, David Vines and Axel Weber (eds), *Financial Crisis : Contagion and Market Volatility*, Cambridge: Cambridge University Press, pp. 9–64.

Allen, F. and D. Gale (1998), 'Optimal financial crises', *The Journal of Finance*, **53** (4), 1245–84.

Allen, F. and D. Gale (2000a), 'Financial contagion', *Journal of Political Economy*, **108** (1), 1–33.

Allen, F. and D. Gale (2000b), 'Optimal currency crises', *Carnegie-Rochester Conference Series on Public Policy*, **53** (1), 177–230.

Andersen, T.M. (1994), 'Shocks and the viability of a fixed exchange rate commitment', *Centre for Economic Policy Research Discussion Paper*, **969**, London, UK.

Andersen, T.M. and O. Risager (1991), 'The role of credibility for the effects of a change in the exchange-rate policy', *Oxford Economic Papers*, **43**, 85–98.

Arellano, C. and E. Mendoza (2002), 'Business cycles in small open economies with credit frictions: an equilibrium approach to emerging market crises', *National Bureau of Economic Research Working Paper*, **8880**, Cambridge, MA: National Bureau of Economic Research.

Aronson, Eliot, Wilson, Timothy D., and Robin M. Akert (1997), *Social Psychology*, New York, NY: Addison Wesley.

Artus, P. (1994), 'Les crises de balance des paiements sont-elles inévitables?', *Revue Economique*, **6**, 1377–1400.

Aumann, R. (1976) 'Agreeing to disagree', *Annals of Statistics*, **4**, 1236–39.

Azariadis, C. (1981), 'Self-fulfilling prophecies', *Journal of Economic Theory*, **25** (3), 380–96.

Bacchetta, P. (1990), 'Temporary capital controls in a balance-of-payments crisis', *Journal of International Money and Finance*, **9**, 246–57.

Bacchetta, P. and E. van Wincoop (1998), 'Capital flows to emerging markets: liberalization, overshooting, and volatility', *National Bureau of Economic Research Working Paper*, **6530**, Cambridge, MA.

Backus, D. and E.J. Driffil (1985a), 'Inflation and reputation', *American Economic Review*, **75**, 530–38.

Backus, D. and E.J. Driffil (1985b), 'Rational expectations and policy credibility following a change in regime', *Review of Economic Studies*, **52**, 211–21.

Backus, D., Foresi, S., and L. Wu (2002), 'Liquidity and contagion in financial markets', mimeo, Fordham University.

Bagehot, W. (1873), *Lombard Street*, London, UK: H.S. King.

Baliño, T., Bennet, A., and E. Borensztein (1999), *Monetary policy in dollarised economies, International Monetary Fund Occasional Paper*, **171**, Washington, DC: International Monetary Fund.

Banerjee, A. (1992), 'A simple model of herd behaviour', *Quarterly Journal of Economics*, **107**, 797–17.

Bank of International Settlements (1998a), *The Maturity, Sectoral and Nationality, Distribution of International Bank Lending, First Semester, 1997*, Basel: Bank of International Settlements.

Bank of International Settlements (1998b), *The Maturity, Sectoral and Nationality, Distribution of International Bank Lending, Second Semester, 1997*, Basel: Bank of International Settlements.

Barlevy, G. and P. Veronesi (2000), 'Information acquisition in financial markets', *Review of Economic Studies*, **67**, 79–90.

Barro, R. and D.B. Gordon (1983), 'Reputation in a model of monetary policy with incomplete information', *Journal of Monetary Economics*, **12**, 101–21.

Baumol, W. (1957), 'Speculation, profitability and stability', *Review of Economics and Statistics*, **39**, 263–71.

Benigno, P. and A. Missale (2001), 'High public debt in currency crises: fundamentals versus signalling effects', *Centre for Economic Policy Research Discussion Paper*, **2862**, London, UK.

Bensaïd, B. and O. Jeanne (1996), 'Fragilité des systèmes de change fixe et contrôle des capitaux', *Economie et Prévision*, **123–124** (2–3), 163–74.

Bensaïd, B. and O. Jeanne (1997), 'The instability of exchange rate systems when raising the nominal interest rate is costly', *European Economic Review*, **41**, 1461–74.

Bensaïd, B. and O. Jeanne (2000), 'Self-fulfilling currency crises and central bank independence', *Scandinavian Journal of Economics*, **102** (4), 605–20.

Berg, A. and E. Borensztein (2000), 'The choice of exchange rate regime and monetary target in highly dollarised economies', *International Monetary Fund Working Paper*, **00/29**, Washington, DC: International Monetary Fund.

Berg, A., Borensztein, E., Milesi-Ferretti, G.M., and C. Patillo (1999), 'Anticipating balance of payments crises: the role of early warning systems', *International Monetary Fund Occasional Paper*, **186**, Washington, DC: International Monetary Fund.

Berg, A. and C. Patillo (1999a), 'Are currency crises predictable?, a test', *International Monetary Fund Staff Papers*, **46** (2), 107–38.

Berg, A. and C. Patillo (1999b), 'Predicting currency crises: the indicators approach and an alternative', *Journal of International Money and Finance*, **18** (4), 561–86.

Berg, A. and C. Patillo (1999c), 'What caused the Asian crises: an early warning system approach', *Economic Notes*, **28** (3), 285–334.

Bertola, G. and L.E.O. Svensson (1993), 'Stochastic devaluation risk and the empirical fit of target-zone models', *Review of Economic Studies*, **60**, 689–712.

Bikhchandani, S., Hirshleifer, D., and I. Welch (1992), 'A theory of fads, fashion, custom and cultural change as informational cascades', *Journal of Political Economy*, **100**, 992–1026.

Bikhchandani, S., Hirshleifer, D., and I. Welch (1998), 'Learning from the behaviour of others: conformity, fads and informational Cascades', *Journal of Economic Perspectives*, **12** (3), 151–70.

Bikhchandani, S., and S. Sharma (2000), 'Herd behavior in financial markets: a review', *International Monetary Fund Working Paper*, 00/48, Washington, DC: International Monetary Fund.

Black, F. (1986), 'Noise', *American Economic Review*, **41**, 529–543.

Blackburn, K., (1988), 'Collapsing exchange rate regimes and exchange rate dynamics: some further examples', *Journal of International Money and Finance*, **7**, 373–85.

Blackburn, K., and M. Sola (1993), 'Speculative currency attacks and balance of payments crises', *Journal of Economic Surveys*, **7** (2), 119–44.

Blanco, H., and P.M. Garber (1986), 'Recurrent devaluation and speculative attacks on the Mexican peso', *Journal of Political Economy*, **94**, 148–66.

Bordo, M.D. (1986), 'Financial crises, banking crises, stock market crashes, and the money supply: some international evidence, 1870–1933', in Forest Capie and G.E. Wood (eds), *Financial Crises and the World Banking System*, London, UK: Macmillan, pp. 190–248.

Bordo, M.D. (1990), 'The lender of last resort: alternative views and historical experience', *Federal Reserve Bank of Richmond Economic Review*, **76** (1), 18–29.

Bordo M.D., B. Eichengreen, D. Klingbiel, and M.S. Martinez-Peria (2001), 'Financial crises : lessons from the last 120 years', *Economic Policy*, **32**, 51–82.

Bordo, Michael D. and Lars Jonung (2000), *Lessons for EMU from the History of Monetary Unions*, London, UK: Insitute of Economic Affairs.

Bordo, M.D. and A.J. Schwartz (1997), 'Why clashes between internal and external stability goals end in currency crisis, 1797–1994', *National Bureau of Economic Research Working Paper*, **5710**, Cambridge, MA.

Bordo, M.D. and A.J. Schwartz (1998), 'Under what circumstances, past and present, have international rescues of countries in financial distress been successful?', *National Bureau of Economic Research Working Paper*, **6824**, Cambridge, MA.

Bordo, M.D. and A.J. Schwartz (2000), 'Measuring real economic bailouts: historical perspectives on how countries in financial distress have fared with and without bailouts', *Carnegie-Rochester Series on Public Policy*, **53** (1), 81–167.

Botman, D.P.J. and H. Jager (2002), 'Coordination of speculation', *Journal of International Economics*, **58** (1), 159–75.

Brandenburger, A. (1992), 'Knowledge and equilibrium in games', *Journal of Economic Perspectives*, **6**, 83–101.

Branson, W.H. (1994), 'Comments on exchange rate credibility before the fall by A. Rose and L. Svensson', *European Economic Review*, **38**, 1217–20.

Brown S.J. (2001), 'Hedge funds: omniscient or just plain wrong', *Pacific-Basin Finance Journal*, **9**, 301–11.

Brown S.J., Goetzmann, W.N., and J. Park (2000), 'Hedge funds and the Asian currency Crisis of 1997', *Journal of Portfolio Management*, **26**, 95–101.

Buch, C.M., and R.P. Heinrich (1999), 'Handling banking crises – the case of Russia', *Economic Systems*, **23** (4), 349–80.

Buiter, W.H. (1987), 'Borrowing to defend the exchange rate and the timing of and magnitude of speculative attacks', *Journal of International Economics*, **23**, 221–39.

Buiter, W.H., Corsetti, G., and P.A. Pesenti (1996), 'Interpreting the ERM crisis: country-specific and systemic issues', *Centre for Economic Policy Research Discussion Paper*, **1466**, London, UK: Centre for Economic Policy Research.

Burnside, C., Eichenbaum, M., and S. Rebelo (2001a), 'Prospective deficits and the Asian currency crisis', *Journal of Political Economy,* **109** (6), 1155–97.

Burnside, C., Eichenbaum, M., and S. Rebelo (2001b), 'On the fiscal implications of twin crises', *World Bank Working Paper*, **8277**, Cambridge, MA, forthcoming in Michael Dooley and Jeffrey Frankel (eds), *Managing Currency Crises in Emerging Markets*, Chicago, Ill: Chicago University Press.

Calvo, G.A. (1983a), 'Staggered contracts and exchange rate policy', in Jeffrey A. Frankel (ed.), *Exchange Rates and International Macroeconomics*, Chicago, Ill: University of Chicago Press.

Calvo, G.A. (1983b), 'Trying to stabilize: some theoretical reflections based on the case of Argentina', in Pedro Aspe Armella, Rudiger Dornbusch and Maurice Obstfeld (eds), *Financial Policies and the World Capital Market: The Problem of Latin American Countries*, Chicago, Ill: University of Chicago Press, pp 199–220.

Calvo, G.A. (1987), 'Balance of payments crises in a cash-in-advance economy', *Journal of Money, Credit and Banking*, **19** (1), 19–32.

Calvo, G.A. (1999), 'Contagion in emerging markets: when Wall Street is a carrier', mimeo, University of Maryland.

Calvo, G.A. and E.G. Mendoza (1996), 'Mexico's balance-of-payments crisis: a chronicle of a death foretold?', *Journal of International Economics*, **41**, 265–283.

Calvo, G.A. and E.G. Mendoza (2000), 'Rational contagion and the globalization of securities markets', *Journal of International Economics*, **51**, 79–113.

Calvo, G.A. and C.M. Reinhart (2002), 'Fear of floating', *Quarterly Journal of Economics*, **117** (2), 379-408.

Calvo, G.A. and C.A. Végh (2000), 'Inflation stabilization and balance of payment crises in developing countries', *National Bureau of Economic Research Working Paper*, **6925**, Cambrige, MA: National Bureau of Economic Research.

Calvo, S. and C.M. Reinhart (1996), 'Capital flows in Latin America: is there evidence of contagion effects?', in Guillermo A. Calvo, Morris Goldstein and Eduard Hochreiter (eds), *Private Capital Flows to Emerging Markets after the Mexican Crisis*, Washington, DC: Institute for International Economics, pp. 151–171.

Campa, J.M. and P.H.K. Chang (1996), 'Arbitrage-based tests of target-zone credibility: evidence from ERM cross-rate options', *American Economic Review*, **86** (4), 726–40.

Campa, J.M., Chang, P.H.K, and J.F. Refalo (2002), 'An option-based analysis of emerging market exchange rate expectations: Brazil's real plan, 1994–1999', *Journal of Development Economics*, **69** (1), 227–53.

Caplin, A. and J. Leahy (1994), 'Business as usual, market crashes, and wisdom after the fact', *American Economic Review*, **84** (3), 548–65.

Caramazza, F. (1993), 'French-German interest rate differentials and time-varying realignment risk', *International Monetary Fund Staff Papers*, **40** (3), 567–83.

Caramazza, F., Ricci, L., and R. Salgado (2000), 'Trade and financial contagion in currency crises', *International Monetary Fund Working Paper*, **00/55**, Cambrige, MA: National Bureau of Economic Research.

Carlsson, H., and E. van Damme, (1993), 'Global games and equilibrium selection', Econometrica, **61**(5), 989–1018.

Cass, D. and K. Shell (1983), 'Do sunspots matter?', *Journal of Political-Economy*, **91**(2), 193–227.

Chan, K.S, and Y.S. Chui (2002), 'The role of (non-)transparency in a currency crisis model', *European Economic Review*, **46**, 397–416.

Chang, R., and G. Majnoni (2000), 'International contagion: implications for policy', *World Bank Working Paper*, **2306**, Washington, DC: World Bank.

Chang, R., and A. Velasco (1998), 'Financial fragility and the exchange rate regime', *National Bureau of Economic Research Working Paper*, **6469**, Cambridge, MA: National Bureau of Economic Research.

Chang, R., and A. Velasco (1999), 'Liquidity crises in emerging markets: theory and policy', *National Bureau of Economic Research Working Paper*, **7272**, Cambridge, MA: National Bureau of Economic Research.

Chang, R., and A. Velasco (2000a), 'Financial crisis in emerging markets: a canonical model', *Journal of Economic Theory*, **90** (2), 1–34.

Chang, R., and A. Velasco (2000b), 'Banks, debt maturity and financial crises', *Journal of International Economics*, **51**, 169–94.

Chang, R., and A. Velasco (2001), 'A model of financial crises in emerging markets', *Quarterly Journal of Economics*, **116** (2001), 489–517.

Chapman, S.A. and M. Mulino (2000), 'Explaining Russia's currency and financial crisis', *Economic Systems*, **24** (4), 365–69.

Chari, V.V., and P. Kehoe (1997), 'Hot money', *National Bureau of Economic Research Working Paper*, **6007**, Cambridge, MA: National Bureau of Economic Research.

Chari, V.V., and P. Kehoe (1998), 'Asking the right questions about the IMF', *Public Affairs*, **13**, 3–26.

Chen, Z., and A. Giovannini (1997), 'The determinants of realignments expectations under the EMS : some empirical regularities', *European Economic Review*, **41**, 1687–707.

Chinn, M.D., Dooley, M.P., and S. Shrestra (1999), 'Latin America and East Asia in the context of an insurance model of currency crises', *Journal of International Money and Finance*, **18**, 659–81.

Claessens, S., (1988), 'Balance-of-payments crises in a perfect foresight optimizing model', *Journal of International Money and Finance*, **7**, 363–72.

Claessens S., Dornbusch, R., and Y.C. Park (2000), 'Contagion: how it spreads and how it can be stopped', *The World Bank Research Observer*, **15** (2), 177–97.

Coeuré, B., and A. Magnier (1996), 'Crédibilité et fondamentaux macro-économiques au sein du SME: un examen empirique', *Economie et Prévision*, **123—124** (2–3), 113–46.

Cole, H.L., and T.J. Kehoe (1996), 'A self-fulfilling model of Mexico's 1994–1995 debt crisis', *Journal of International Economics*, **41**, 309–30.

Cole, H.L., and T.J. Kehoe (2000), 'Self-fulfilling debt crises', *Review of Economics Studies*, **67**, 91–116.

Collins, S.M. (1996), 'On becoming more flexible: exchange rate regimes in Latin America and the Caribbean', *Journal of Development Economics*, **51** (1), 117–38.

Connoly, M. (1986), 'The speculative attack on the peso and the real exchange rate', *Journal of International Money and Finance*, **5** (supplement), S117–S130.

Connoly, M., and D. Taylor (1984), 'The exact timing of the collapse of an exchange rate regime and its impact on the relative price of traded goods', *Journal of Money, Credit and Banking*, **16** (2), 194-207.

Corsetti, G., Dasgupta, A., Morris, S., and H.S. Shin (2000), 'Does one Soros make a difference ? a theory of currency crises with large and small traders', *Centre for Economic Policy Research Discussion Paper*, **2610**, London, UK: Centre for Economic Policy Research.

Corsetti, G. and B. Mackowiak (2001), 'Nominal debt and the dynamics of currency crises', *Centre for Economic Policy Research Discussion Paper*, **2929**, London, UK: Centre for Economic Policy Research.

Corsetti, G., Pesenti, P., and N. Roubini (1999a), 'Paper tigers? a model of the Asian Crisis', *European Economic Review*, **43** (7), 1211–36.

Corsetti, G., Pesenti P., and N. Roubini (1999b). 'What caused the Asian currency and financial crisis?', *Japan and the World Economy*, **11** (3), 305–73.

Corsetti, G., Pesenti, P., and N. Roubini (2002), 'The role of large players in currency crises', in Sebastian Edwards and Jeffrey A. Frankel (eds), *Preventing Currency Crises in Emerging Markets*, Chicago, Ill : The University of Chicago Press, pp. 197–258.

Corsetti, G., Pesenti, P., Roubini, N., and C. Tille (2000), 'Competitive devaluations: toward a welfare-based approach', *Journal of International Economics*, **51** (1), 217–41.

Cukierman, A. (1992), *Central Bank Strategy, Credibility, and Independence: Theory and Evidence*, Cambridge, MA: The MIT Press.

Cukierman, A., Goldstein, I., and Y. Spiegel, (2002), ' The choice of exchange rate regime and speculative attacks', Tel Aviv University Working Paper.

Cumby, R.E. and S. van Wijnbergen (1989), 'Financial policy and speculative runs with a crawling peg: Argentina 1979–1981', *Journal of International Economics*, **27**, 111–27.

Daniel, B.C. (2000), 'The timing of exchange rate collapse', *Journal of International Money and Finance*, **19**, 765–84.

Daniel, B.C. (2001), 'A fiscal theory of currency crises', *International Economic Review*, **42**, 969–88.

Davies, G. and D. Vines (1995), 'Equilibrium currency crises: are multiple equilibria self-fulfilling or history dependent?', *Centre for Economic*

Policy Research Discussion Paper, **1239**, London, UK: Centre for Economic Policy Research.

De Bandt, O. and P. Hartmann (2000), 'Systemic risk: a survey', *Centre for Economic Policy Research Discussion Paper*, **2634**, London, UK: Centre for Economic Policy Research.

Dekle, R., Hsiao, C., and S.Wang (2001), 'Do high interest rates appreciate exchange rates during crisis? The Korean evidence', *Oxford Bulletin of Economics and Statistics*, **63** (3), 359–80.

De Kock, G. and V. Grilli (1993), 'Fiscal policies and the choice of exchange rate regimes', *The Economic Journal*, **103**, 347–98.

Dellas, H. and A.C. Stockman (1993), 'Self-fulfilling expectations, speculative attacks and capital controls', *Journal of Money, Credit and Banking*, **25** (4), 721–30.

DeLong, J.B., Shleifer, A., Summers, L. and R. Waldmann (1990), 'The economic consequences of noise traders', *Journal of Political Economy*, **98**, 703–38.

Demirgüç-Kunt, A. and E. Detragiache (1998), 'The determinants of banking crises in developing and developed countries', *International Monetary Fund Staff Papers*, **45** (1), 81–109.

Desai, P. (2000), 'Why did the ruble collapse in August 1998 ?', *American Economic Review*, **90** (2), 49–52.

Diamond, D.D.W. and P.H. Dybvig (1983), 'Bank runs, deposit insurance, and liquidity', *Journal of Political Economy*, **91**, 401–19.

Diebold F., Lee, J.H, and G. Weinbach, (1994), 'Regime switching with time varying transition probabilities', in Colin Hargreaves (ed.), *Non-stationary Time Series Analysis and Cointegration*, Oxford, UK: Oxford University Press.

Djajic, S. (1989), 'Dynamics of the exchange rate in anticipation of pegging', *Journal of International Money and Finance*, **8**, 559–71.

Dooley, M.P. (1996), 'The Tobin tax: good theory, weak evidence, questionable policy', in M. ul Haq, I. Kaul, I. Grunberg (eds), *The Tobin Tax, Coping with Financial Volatility*, Oxford, UK: Oxford University Press, 83–106.

Dooley, M.P. (1997), 'A model of crises in emerging markets', *National Bureau of Economic Research Working Paper*, **6300**, Cambridge, MA: National Bureau of Economic Research.

Dornbusch, R. (1976), 'Expectations and exchange rate dynamics', *Journal of Political Economy*, **84**, 1161–76.

Dornbusch, R. (1987), 'Collapsing exchange rate regimes', *Journal of Development Economics*, **27**, 71–83.

Dornbusch, R., Goldfajn, I., and R.O. Valdés (1995), 'Currency crises and collapses', *Brookings Papers on Economic Activity*, **2**, 219–93.

Drazen, A. (1999), 'Political contagion in currency crises', *National Bureau of Economic Research Working Paper*, **7291**, Cambridge, MA: National Bureau of Economic Research.

Drazen, A. (2000a), 'Interest rate defense and borrowing defense against speculative attacks', *Carnegie-Rochester Conference Series on Public Policy*, **53** (2), 303–48.

Drazen, Allan (2000b), *Political Economy in Macroeconomics*, Princeton, NJ: Princeton University Press.

Drazen, A. and E. Helpman (1987), 'Stabilization with exchange rate management', *Quarterly Journal of Economics*, **52**, 835–55.

Drazen, A. and P. Masson (1994), 'Credibility of policies versus credibility of policymakers', *Quarterly Journal of Economics*, **104**, 735–54.

Easterly, William (2001), *The Elusive Quest for Growth: Economists' Adventures and Misadventures in the Tropics*, Cambridge, MA: MIT Press.

Edison, H. (1997), 'The reaction of exchange rates and interest rates to news releases', *International Journal of Financial Economics*, **2**, 87–100.

Edwards, Sebastian (1989), *Real Exchange Rates, Devaluation and Adjustment: Exchange Rate Policy in Developing Countries*, Cambridge, MA: MIT Press.

Edwards, S. (1996), 'The determinants of the choice between fixed and flexible exchange rate regimes', *National Bureau of Economic Research Working Paper*, **5756**, Cambridge, MA: National Bureau of Economic Research.

Edwards, S. (1999), 'On crisis prevention : lessons from Mexico and East Asia', *National Bureau of Economic Research Working Paper*, **7233**, Cambridge, MA: National Bureau of Economic Research.

Edwards, S. (2001a), 'Dollarization and economic performance : an empirical investigation', *National Bureau of Economic Research Working Paper*, **8274**, Cambridge, MA: National Bureau of Economic Research.

Edwards, S. (2001b), 'Dollarisation: myths and realities', Journal of Policy Modeling, **23** (3), 249–65.

Edwards, S. and P.J. Montiel (1989), 'Devaluation crises and the macroeconomic consequences of postponed adjustment in developing countries', *International Monetary Fund Staff Papers*, **36**, 875–903.

Edwards, S. and M. Savastano (1999), 'Exchange rates in emerging economies: What do we know? What do we need to know?', *National Bureau of Economic Research Working Paper*, **7228**, Cambridge, MA.

Eichengreen, B. (2000), 'The EMS crisis in retrospect', *National Bureau of Economic Research Working Paper*, **8035**, Cambridge, MA.

Eichengreen, B. and D. Mathieson (1998), 'Hedge funds and financial markets dynamics', *International Monetary Fund Occasional Paper*, **166**, Washington, DC.

Eichengreen, B. and A.K. Rose (1998), 'Staying afloat when the wind shifts: external factors and emerging-market banking crises', *National Bureau of Economic Research Working Paper*, **6370**, Cambridge, MA: National Bureau of Economic Research.

Eichengreen, B. and A.K. Rose (2000), 'The empirics of currency and banking crises', *Wirtschaftspolitische Blatter*, **47** (4), 395–402.

Eichengreen, B., Rose, A.K., and C. Wyplosz (1996a), 'Contagious currency crises', *Centre for Economic Policy Research Discussion Paper*, **1453**, London, UK.

Eichengreen, B., Rose A.K., and C. Wyplosz (1996b), 'Exchange market mayhem: the antecedents and aftermath of speculative attacks', *Economic Policy,* **21**, 251–312.

Eichengreen, B., Tobin, J., and C. Wyplosz (1995), 'Two cases for sand in the wheels of international finance', *The Economic Journal*, **105**, 162–72.

Eichengreen, B., and C. Wyplosz (1993), 'The unstable EMS', *Brookings Papers on Economic Activity*, **1**, 51–143.

Eichengreen, B., and C. Wyplosz (1996), 'Taxing international financial transactions to enhance the operation of the international monetary system', in Mahbub ul Haq, Inge Kaul and Isabelle Grunberg (eds), *The Tobin Tax, Coping with Financial Volatility*, Oxford, UK : Oxford University Press, pp. 15–39.

Evrensel, A.Y. (2002), Effectiveness of IMF-supported stabilization programs in developing countries, *Journal of International Money and Finance*, **21**, 565–87.

Farmer, Roger (2001), *The Macroeconomics of Self-fulfilling Prophecies*, Cambridge, MA: The MIT Press.

Femminis, G. (2002), 'Currency attack with multiple equilibria and imperfect information: the role of wage-setters', *Centre for Economic Policy Research Discussion Paper*, **3291**, London, UK.

Fielding, D. and P. Mizen (2001), 'Seigniorage revenue, deficits and self-fulfilling currency crises', *Journal of Development Economics*, **65** (1), 81–93.

Fischer, S. (1999), 'On the need for an international lender of last resort', *American Economic Review*, **13** (4), 85–104.

Fischer, S. (2002), 'Financial crises and the reform of the International Financial System', *National Bureau of Economic Research Working Paper*, **9297**, Cambridge, MA: National Bureau of Economic Research.

Flood, R.P. and P.M. Garber (1984a), 'Gold monetization and gold discipline', *Journal of Political* Economy, **92**, 90–107.

Flood, R.P. and P.M. Garber (1984b), 'Collapsing exchange rate regimes: some linear examples', *Journal of International Economics*, **17**, 1–13.

Flood, R.P., Garber, P.M., and C. Kramer (1996), 'Collapsing exchange rate regimes: another linear example', *Journal of International Economics*, **41**, 223–34.

Flood, R.P. and R.J. Hodrick (1986), 'Real aspects of exchange rate regime choice with collapsing fixed rates', *Journal of International Economics*, **21**, 215–32.

Flood, R.P. and O. Jeanne (2000), 'An interest rate defense of a fixed exchange rate ?', *International Monetary Fund Working Paper*, **00/159**, Washington, DC: International Monetary Fund.

Flood, R.P. and N.P. Marion (1997), 'Policy implications of second generation crisis models', *International Monetary Fund Staff Papers*, **44** (3), 383–90.

Flood, R.P. and N.P. Marion (1998a), 'Perspectives on the recent currency crisis literature', *National Bureau of Economic Research Working Paper*, **6380**, Cambridge, MA: National Bureau of Economic Research.

Flood, R.P. and N.P. Marion (1998b), 'Self-fulfilling risk predictions: an application to speculative attacks', *International Monetary Fund Working Paper*, **98/124**, Washington, DC: International Monetary Fund.

Flood, R.P. and N.P. Marion (2001), 'A model of the joint distribution of banking and exchange-rate crises', *International Monetary Fund Working Paper*, **01/213**, Washington, DC: International Monetary Fund.

Fourçans, A. and R. Franck (2002), 'The speculators' behaviour in a model of self-fulfilling currency crises', *ESSEC Business School Working Paper*.

Franco, G.H.B. (2000), 'The Real plan and the exchange rate', Essays in International Finance, **217**, Princeton University.

Frankel, J.A. (1996), 'How well do markets work: might a Tobin tax help ?', in Mahbub ul Haq, Inge Kaul, Isabelle Grunberg (eds), *The Tobin Tax, Coping with Financial Volatility*, Oxford, UK : Oxford University Press, pp. 41–81.

Frankel, J.A. (1998), 'The Asian model, the miracle, the crisis', *Speech delivered at the U.S. International Trade Commission*, Washington DC, 16 April.

Frankel, J.A. (1999), 'No single currency regime is right for all countries or at all times', *National Bureau of Economic Research Working Paper*, **7338**, Cambridge, MA.

Frankel, J.A. and A.K. Rose (1996), 'Currency crashes in emerging markets: an empirical treatment', *Journal of International Economics*, **41**, 351–66.

Frankel, J.A. and S.L. Schmukler (2000), 'Country funds and asymmetric information', *International Journal of Finance and Economics*, **5**, 177–95.

Fratzscher, M. (1998), 'Why are currency crises contagious ? A comparison of the Latin American crisis of 1994–1995 and the Asian crisis of 1997–1998', *Weltwirtschafliches Archiv*, **134** (4), 664-691.

Friedman, Milton (1953), *Essays in Positive Economics*, Chicago, Ill: University of Chicago Press.

Friedman, M. (1969), The optimum quantity of money, in *The Optimum Quantity of Money and Other Essays*, Chicago, Ill : Aldine, pp. 1-50.

Froot K.A., Scharftein, S., and J. Stein (1992), 'Herd on the street: informational inefficiencies in a market with short-term speculation', *Journal of Finance*, **47**, 1461–84.

Funke, N. (1996), 'Vulnerability of fixed exchange rate regimes: the role of economic fundamentals', *Organisation for Economic Cooperation and Development Economics Studies*, **26** (1), 157–76.

Furman, J. and J.E. Stiglitz (1998), 'Economic crises: evidence and insights from East Asia', *Brookings Papers on Economic Activity*, **2**, 1–135.

Garber, P.M. (1996a), 'Comments on "Are currency crises self-fulfilling?" by P. Krugman', in Ben S. Bernanke and Julio Rotemberg (eds), *National Bureau of Economic Research Macroeconomics Annual*, Cambridge, MA: MIT Press, pp. 389–93.

Garber, P.M. (1996b), 'Issues of enforcement and evasion in a tax on foreign transactions', in Mahbub ul Haq, Inge Kaul and Isabelle Grunberg (eds), *The Tobin Tax, Coping with Financial Volatility*, Oxford, UK: Oxford University Press, pp. 129–42.

Garber, P.M. (1998), 'Derivatives in capital flows', *National Bureau of Economic Research Working Paper*, **6623**, Cambridge, MA: National Bureau of Economic Research.

Garber, P.M. (2000), 'Comments on "Balance sheets, the transfer problem, and financial crises" by P. Krugman', in Peter Isard, Assaf Razin and Andrew K. Rose (eds), *International Finance and Financial Crises, Essays in Honor of Robert P. Flood Jr*, Boston, MA: Kluwer Academic Publishers, pp. 45–8.

Garber, P.M. and M.G. Spencer (1995), 'Foreign exchange hedging and the interest rate defense', *International Monetary Fund Staff Papers*, **42** (3), 490–516.

Garber, P.M. and L.E.O. Svensson (1994), 'The operation and collapse of fixed exchange rate regimes', *National Bureau of Economic Research Working Paper*, **4971**, Cambridge, MA: National Bureau of Economic Research.

Garber, P.M. and M.P. Taylor (1995), 'Sand in the wheels of foreign exchange markets: a sceptical note', *The Economic Journal*, **105**, 173–80.

Garretsen, H., Knot, K., and E. Nijsse (1998), 'Learning about fundamentals: the widening of the French ERM bands in 1993', *Weltwirtschafliches Archiv*, **134** (1), 25–41.

Geanakoplos, J. (1992), 'Common knowledge', *Journal of Economic Perspectives*, **6** (4), 53–82.

Gelos, G. and R. Sahay (2000), 'Financial market spillovers in transition economies', *International Monetary Fund Working Paper*, **00/71**, Washington DC.

Gerlach, S. and F. Smets (1995), 'Contagious speculative attacks', *European Journal of Political Economy*, **11**, 5–63.

Gicquiau, H. (1998), 'L'industrie russe d'aujourd'hui', *Le Courrier des Pays de l'Est*, **427**, February, 3-16.

Girton, L. and D. Roper (1977), 'A monetary model of exchange market pressure applied to the postwar Canadian experience', *American Economic Review*, **67**, 537–48.

Glick, R. and M. Hutchinson (1999), 'Banking and currency crises: How Common are Twins?', *Federal Reserve Bank of San Francisco Center for Pacific Basin Monetary and Economic Studies, Economic Research Department Working Paper*, **99-07**, San Francisco, CA: Federal Reserve Bank of San Francisco.

Glick, R. and A.K. Rose (1998), 'Contagion and trade: why are currency crises regional?', *National Bureau of Economic Research Working Paper*, **6806**, Cambridge, MA: National Bureau of Economic Research.

Goh, A.T. and J. Olivier (2002), 'Financing decisions of firms and Central Bank policy', *Journal of International Economics*, **56** (2), 411–44.

Goldberg, L.S. (1991), 'Collapsing exchange rate regimes : shocks and Biases', *Journal of International Money and Finance*, **10**, 252–63.

Goldberg, L.S. (1994), 'Predicting exchange rate crises: Mexico revisited', *Journal of International Economics*, **36**, 413–30.

Goldfajn, I. and P. Gupta (1999), 'Does monetary policy stabilize the exchange rate following a currency crisis?', *International Monetary Fund Working Paper*, **99/42**, Washington, DC: International Monetary Fund.

Goldfajn, I. and R.O. Valdès (1996), 'The aftermath of appreciations', *National Bureau of Economic Research Working Paper*, **5650**, Cambridge, MA: National Bureau of Economic Research.

Goldfajn, I. and R.O. Valdès (1998), 'Are currency crisis predictable?', *European Economic Review*, **42**, 873–85.

Goodhart, C. and H. Huang (2000), 'A simple model of an international lender of last resort', *Economic Notes*, **29** (1), 1–10.

Gould, D. and S.B. Kamin (2000), 'The impact of monetary policy on exchange rates during financial crises', *Board of Governors of the Federal Reserve System International Finance Discussion Paper*, **669**, Board of Governors of the Federal Reserve System: Washington DC.

Grilli, V. (1986), 'Buying and selling attacks on fixed exchange rate systems', *Journal of International Economics*, **20**, 143–56.

Grilli, V. (1990), 'Managing exchange rate crises : evidence from the 1890's', *Journal of International Money and Finance*, **9**, 258–75.

Gros, D. (1992), 'Capital controls and foreign exchange market crises in the EMS', *European Economic Review*, **36**, 1533–44.

Grossman, S.J. (1976), 'On the efficiency of competitive stock markets where traders have diverse information', *Journal of Finance*, **31**, 573–85.

Grossman, S.J. and J.E. Stiglitz (1980), 'On the impossibility of informationally efficient markets', *American Economic Review*, **70**, 393–408.

Hamilton, J.D. (1990), 'Analysis of time series subject to changes in regime', *Journal of Econometrics*, **45**, 39–70.

Hamilton, James D. (1994), *Time Series Analysis*, Princeton NJ: Princeton University Press.

Hamilton, J.D. (1996), 'Specification testing in Markov-switching time-series models', *Journal of Econometrics*, **70**, 127–57.

Hanke, Steve H., Jonung, Lars, and Kurt Schuler (1993), *Russian Currency and Finance: A Currency Board Approach to Reform*, London, UK: Routledge.

Heinemann, F. (2000), 'Unique equilibrium in a model of self-fulfilling currency attacks', *American Economic Review*, **90** (1), 316–18.

Heinemann, F. (2002), 'Exchange rate attack as a coordination game: theory and experimental evidence', *Oxford Review of Economic Policy*, **18** (4), 462–78.

Heinemann, F. and G. Illing (2002), 'Speculative attacks: unique equilibrium and transparency', *Journal of International Economics*, **58** (2), 429–50.

Hellwig, M.F. (1980), 'On the aggregation of information in competitive markets', *Journal of Economic Theory*, **22**, 477–98.

Helpman, H. and A. Razin (1987), 'Exchange rate management: intertemporal tradeoffs', *American Economic Review*, **77**, 107–23.

Hirshleifer, J. (1975), 'Speculation and equilibrium: information, risk and markets', *Quarterly Journal of Economics*, **89**, 519–42.

Horn, H. and T. Persson (1988), 'Exchange rate policy, wage formation and credibility', *European Economic Review*, **32**, 1621–36.

Huang, H. and C. Xu (2000), 'Financial institutions, financial contagion, financial crises', *International Monetary Fund Working Paper*, **00/91**, Washington DC.

Illiarionov, A. (2000), 'Myths and lessons of the August crisis', *Problems of Economic Transitions*, **43** (5), 86–95.

International Monetary Fund (1997), *Annual Report*, Washington DC: International Monetary Fund.

International Monetary Fund (1998a), *World Economic Outlook*, Washington DC: International Monetary Fund.

International Monetary Fund (1998b), *Annual Report*, Washington DC: International Monetary Fund.

International Monetary Fund (2001), *World Economic Outlook*, Washington DC: International Monetary Fund.

Irwin G. and D. Vines (1995), 'The macroeconomics of the Mexican crisis: a simple two-period model', *Centre for Economic Policy Research Discussion Paper*, **1241**, London, UK.

Irwin G. and D. Vines (1999), 'A Krugman–Dooley–Sachs third-generation model of the Asian financial crisis', *Centre for Economic Policy Research Discussion Paper*, **2149**, London, UK.

Isard, Peter (1995), *Exchange Rate Economics*, Cambridge, UK: Cambridge University Press.

Jeanne, O. (1996a), 'Les modèles de crises de change: un essai de synthèse en relation avec la crise du franc de 1992–1993', *Economie et Prévision*, **123–124** (2–3), 147–62.

Jeanne, O. (1996b), 'Would a Tobin tax have saved the EMS ?', *Scandinavian Journal of Economics*, **98** (4), 503–20.

Jeanne, O. (1997), 'Are currency crises self-fulfilling? A test', *Journal of International Economics*, **43** (3–4), 263–286.

Jeanne, O. (1999), 'Currency crises: a perspective on recent theoretical developments', *Centre for Economic Policy Research Discussion Paper*, **2170**, London, UK.

Jeanne, O. (2000), 'Currency crises: a perspective on recent theoretical developments', *Special Papers in International Economics, International Finance Section*, **20**, Princeton University.

Jeanne, O. and P. Masson (2000), 'Currency crises, sunspots and Markov-switching regimes', *Journal of International Economics*, **50**, 327–50.

Jeanne, O. and J. Zettelmeyer, (2001), 'International bailouts, moral hazard and conditionality', *Economic Policy*, **16** (33), 407–32.

Kajanoja, L. (2001), 'Self-fulfilling features in European currency crises: further evidence based on regime switching models', mimeo, Helsinki University.

Kaldor, N. (1939), 'Speculation and economic stability', *Review of Economics Studies*, **7**, 1–27.

Kaminsky, G.L. (1999), 'Currency and banking crises: The early warning signs of distress', *International Monetary Fund Working Paper*, **99/178**, Washington DC.

Kaminsky, G.L., Lizondo, S., and C.M. Reinhart (1997), 'Leading indicators of currency crises', *International Monetary Fund Working Paper*, **97/79**, Washington DC.

Kaminsky, G.L. and C.M. Reinhart (1998), 'Financial crises in Asia and Latin America: then and now', *American Economic Review*, **88** (2), 444–8.

Kaminsky, G.L. and C.M. Reinhart (1999), 'The twin crises: the causes of banking and balance-of-payments problems', *American Economic Review*, **89** (3), 473–500.

Kaminsky, G.L. and C.M. Reinhart (2000), 'On crises, contagion, and confusion', *Journal of International Economics*, **51**, 145–68.

Kaminsky, G.L. and S.L. Schmukler (1999), 'What triggers markets jitters? A chronicle of the Asian crisis', *Journal of International Money and Finance*, **18**, 537–60.

Kaplan, E. and D. Rodrik (2002), 'Did the Malaysian capital controls work?', in Sebastian Edwards and Jeffrey A. Frankel (eds), *Preventing Currency Crises in Emerging Markets*, Chicago, Ill : The University of Chicago Press, pp. 393–440.

Kareken, J. and N. Wallace (1981), 'On the indeterminacy of equilibrium exchange rates', *Quarterly Journal of Economics*, **96** (2), 207–22.

Karni, E. and D. Levine (1994), 'Social attributes and strategic equilibrium: a restaurant bargaining game', *Journal of Political Economy*, **102** (4), 822–40.

Kaufman, G. (1991), 'Lender of last resort: a contemporary perspective', *Journal of Financial Services Research*, **5**, 95–110.

Kenen, P.B. (1995), 'Capital controls, the EMS and EMU', *The Economic Journal*, **105**, 181–92.

Kenen, P.B. (1996), 'The feasibility of taxing foreign exchange rate transactions', in Mahbub ul Haq, Inge Kaul, Isabelle Grunberg (eds), *The Tobin Tax, Coping with Financial Volatility*, Oxford, UK: Oxford University Press, pp. 109–28.

Keynes, J.M. (1937), 'The general theory of employment', *Quarterly Journal of Economics*, **51**, 220–33.

Kiguel, M. and N. Liviatan (1992), 'The business cycle associated with exchange rate based stabilization', *World Bank Economic Review*, **6**, 279–305.

King, M.A. and S. Wadhwani (1990), 'Transmission of volatility between stock markets', *Review of Financial Studies*, **3** (1), 5–33.

Klein, M. and N.P. Marion (1997), 'Explaining the duration of exchange rate pegs', *Journal of Development Economics*, **54** (2), 387–404.

Kodres, L.E. and M. Pritsker (2002), 'A rational expectations model of financial contagion', *Journal of Finance*, **57** (2), 769–99.

Kraay, A. (2003), 'Do high interest rates defend currencies during speculative attacks ?', Journal of International Economics, **59** (2), 297–321.

Krueger, A.O. (2000), 'Conflicting demands on the International Monetary Fund', *American Economic Review*, **90** (2), 38–47.

Krugman, P. (1979), 'A model of balance-of-payments crises', *Journal of Money, Credit and Banking*, **11** (3), 311–25.

Krugman, P. (1991), 'Target zone and exchange rate dynamics', *Quarterly Journal of Economics*, **106** (3), 669–82.

Krugman, P. (1996), 'Are currency crises self-fulfilling?', in Ben S. Bernanke and Julio Rotemberg (eds), *NBER Macroeconomics Annual*, Cambridge, MA: MIT Press, pp. 345–78

Krugman, P. (1998), '*What happened to Asia?*' mimeo, MIT.

Krugman, P. (2000), 'Balance sheets, the transfer problem, and financial crises', in Peter Isard, Assaf Razin and Andrew K. Rose (eds), *International Finance and Financial Crises, Essays in Honor of Robert P. Flood Jr*, Boston, MA: Kluwer Academic Publishers, pp. 31–43.

Kumhof, M. (2000), 'A quantitative exploration of the role of short-term domestic debt in balance-of-payments crises', *Journal of International Economics*, **51**, 195–215.

Kydland, F. and E. Prescott (1977), 'Rule rather than discretion: The inconsistency of optimal plans', *Journal of Political Economy*, **85**, 473–92.

La Chapelle Bizot, B. (2000), 'La dette des pays en developpement (1982-2000): vers une nouvelle gouvernance financière', *Notes et études documentaires de la Documentation Française*, **5124**, Paris.

Lagunoff, R. and S.L. Schreft (2001), 'A model of financial fragility', *Journal of Economic Theory*, **99** (1–2), 220–264.

Lahiri, A. and C.A. Végh (2003), 'Delaying the inevitable: interest rate defence and balance-of-payments crises', *Journal of Political Economy*, **111** (2), 404–24.

Lane, T., Ghosh, A., Hamann, J, Philipps, S., Schulze-Ghattas, M., and T. Tsikata (1999), 'IMF-supported programs in Indonesia, Korea and Thailand: a preliminary assessment', *International Monetary Fund Occasional Paper*, **178**, Washington DC.

Lane, T. and S. Philipps (2000), 'Does IMF financing result in moral hazard?', *International MonetaryFund Working Paper*, **00/168,** Washington DC.

LeBaron, B. and R. McCulloch (2000), 'Floating, fixed or super-fixed: dollarization joins the menu of exchange-rate options', *American Economic Review*, **90** (2), 32–7.

Levy-Yeyati, E. and A. Ubide (1998), 'Crises, contagion and the closed-end country fund puzzle', *International Monetary Fund Working Paper*, **98/143**, Washington, DC: International Monetary Fund.

Lingle, Christopher (1998), *The Rise and Decline of the East Asian Century, False Starts on the Path to the Global Millennium*, Third Edition, Hong Kong: Asia 2000.

Loisel, O. and P. Martin (2001), 'Coordination, cooperation, contagion and currency crises', *Journal of International Economics*, **53**, 399–419.

Lux, T. (1995), 'Herd behaviour, bubbles and crashes', *The Economic Journal*, **105**, 881–96.

Lyrio, M. and H. Dewachter (2000), 'Multiple equilibria and the credibility of the Brazilian crawling peg, 1995–1998', *International Finance*, **3** (1), 1–23.

Madrigal, V. (1996), 'Non-fundamental speculation', *Journal of Finance*, **51**, 553–78.

Mankiw, N.G. (1987), 'The optimal collection of seigniorage: theory and evidence', *Journal of Monetary Economics*, **20**, 327–41.

Marion, N.P. (2000), 'Some parallels between currency and banking crises', in Peter Isard, Assaf Razin and Andrew K. Rose (eds), *International Finance and Financial Crises*, Essays in Honor of Robert P. Flood Jr, Boston, MA: Kluwer Academic Publishers, pp. 1–29.

Marshall, Alfred (1923), *Industry and Trade*, 3rd edition, London, UK: MacMillan.

Martinez-Peria, M.S. (1999), 'A regime switching approach to studying speculative attacks: a focus on European monetary system crises', *World Bank Policy Research Working Paper*, **2132**, Washington, DC: World Bank.

Masson, P.R. (1995), 'Gaining and losing ERM credibility: the case of the United Kingdom', *The Economic Journal*, **105**, 571–82.

Masson, P.R. (1998), 'Contagion: monsoonal effects, spillovers, and jumps between multiple equilibria', *International Monetary Fund Working Paper*, **98/142**, Washington, DC: International Monetary Fund.

Masson, P. (1999), 'Contagion: macroeconomic models with multiple equilibria', *Journal of International Money and Finance*, **18**, 587–602.

Masson, P. and M. Mussa (1997), 'The role of the IMF', *International Monetary Fund Pamphlet Series*, **50**, Washington, DC: International Monetary Fund.

Melick, W.R. (1996), 'Estimation of speculative attack models: Mexico yet again', *Bank of International Settlements Working Paper*, **109**, Basel, Switzerland: Bank of International Settlements.

Meltzer, Alan H. (ed.) (2000), *Report of the International Financial Institution Advisory Commission*, Washington, DC: Government Printing Office.

Mendoza, E.G. (1995) 'The terms of trade, the real exchange rate and economic fluctuations', *International Economic Review*, **36**, 101–37.

Mendoza, E.G. and L.L. Tesar (1998), 'The international ramifications of tax reforms: supply side economics in a global economy', *American Economic Review*, **88** (1), 226–45.

Mendoza, E.G. and M. Uribe (1997), 'The syndrome of exchange-rate based stabilizations and the uncertain duration of currency pegs', *Institute for*

Empirical Macroeconomics Discussion Paper, **121**, Federal Reserve Bank of Minneapolis.

Mendoza, E.G. and M. Uribe (2000), 'Devaluation risk and the business-cycle implications of exchange rate management', *Carnegie Rochester Conference Series on Public Policy*, **53**, 239–96.

Méon, P.G. (2001), 'A model of exchange rate crises with partisan governments', *Journal of Macroeconomics*, **23** (1), 517–35.

Méon, P.G. and J.M. Rizzo (2002), 'The viability of fixed exchange rate commitments: does politics matter? A theoretical and empirical investigation', *Open Economies Review*, **13** (2), 111–32.

Metz, C. (2002), 'Private and public information in self-fulfilling currency crises', *Journal of Economics*, **76** (1), 65–85.

Milesi-Feretti, G.M. and A. Razin (1998), 'Current account reversals and currency crises: empirical regularities', *International Monetary Fund Working Paper*, **98/99**, Washington, DC: International Monetary Fund.

Miller, V. (1996), 'Exchange rate crises with domestic bank runs: evidence from the 1890s', *Journal of International Money and Finance*, **15** (4), 637–56.

Miller, V. (1998), 'The double-drain with a cross-border twist: more on the relationship between banking and currency crisis', *American Economic Review*, **88** (2), 444–48.

Miller, V. (1999), 'The timing and size of bank-financed speculative attacks', *Journal of International Money and Finance*, **18**, 459–70.

Miotti, E.L., Quenan, C. and N. Ricoeur-Nicolaï (1999), 'L'Amérique Latine dans la crise financière internationale', *Problèmes d'Amérique Latine*, **33** (April–June), 95–125.

Mizen, P. (1999), 'Can foreign currency deposits prop up a collapsing exchange-rate regime', *Journal of Development Economics*, **58**, 553–62.

Moreno, R. and B. Trehan (2000), 'Common shocks and currency crises', *Federal Reserve Bank of San Francisco Working Paper*, **2000-05**, San Francisco, CA: Federal Reserve Bank of San Francisco.

Morris, S. and H.S. Shin (1998a), 'Unique equilibrium in a model of self-fulfilling currency attacks', *American Economic Review*, **88** (3), 587-597.

Morris, S. and H.S. Shin (1998b), 'A theory of the onset of currency attacks', *Centre for Economic Policy Research Discussion Paper*, **2025**, London, UK: Centre for Economic Policy Research.

Morris, S. and H.S. Shin (2000), 'Rethinking multiple equilibria in macroeconomic modelling', in Ben S. Bernanke and Kenneth Rogoff (eds), *NBER Macroeconomics Annual 2000*, Cambridge, MA: MIT Press, pp. 139–61.

Nagy, Piroska Mohácsi (2000), *The Meltdown of the Russian State: The Deformation and Collapse of the State in Russia*, Northampton, MA, USA and Cheltenham, UK: Edward Elgar.

Naisbitt, John (1995), *Megatrends Asia: The Eight Megatrends that are Changing the World*, London, UK: Nicholas Brealey.

Obstfeld, M. (1984), 'Balance-of-payments crises and devaluation', *Journal of Money, Credit and Banking*, **16** (2), 208–17.

Obstfeld, M. (1985), 'The capital inflows problem revisited: a stylized model of southern cone disinflation', *Review of Economic Studies*, **52**, 605–25.

Obstfeld, M. (1986a), 'Speculative attack and the external constraint in a maximizing model of the balance of payments', *Canadian Journal of Economics*, **19** (1), 1–22.

Obstfeld, M. (1986b), 'Rational and self-fulfilling balance-of-payments crises', *American Economic Review*, **76** (1), 72–81.

Obstfeld, M. (1986c), 'Capital controls, the dual exchange rate and devaluation', *Journal of International Economics*, **20**, 1-20.

Obstfeld, M. (1991), 'Destabilizing effects of exchange rate escape clauses', *National Bureau of Economic Research Working Paper*, **3603**, Cambridge, MA: National Bureau of Economic Research, reprinted in (1997), *Journal of International* Economics, **43** (1–2), 61–77.

Obstfeld, M. (1994), 'The logic of currency crises', *National Bureau of Economic Research Working Paper*, 4640, Cambridge, MA: National Bureau of Economic Research.

Obstfeld, M. (1996), 'Models of currency crises with self-fulfilling features', *European Economic Review*, **40** (3–5), 1037–47.

Obstfeld, Maurice and Kenneth Rogoff (1996), *Foundations of International Macroeconomics*, Cambridge, MA: MIT Press.

Organisation of Economic and Commerce Development (2000), *Fédération de Russie*, Collection 'Etudes économiques de l'OCDE', Paris: OCDE.

Osakwe, P.N. and L.L. Schembri (2002), 'Real effects of collapsing exchange rate regimes: an application to Mexico', *Journal of International Economics*, **57**, 299–325.

Otani, K. (1989), 'A collapse of a fixed rate regime with a discrete realignment of the exchange rate', *Journal of the Japanese and International Economies*, **3**, 250–69.

Otker, I. and C. Pazarbasioglu (1997a), 'Likelihood versus timing of speculative attacks: a case study of Mexico', *European Economic Review*, **41**, 837–845.

Otker, I. and C. Pazarbasioglu (1997b), 'Speculative attacks and macroeconomic fundamentals: evidence from some European currencies', *European Economic Review*, **41**, 847–60.

Ozkan, F.G. and A. Sutherland (1994), 'A model of the ERM crisis', *Centre for Economic Policy Research Discussion Paper*, **879**, London, UK: Centre for Economic Policy Research.

Ozkan, F.G. and A. Sutherland (1995), 'Policy measures to avoid a currency crisis', *The Economic Journal*, **105**, 510–19.

Ozkan, F.G. and A. Sutherland (1998), 'A currency crisis model with an optimizing policymaker', *Journal of International Economics*, **44**, 339–64.

Pastine, I. (2002), 'Speculation and the decision to abandon a fixed exchange rate regime', *Journal of International Economics*, **57** (1), 197–229.

Peek, J. and E.S. Rosengren (2000), 'Implications of the Globalization of the Banking Sector: The Latin American Experience', *Federal Reserve Bank of Boston New England Economic Review*, **September–October**, 45–62.

Penati, A. and G. Pennachi (1989), 'Optimal portfolio choice and the collapse of fixed exchange rate regime', *Journal of International Economics*, **27**, 1-24.

Pesenti, P. and C. Tille (2000), 'The economics of currency crises and contagion: an introduction', *Federal Reserve Bank of New York Economic Policy Review*, **6** (3), 3–16.

Plott, C.R. and J. Smith (1999), 'Instability of equilibria in experimental markets: upward-sloping demands, externalities and fad-like incentives', *Southern Economic Journal*, **65** (3), 405–26.

Pomerleano, M. (1998), 'The East Asian crisis and corporate finances: the untold microeconomic story', *Emerging Markets Quarterly*, **2** (4), 14–27.

Prati, A. and M. Sbrascia (2002), 'Currency crises and uncertainty about fundamentals', *International Monetary Fund Working Paper*, **02/3**, Washington, DC: International Monetary Fund.

Pritsker, M. (2000), 'The channels for financial contagion', mimeo, Board of the Governors of the Federal Reserve System.

Radelet, S. and J. Sachs (1998a), 'The East Asian financial crisis: diagnosis, remedies, prospects', *Brookings Papers on Economic Activity*, **1**, 1–90.

Radelet, S. and J. Sachs (1998b), 'The onset of the East Asian crisis', *National Bureau of Economic Research Working Paper*, **6680**, Cambridge, MA: National Bureau of Economic Research.

Rangvid J. (2001), 'Second-generation models of currency crises', *Journal of Economic Surveys*, **15** (5), 613–46.

Reagle, D. and D. Salvatore (2000), 'Forecasting financial crises in emerging market economies', *Open Economies Review*, **11**, 247–59.

Rochet, J.C. and X. Vives (2002), 'Coordination failures and the lender of last resort: was Bagehot right after all?, *Centre for Economic Policy Research Discussion Paper*, **3233**, London, UK: Centre for Economic Policy Research.

Rogoff, K. (1985), 'The optimal degree of commitment to an intermediate monetary target', *Quarterly Journal of Economics*, **100**, 1169–90.

Rogoff, K. (2002), 'An open letter to Joseph Stiglitz', Washington, DC: International Monetary Fund.

Rohwer, Jim (1995), *Asia Rising: Why America Will Prosper as Asia's Economies Boom*, New York: Simon & Schuster.

Rose, A.K. and L.E.O. Svensson (1994), 'European exchange rate credibility before the fall', *European Economic Review*, **38**, 1185–216.

Roubini, N. (1998), 'The case against currency boards: debunking 10 myths about the benefits of currency boards', mimeo, New York University.

Rucker, L. and M.A. Crosnier (2000), 'Russie 1999–2000: une nouvelle dynamique', *Le Courrier des Pays de l'Est*, **1010**, November–December, 105–23.

Saboia, J (2000), 'Bresil, deconcentration industrielle dans les annees 1990: une approche regionale', *Problèmes d'Amerique Latine*, **39**, October–December, 89–108.

Sachs, J. (1995), 'Do we need an international lender of last resort?', Frank D. Graham Lecture, Princeton University.

Sachs, J., Tornell, A., and A. Velasco (1996a), 'Financial crises in emerging markets: the lessons from 1995', *Brookings Papers on Economic Activity*, **1**, 147–215.

Sachs, J., Tornell, A., and A. Velasco (1996b), 'The Mexican peso crisis: sudden death or death foretold ?', *Journal of International Economics*, **41**, 265–283.

Salant, S.W. (1983), 'The vulnerability of price stabilization schemes to speculative attack', *Journal of Political Economy*, **91** (1), 1–38.

Salant, S.W. and D. Henderson (1978), 'Market anticipations of government policies and the price of gold', *Journal of Political Economy*, **86**, 627–48.

Sapir, Jacques (1996), *Le Chaos Russe*, Paris: La Découverte.

Sapir, Jacques (1998), *Le Krach Russe*, Paris: La Découverte.

Sargent, T.J. and N. Wallace (1973), 'The stability of models of money and growth with perfect foresight', *Econometrica*, **41**, 1043–48.

Sargent, T.J. and N. Wallace (1981), 'Some unpleasant monetarist arithmetic', *Federal Reserve Bank of Minneapolis Quarterly Review*, **5**, 1-17.

Sarno, Lucio and Mark P. Taylor (2002), *The Economics of Exchange Rates*, Cambridge, UK: Cambridge University Press.

Savastano, M. (1992), 'Collapse of a crawling peg regime in the presence of a government budget constraint', *International Monetary Fund Staff Papers*, **39** (1), 79–100.

Sbracia, M. and A. Zaghini (2001), 'Expectations and information in second-generation models of currency crises', *Economic Modeling*, **18**, 203–22.

Scharfstein, D.S. and J.C. Stein (1990), 'Herd behavior and investment', *American Economic Review*, **80**, 465–79.

Schinasi, G.J. and R.T. Smith (2000), 'Portfolio diversification, leverage and financial contagion', *IMF Staff-Papers*, **47** (2), 159–76.

Schneider, M. and A. Tornell (2001), 'Boom–bust cycles and the balance-sheet effect', Working Paper, UCLA.

Schuler, K. (1996), *Should Developing Countries Have Central Banks?*, London, UK: Institute of Economic Affairs.

Schwartz, A.J. (1993), 'Currency boards: their past, present and possible future role', *Carnegie-Rochester Conference Series on Public Policy*, **39**, 147–84.

Schwartz, A.J. (1998), 'International financial crises: myths and realities', *Cato Journal*, **17** (3), 251–256.

Sevic, Zeljko (2002), *Banking Reforms in Southeast Europe*, Cheltenham, UK and Northampton, MA, USA: Edward Elgar.

Shiller, R.J. (1995), 'Conversation, information and herd behavior', *American Economic Review*, **85** (2), 181–85.

Söderlind, P. (2000), 'Market expectations in the UK before and after the ERM crisis', *Economica*, **67**, 1–18.

Söderlind, P. and L.E.O. Svensson (1997), 'New techniques to extract market expectations from financial instruments', *Journal of Monetary Economics*, **40**, 383–429.

Stiglitz, Joseph (2002), *Globalisation and its Discontents*, New York, NY: W.W. Norton & Company.

Summers, L.H. (2000), 'International financial crises: causes, prevention, and cures', *American Economic Review*, **90** (2), 1–16.

Sutherland, A. (1995), 'Currency crisis models: bridging the gap between new and old approaches', in Christian Bordes, Eric Girardin and Jacques Melitz (eds), *European Currency Crises and After*, Manchester UK: Manchester University Press, pp. 57–82.

Svensson, L.E.O. (1992a), 'The foreign exchange risk premium in a target zone with devaluation risk', *Journal of International Economics*, **33**, 21–40.

Svensson, L.E.O. (1992b), 'An interpretation of recent research on exchange rate target zones', *Journal of Economic Perspectives*, **6** (4), 119–44.

Svensson, L.E.O. (1993), 'Assessing target zone credibility – mean reversion and devaluation expectations in the ERM, 1979-1992', *European Economic Review*, **37**, 765–802.

Tarashev, N.(2001), 'Currency crises and the informational role of interest rates', mimeo, Princeton University.

Thomas, A. (1994), 'Expected devaluation and economic fundamentals', *International Monetary Fund Staff Papers*, **41** (2), 262–85.

Thornton, H. (1802), *An Enquiry into the Nature and Effects of Paper Credit of Great Britain*, London, UK: Hatchard.

Tirole, J. (1982), 'On the possibility of speculation under rational expectations', *Econometrica*, **50**, 1163–81.

Tirole, Jean (2002), *Financial Crises, Liquidity and the International Financial System*, Princeton, NJ: Princeton University Press.

Tobin, J. (1978), 'A proposal for international monetary reform', *Eastern Economic Journal*, **4**, 153–59.

Toda, H. and P.C.B Philipps (1993), 'Vector autoregression and causality', *Econometrica*, **61**, 1367–93.

Toda, H and P.C.B. Philipps (1994), 'Vector autoregressions and causality: a theoretical overview and simulation study', *Econometric Reviews*, **13**, 259–85.

Tornell, A. (1999), 'Common fundamentals in the Tequila and Asian crises', *National Bureau of Economic Research Working Paper*, **7139**, Cambridge, MA.

Tronzano, M. (2001), 'Macroeconomic fundamentals and exchange rate credibility. Further evidence on the Italian experience from a regime-switching approach', *Scottish Journal of Political Economy*, **48** (4), 442–60.

Uribe, M. (2002), 'The price-consumption puzzle of currency pegs', *Journal of Monetary Economics*, **49** (3), 533–69.

Van Rijckeghem, C. and B. Weder (2000), 'Spillovers through banking centers, a panel data analysis', *International Monetary Fund Working Paper*, **00/88**, Washington DC: International Monetary Fund.

Van Rijckeghem, C. and B. Weder (2001), 'Source of contagion: finance or trade', *Journal of International Economics*, **54** (2), 293–308.

Van Wijnbergen, S. (1991), 'Fiscal deficits, exchange rate crises, and inflation', *Review of Economic Studies*, **58**, 81–92.

Végh, C. (1992), 'Stopping high inflation: an analytical overview', *IMF Staff Papers*, **39**, 626–96.

Velasco, A. (1987), 'Financial crises and balance of payments crises', *Journal of Development Economics*, **27**, 263–83.

Velasco, A. (1996), 'Fixed exchange rates: credibility, flexibility and multiplicity', *European Economic Review*, **40**, 1023–35.

Ventura, J. (2002), 'Comment on "The role of large players in currency crises" by G. Corsetti, P. Pesenti, and N. Roubini', in Sebastian Edwards and Jeffrey A. Frankel (eds), *Preventing Currency Crises in Emerging Markets*, Chicago, Ill: The University of Chicago Press, pp 258-267.

Verrechia, R. (1982), 'Information acquisition in a noisy rational expectations economy', *Econometrica*, **50**, 1415–30.

Vitale, P. (2000), 'Speculative noise trading and manipulation in the foreign exchange market', *Journal of International Money and Finance*, **19**, 689–712.

Wallace, N. (1990), 'Why markets in foreign exchange are different from other markets', *Federal Reserve Bank of Minneapolis Quarterly Review*, **14** (1), 12–18.

Wang, J. (1993), 'A model of intertemporal asset prices under asymmetric information', *Review of Economic Studies*, **60**, 249–82.

Wang, J. (1994), 'A model of competitive stock trading volume', *Journal of Political Economy*, **102**, 127–68.

Weber, A.A. (1991), 'Stochastic process switching and intervention in exchange rate target zones: empirical evidence from the EMS', *Centre for Economic Policy Research Discussion Paper*, **554**, London, UK.

Weber, A.A. (1998), 'Sources of currency crises: an empirical analysis', *Osterreichisches Nationalbank Working Paper*, **25**.

Wei, S.J. and J. Kim (1997), 'The big players on the foreign exchange market: do they trade on information or noise ?', *National Bureau of Economic Research Working Paper*, **6256**, Cambridge, MA.

Williams, J. (1936), 'Speculation and the carryover', *Quarterly Journal of Economics*, **50**, 436–55.

Williamson, John (1995), *What Role for Currency Boards?*, Washington DC: Institute for International Economics.

Willman, A. (1988), 'The collapse of the fixed exchange rate regime with sticky wages and imperfect substitutability between domestic and foreign bonds', *European Economic Review*, **32**, 1817–38.

Willman, A. (1989), 'Devaluation expectations and speculative attacks on the currency', *Scandinavian Journal of Economics*, **97** (1), 97–16

Woodruff, David (1999), *Money Unmade: Barter and the Fate of Russian Capitalism*, Ithaca and London: Cornell University Press.

World Bank (1993), *The East Asian Miracle: Economic Growth and Public Policy*, Washington DC : World Bank.

World Bank (1998), *East Asia: The Road to Recovery*, Washington DC : World Bank.

World Bank (1999), *Global Economic Prospects and the Developing Countries : Beyond Financial Crisis*, Washington DC: World Bank.

Wyplosz, C. (1986), 'Capital controls and balance of payments crises', *Journal of International, Money and Finance*, **5**, 167–79.

Zettelmeyer, J. (2000), 'Can official crisis lending be counterproductive in the short-run?', *Economic Notes*, **29** (1), 13–29.

Index